Jack Benny's Lost Radio Broadcasts

Volume One: May 2 – July 27, 1932

TONIGHT AT 8.45

Eastern Standard Time

STATION WHAM

A new radio program of sparkling wit and music with

Jack Benny

as master of ceremonies, Ethel Shutta and

George Olsen

and his famous music

Every Monday at 8.45 P. M. and Wednesday 8.30 P. M. over Station WHAM and associated N. B. C. stations Eastern Standard Time.

CANADA DRY

The Champagne of Ginger Ales

Jack Benny's Lost Radio Broadcasts

Volume One: May 2 – July 27, 1932

by Jack Benny and Harry Conn

Edited and with an introduction by Kathryn Fuller-Seeley

BearManor Media

2020

The Jack Benny Program Radio Scripts, 1932–1936
by Jack Benny and Harry Conn

Introduction © 2020 Kathryn Fuller-Seeley

All rights reserved.

No portion of this publication may be reproduced, stored, and/or copied electronically (except for academic use as a source), nor transmitted in any form or by any means without the prior written permission of the publisher and/or author.

Published in the United States of America by:

BearManor Media
4700 Millenia Blvd.
Suite 175 PMB 90497
Orlando, FL 32839
bearmanormedia.com

Printed in the United States.

Typesetting and layout by John Teehan

Back cover illustration: Jack Benny, George Olsen and Ethel Shutta, ca. 1932
Front cover illustration: Young and Rubicam advertisement, *Fortune*, June 1935

ISBN—978-1-62933-578-0

Table of Contents

Introduction 1

May 2, 1932 11
May 4, 1932 19
May 9, 1932 27
May 11, 1932 33
May 16, 1932 41
May 18, 1932 49
May 23, 1932 57
May 25, 1932 67
May 30, 1932 75

June 1, 1932 85
June 6, 1932 95
June 8, 1932 105
June 13, 1932 115
June 15, 1932 125
June 20, 1932 137

June 22, 1932 147

June 27, 1932 155

June 29, 1932 165

July 4, 1932 175

July 6, 1932 185

July 11, 1932 195

July 13, 1932 207

July 18, 1932 219

July 20, 1932 229

July 25, 1932 239

July 27, 1932 249

Introduction

JACK BENNY, RADIO'S GREATEST COMEDIAN, broadcast 931 half-hour episodes of his program between 1932 and 1955. His show is renowned for the character Benny created — the eternally 39-year old "fall guy," the vain cheapskate who was constantly the butt of jokes launched by his zany cast of underlings – announcer, bandleader, tenor, quasi-secretary and valet. The ancient Maxwell jalopy, the vault, the show's catchphrases and running gags are dear to all who love old-time radio. Yet Benny's comic world did not launch fully formed when he began his NBC program on May 2, 1932. Originally billed as the "Canada Dry humorist," Benny's initial duty was to provide brief monologues between six tunes performed by prominent New York bandleader George Olsen's musicians and sung by his wife, Ziegfeld Follies chanteuse Ethel Shutta.

How did Jack Benny's program evolve from stand-up routines to lively ensemble situation comedy? For nearly 90 years, it has been very difficult for radio fans to learn. Of the first five seasons of live broadcasts, 177 episodes have no available recordings and many of the remainder are only fragmentary or in poor shape. Most of the fragile transcription discs of the episodes that Benny received have decayed over the years.

I am delighted to present the scripts of these early 'lost' Jack Benny radio programs, transcribed from the originals housed in the Jack Benny Papers, in Special Collections at the UCLA library, for your reading pleasure. Of the 26 scripts presented here, only a recording of the first episode (May 2) is known to exist. Indeed, four of these scripts were missing from Jack Benny's own collection, including the most significant one which introduced the Mary Livingstone character to the show. Fortuitously, they have been located in the "NBC Masterfile" collection at the Library of Congress, and are included.

THE EARLIEST EPISODES

The Canada Dry Program, featuring Jack Benny, George Olsen and Ethel Shutta (pronounced shu-TAY), debuted on Monday May 2, 1932 at 9:30 pm Eastern time on the NBC Blue network. Broadcast twice a week (Mondays and Wednesdays) the program was produced in a small-glass-walled studio that NBC had erected in the former Roof Garden of the New Amsterdam Theatre in Manhattan, that had been home to Ziegfeld summer midnight shows in the 1920s. No studio audience added laughter and applause to the live broadcasts.

The show had been assembled for Canada Dry Ginger Ale by NBC executive Bertha Brainard as a new direction in sponsorship for the company, which had previously underwritten a dramatic (and violent) adventure series set in the Canadian Rockies. Advertising agency N. W. Ayer & Son billed the new show as "30 minutes of music and quips" featuring Olsen and Shutta. Already widely familiar to radio listeners, they were considered to be the main attraction. The music would be interspersed with brief monologue segments performed by 38-year-old Jack Benny, a Midwestern-voiced, genially-self-deprecating vaudeville veteran known around New York as "that sleekly bored joker" and a "Broadway Romeo."

Neither Brainard nor the admen were not especially enthusiastic about the choice of Jack Benny. They were uncertain about what styles and types of performers would work on the radio—some preferred the loud brashness and quickness of other comics and the stentorian tones of tuxedoed announcers. NBC had actually approached literary humorist Irvin S. Cobb prior to contacting Benny, but Cobb's salary demands were too high. Executives probably noted the affinities Benny's vaudeville act had with aural presentation—Benny produced most of his humor through low-key language and smooth, superbly timed delivery of his lines. He was not a primarily physical or visual comedian getting laughs through broad facial expressions, costume, or slapstick body movements. Benny engaged in quiet, intimate joking, confiding in the audience as if it were a small group, similar to the methods of popular "crooning" singers Bing Crosby and Rudy Vallee. On the other hand, Benny's droll stare out at the vaudeville audience, with hand to his cheek, which silently communicated his frustration and won viewers' sympathy, would be lost on radio listeners. (It would only reemerge in the early 1950s to embellish his comedy routines on television.)

The new Canada Dry show joined a rapidly increasing number of variety-comedy programs on primetime network radio. While music had been the dominant program form of the previous five years, the entertainment trade press noted that comedy was growing as a less expensive option for sponsors weary of paying for high-priced orchestras and temperamental crooners. New shows in the 1932 season featured not only newcomer Jack Benny but also other vaudevillians such as George Burns and Gracie Allen, George Jessel, Fred Allen, and Jack Pearl. The new entrants joined such already-popular variety programs as those hosted by Rudy Vallee for Fleischmann's Yeast, Ed Wynn for Texaco, and Eddie Cantor for Chase and Sanborn Coffee.

As Benny began the twice-weekly broadcasts of Canada Dry's new musical comedy radio show in May 1932, it seemed that not only he, but the sponsor, ad agency, and network were almost shockingly naïve about how much labor Benny's role might entail. The orchestra and vocalist had large musical catalogs from which they could draw new tunes to perform, but if Benny was to do more than introduce the title of the next song, he was going to need fresh material every episode. The executives must have assumed Benny ad-libbed or wrote his own humorous asides. As a popular emcee, Benny had experience in creating short gags and exchanges with vaudeville performers, but he was used to repeating similar patter for different audiences the whole week of the engagement, either getting new performers to work with or a new city to play in the following week.

The first live Canada Dry episode demonstrated the promise and the drawback of the concept. In seven short monologues interspersed between the songs, Benny presented himself as a suave, urban, and thoroughly Americanized fellow who was witty and personable, a wisecracker who was self-centered but who self-deprecatingly understood that his attempts at boastful egotism would end in mild humiliation. Benny exchanged a little banter with Olsen and Shutta as he introduced them. Nervous awkwardness of the new endeavor was apparent in Benny's doing most of the talking and their very brief responses to standard vaudeville jokes, such as ribbing the age of Olsen's automobile. Benny always worked from a script; he wanted a written structure to guide him to make sure he was organized and that the wording of the jokes could be carefully pored over and crafted into polished gems. He delivered his lines, though, in such an easy, nonchalant manner that listeners may have thought he was speaking off-the-cuff. Even in this first episode, he wove the middle-of-the-program advertising messages into his monologues, entwining a playful (and fairly unusual) mocking tone toward the product in the same way he told self-deprecating stories about himself.

In the second and third episodes, with a dash of desperation, Benny provided brief descriptions of his fellow radio performers that again drew on standard vaudeville insult-humor patter—Olsen was penurious, Shutta lied about her age, the boys in the band were drunkards, and announcer Ed Thorgerson resembled a Hollywood playboy with slicked-back hair and a mustache that looked like he had swallowed all of Mickey Mouse except the tail. The others were given few lines to speak. Benny appealed to his unseen listeners directly, asking if there was anybody out there and reintroduced himself halfway through the show.

Variety's reviewer in May 1932 sensed Benny's nervousness, but noted encouragingly, "there's no reason why a clever, intimate comedian of Benny's type shouldn't hit over the air. Essentially he has everything it takes, from an excellent speaking voice to the right kind of delivery." Nevertheless, the reviewer was unenthusiastic about Benny's integration of the separate elements of music, comedy, and advertising in the show, recommending that Olsen "should leave all the talking to Benny." *Billboard's* review of the new program noted that Benny's nonchalant style of humor and delivery was different from what other comics were offering on air. "A taste for his style has to be acquired," cautioned the reviewer, who also noticed the reliance on old vaudeville patter—"On this particular program he rang in some of his old material, but no doubt new to radio fans."

Soon, Benny queasily realized he had used up nearly every monologue he had perfected over fifteen years in vaudeville. Years later, Jack Benny confessed his radio panic: "In vaudeville you had one show and that was it. You changed it whenever you felt like it. And in this, when you realized that every week you needed a new show, this got a little bit frightening." In another interview, he recalled: "I didn't have any idea how important it was to have good material, and how hard it was to get. The first show was a cinch—I used about half of all the gags I knew. The second show consumed all the rest, and I faced the third absolutely dry."

Established performers appearing on the airwaves similarly expressed terror at the speed with which the live broadcasts to huge audiences consumed a career's worth of material in just a few hours. Radio scriptwriter Dave Freedman devised one method to address radio comics' problem, hiring a staff of young assistants who combed through every source of humor in the library—joke books, magazine articles, and nineteenth-century literature—to cull every possible jest, quip, and comic exchange. They organized these jokes into vast files on every conceivable topic that Freedman could then dip into, rearrange a few particulars, and assemble into scripts churned out for a half-dozen different radio comedy shows each week.

By the end of the second week on air, Jack Benny sought out Harry Conn, a tap-dancing former vaudevillian who had turned to full-time writing, penning routines for dozens of comedians, including Benny. In the spring of 1932, Conn was working on the Burns and Allen staff, but was lured to the new show. Benny decided to rely solely on Conn, paying Conn's substantial salary out of his own pocket. The two quickly became partners, co-writers and co-editors, working closely together week in and out. To Conn's chagrin, the radio network would not allow writers to get on-air credit, however, so Benny always remained the sole focus of public and critical acclaim.

With Conn on board, the Canada Dry scripts started to become more adventurous. Instead of Benny spieling out a long joke soliloquy, George Olsen now was given more straight lines as he and Benny engaged in conversation. Everyone else in the studio—from orchestra members and Conn to Benny's personal assistant Harry Baldwin—was pulled to the mike to voice fictional guests. Benny and Conn began experimenting with creating a richer fictional world for the program, creating sketch routines that briefly moved away from the microphone. On May 23, they finessed the problem of segueing by endowing announcer Ed Thorgerson with a magical ability to tune an on-air radio into conversation made by the Benny, Olsen, Shutta and band members at a soda fountain located in the building's lobby. The scene may have only lasted two minutes, but when Benny "returned" to the studio after the next song, he jokingly assumed that he had to explain to the audience what they had done.

Subsequent episodes of the Canada Dry program contained a three- to five-minute sketch occurring in a fictional place away from the immediacy of the studio space. Some involved Jack traveling to a special event and reporting on it (essentially still performing a monologue). Jack "attended" the Dempsey-Sharkey prize fight at Madison Square Garden, and parodied radio sports coverage, giving play-by-play action. On July 6 the cast visited the zoo and gathered testimonials from the animals about how much they enjoyed drinking Canada Dry. Meanwhile, Jack continued to rib George Olsen about being a spendthrift. Back at the soda fountain, George offered to treat Jack to a glass of ginger ale, but had forgotten his wallet, so Jack ended up picking up the check for the entire orchestra's order.

EXPERIMENTATION WITH TOPICS AND CHARACTERS

Benny and Conn devised a mixture of comic monologues, repartee, pun tossing, and fictional adventures between the musical numbers, avoiding rigid formulas. Some of their experimental ideas were solidly successful, while some were problematic and abandoned as unworkable. Others ended perhaps at the behest of their sponsor.

Benny employed an aggressive absurdist-comic approach to the Canada Dry commercials from the start, and it was controversial. Folklore has said that the sponsor was appalled. Even Variety's review of initial episode warned that the comic advertising was disturbing: "Plug angle was considerably overdone here, with Benny handling it throughout. He pulled some pretty obvious puns, such as "drinking Canada Dry." ... Right now, the subtle spotting of the plug should be handled with silk gloves." But Benny kept on mercilessly ribbing the product, reportedly receiving encouragement from fan mail which started pouring in to the show. Perhaps Benny was reading *Ballyhoo*, a satirical magazine in vogue at the time which mercilessly pilloried the excesses of product advertising.

On May 9, Jack announced the beginning of a write-in contest, in which listeners would submit testimonials to the deliciousness of Canada Dry Ginger Ale. Benny's radio show was followed by a musical program for San Felipe cigars, which was then currently conducting a jingle-writing competition with prizes valued at $70,000. Advertising agencies who created the radio programming loved these contests, for they generated thousands of listener responses that agencies could use to demonstrate the radio program's popularity and justify the hefty expense of radio sponsorship to their clients. The Federal Radio Commission and NBC worked to eliminate contests, however, as they added a tawdry, hucksterish element to a network broadcasting that was trying to seem more culturally elevated. Benny's increasingly absurd contest rules exposed the crassness of these gimmicks and made his sponsor seem insincere and foolish. The *Pittsburgh Press*' reviewer however, praised Benny for his clever parodies, calling them a delightful new twist in radio humor. The outrageous Canada Dry middle commercials are a highlight of this earliest portion of Benny's radio career (see the Kentucky factory experiment on May 25 and the foot race between a talking glass of Canada Dry and a bottle of ketchup on May 30). Benny would continue to innovate new techniques of advertising humor with Jell-O and Lucky Strike cigarette commercials in the years to come.

Benny and Conn gingerly dipped a toe into political satire. The upcoming presidential election must have been a topic difficult for radio jokesters to avoid, as the candidates' sloganeering filled the newspapers. Conn and Benny brought a touch of cynical humor and an absurdity to their political skits, weaving Roosevelt and Hoover's names into Benny's monologues similarly to the way they talked about current celebrities such as Clark Gable and Greta Garbo. In early June, Benny made a mild joke about ex-servicemen descending on Washington in the Bonus March, and the *Pittsburgh Press*' radio critic took him to task for making fun of a serious subject. On June 20, Benny announced that he was going to dive into politics. After a barrage of digressive jokes and puns, and a song (Olsen's band performed a tune entitled "Everything's' Going to be Okay, America"), Benny briefly brought on "The Canada Dry candidate for president, Trafalgar Bee-Fuddle… The man who broke his umbrella and is neither wet nor dry…" After an absurd stump speech, Bee-Fuddle was summarily shot.

The two writers also experimented in those first months on the radio with added voices. On May 25, Benny interviewed the janitor of the building, Mr. Philander Kvetch, played by band member Bobby Moore, who only responded to questions in gurgles of baby talk. On June 1, Kvetch briefly returned, speaking in a heavy German accent. This time the part was probably played by Harry Conn. On June 15, Conn was an Italian-American tough guy attending the boxing match. On July 13, Jack talked to a group of Scottish gentlemen who would be judging the latest Canada Dry contest; all the Scots were played by Conn (including a Scottish terrier who simply woofed). Ethnic characters were a favorite staple in Conn's bag of comedy writing tricks; although use of foreign accents was a creaky throwback to earlier vaudeville days of Gallagher and Sheen, or an insensitive burlesquing of immigrants, it's probable that Conn saw the ethnic-accented caricature of American voices to be a bit of "verbal slapstick" or unexpected aural comedy costuming for the airwaves. Despite Conn's favoring of ethnic voices, he rarely appeared on-air as a performer again.

In the show's second month, Jack began to talk about hiring an assistant to handle all the mail the program was receiving in response to the outrageous Canada Dry contests. This search continued over the next month, as Jack acquired first an inefficient male secretary, then an incompetent female secretary named Garbo. In the final script of this volume, at the date on which the program was renewed for another thirteen weeks, Benny's wife Sadye Marks Benny (his sometime assistant on the vaudeville stage) became incorporated into the radio program, as a young woman named "Mary Livingstone," a fan of the program from the small town of Plainfield, New Jersey. She assumed the role of Jack's lackadaisical part-time secretary on the radio show, and soon would become a central character.

Several long-lasting themes of Benny's radio comedy appear in these earliest radio episodes (some were holdovers from his vaudeville humor), such as:

- Mentioning Waukegan and his family; brother in law Leonard Fenchel gets two plugs, and his father in Waukegan IL a shout-out on June 22.
- Playing the violin terribly. Starts June 6 when Olsen dares Jack to play and band boys make fun of him. Jack hits a sour note, although he finishes number OK and there is applause from band. On July 25 the band misbehaves when Benny takes the baton.
- Claiming that his movies were terrible. On May 25 Ethel asks him about his film career and he jokes that she's the only one who saw *The Medicine Man*.
- "What are you laughing at?" Jack asks cast members June 27 and July 13, even before Mary is on board.
- Bad poetry – begins with the Canada Dry contest limericks and songs.
- Train announcer with crazy stops, starts June 27 when a ticket puncher-conductor is asked about the punches in the Sharkey-Schmelling fight; and again, train announcer on July 11's amateur night.

Other program elements of the first radio weeks that would NOT continue in coming years

- Jack's girlfriend in Newark, from his vaudeville routine on May 2; on June 13 her name is revealed as Molly as she repeatedly phones Jack during the show. Jack tells her to stop calling, but does blow kisses into the phone; on June 29 she doesn't have a name but is his BABY who calls on Babies' Night who is 29 (which was about the age of his real wife Sadye Marks Benny.)
- Lengthy monologues, as the program soon becomes dominated by dialogue and interaction. We will encounter them again in Benny's early TV episodes (1950-1955), when he stands alone on a small stage.
- Politics/current events – there's a mild Bonus marchers joke on June 8; Prosperity around the corner joke on June 15, and other small Depression references. The political party presidential nominating conventions are mentioned in June.
- Programs twice a week – only during the Canada Dry sponsorship.
- Jack speaking German and other dialects. On July 6 Jack pretends he had been in a circus in Potsdam; at other times he switches to Irish brogue or Scotch accent.
- Accusing others of being cheap, especially George Olsen; Benny is not yet the 'fall guy.'
- Four or more announcers over the period, including Ed Thorgerson, George Hicks, Alois Havrilla and Jimmy Wallingford. It must have been more difficult to write comedy lines if Benny and Conn did not know who would be voicing them.
- A major female character apart from Mary; Ethel Shutta's character is sophisticated and flirts with Jack.
- Fireworks on the radio on July 4th. Too bad Benny never broadcast in July again.

These Jack Benny program scripts are located in the collection of business and personal papers Benny donated to UCLA in the 1960s, and they are housed in the Special Collections library. The researcher needs to arrange days in advance for them to be brought onsite. Each episode's cover page is typed on ad agency NW Ayer & Sons letterhead, and Jack Benny signed his name in pencil on each cover. These copies are probably the final "as aired" version and do not reflect the changes that resulted from Benny and Conn's polishing of drafts up to airtime.

Nevertheless, we have worked to transcribe the notations typed into the scripts that helped guide the performers in pauses and verbal emphasis. After Harry Conn joined the program the number of underlined and capitalized words and ellipses for pauses greatly increased. Although Conn's name is nowhere found on these scripts, his influence was immediately felt. Benny and Conn left us very little evidence of how they worked together (writing notes, outlines or earlier drafts). But accusations they hurled at each other in the heated exchange when the pair "broke up" in 1936 indicate that Harry thought Jack rushed the lines he and his cast exchanged; Harry constantly cautioned him to slow down. Jack felt that Harry downplayed the huge contributions Jack made to script editing, cast direction and performance that made the resulting program such a success. I invite you to learn more about Benny's broadcasting career in my book *Jack Benny and the Golden Age of Radio Comedy*.

In sum, these Canada Dry scripts from Summer 1932 demonstrate that Jack Benny initially struggled on his radio program (coming up with enough new material for each episode), but ultimately thrived in the new medium by developing new approaches to comedy. Benny and scriptwriter Harry Conn began to craft a personality-based radio variety program, drawing on Benny's vaudeville style and exploring new (to them) comic constructions of what contemporary critics termed *character comedy* and comedy *situations*. Experimenting as the program progressed from week to week, Benny and Conn expanded the narrative world of the show. They began developing comic identities for the major performers (orchestra leader, vocalist, and announcer) who stood around the microphone. Framing the group as workers putting on a radio show, Benny and Conn developed a personality for each of them that blended reality and fiction. The cast became a stable of recognizable, quirky-yet-likeable continuing characters who could bounce off each other in informal exchanges in the studio or interact in situations from visiting the zoo or having dinner at a cast member's home to performing a parody of a popular new film. This variety greatly reduced Benny and Conn's reliance on pat monologues and standard joke telling. What they developed was a forerunner of the situation comedy, a genre that would become much more prominent only fifteen years later in radio and television broadcasting.

Endnotes

1. Review of Canada Dry program, Variety, May 10, 1932, 58.
2. "Canada Dry Program," *Billboard*, May 14, 1932, 17.
3. "Stars Shine Best When Polished," *Broadcasting and Television*, October 1956, 122.
4. Jerome Beatty, "Unhappy Fiddler," *American Magazine*, December 1944, 142.
5. Review of Canada Dry program, *Variety*, May 10, 1932, 58.

Jack Benny Resources:

Benny, Jack and Joan Benny, *Sunday Nights at Seven: The Jack Benny Story* (Warner Books, 1990)

Fuller-Seeley, Kathryn, *Jack Benny and the Golden Age of American Radio Comedy* (University of California Press, 2017)

International Jack Benny Fan Club (www.jackbenny.org and on Facebook)

Leibowitz, Laura, *Jack Benny Forever, 2nd edition, Volume 1, Radio May 1932–May 1942* (2004)

Leibowitz, Laura, *Jack Benny Forever, 2nd edition, Volume 2 Radio October 1942–May 1955* (2006)

Leibowitz, Laura, *Jack Benny Forver, 2nd edition, Volume 3 Television* (2011)

Old Time Radio Researchers Group (https://otrrpedia.net/hotrod.html) Jack Benny radio shows digitized to enjoy for free, as well as through www.archive.org and other websites

May 2, 1932

STATION	WJZ AND BLUE NETWORK	PROGRAM	CANADA DRY GINGER ALE, INC.
		DATE	MONDAY, MAY 2, 1932
		TIME	9.30 - 10:00 P.M. (E.D.T.)

(2ND REVISION)

1.	I BEG YOUR PARDON, MA'AMSELLE	RAVZL	WITMARK	ORCHESTRA
2.	I FOUND A MILLION DOLLAR BABY	WARREN	REMICK	ORCHESTRA AND MISS SHUTTA
3.	I LOVE A PARADE	ARLEN	HARMS	ORCHESTRA AND TRIO
4.	PARADISE	MACIO HERB BROWN	FEIST	ORCHESTRA
5.	THAT'S HOW WE MAKE MUSIC			ORCHESTRA
6.	COME WEST, LITTLE GIRL, COME WEST ("WHOOPEE")	WALTER DONALDSON	DONALDSON DOUGLAS & GUMBLE	ORCHESTRA TRIO AND MISS SHUTTA
7.	DRUMS IN MY HEART	YOUMANS	MILLER MUSIC CORP.	ORCHESTRA

SIGNATURE:

ANNOUNCER	Tonight Canada Dry, the champagne of ginger ales, presents a series of programs to advertise the new made-to-order Canada Dry, which you can now buy by the glass at drug stores and soda fountains. This series will feature George Olsen and his music, Miss Ethel Shutta, the star of many Broadway successes, and that suave comedian, dry humorist and famous Master of Ceremonies — – Jack Benny.
BENNY	Thank you, Mr. Thorgerson. That's pretty good from a man who doesn't even know me. Ladies and Gentlemen, this is Jack Benny talking, and making my first appearance on the air professionally. By that I mean, I am finally getting paid, which will be a great relief to my creditors. I really don't know why I am here. I'm supposed to be a sort of Master of Ceremonies and tell you all about the things that will happen, which would happen anyway. I must introduce the different artists, who could easily introduce themselves, and also talk about the Canada Dry made-to-order by the glass, which is a waste of time, as you know all about it. You drink it, like it, and don't want to hear about it. So ladies and gentlemen, a Master of Ceremonies is really a fellow who is unemployed and gets paid for it. I think you will like the entertainment arranged for tonight—I hope. Of course, I haven't seen any of the program myself, but I have spoken to the artists individually and they seem to think it is awfully good. The first number will be a selection by George Olsen and his orchestra. I think this being our first program together, it is no more than fair that I have you meet Mr. Olsen personally. He is really a very charming fellow and one of the directors who comes to and from work on roller skates. I might add that Mr. Olsen is very, very handsome—I told you, George, I'd get that in—but as long as we are both on the air I won't have to worry about that. Oh, George, come here—I want you to say "hello" to the folks.
OLSEN	Hello, everybody!
BENNY	That was George Olsen, ladies and gentlemen. He rehearsed that speech all week. You know this is really all play with George, he doesn't have to work at all. I might say that Mr. Olsen is one of the wealthiest conductors in America. You know what I mean—he owns his own car. Of course, the other boys are in debt, too. George, what kind of a car have you?
OLSEN	Saxon.

BENNY	What?
OLSEN	Saxon.
BENNY	A Saxon! Well, that was my fault for asking. Is it a new one?
OLSEN	Oh, yes, a very late model.
BENNY	Well, you must have been in this country a long time.
OLSEN	What kind of a car have you got, Jack?
BENNY	A bicycle built for two. Now you can't go back any further than that. Well, George, I think we ought to get started. What's the first number?
OLSEN	"I Beg Your Pardon, Ma'amselle".
BENNY	What's that?
OLSEN	"I Beg Your Pardon, Ma'amselle." It's a little French number. Do you like French numbers, Jack?
BENNY	Do I? Mon Dieu, Mon Dieu.

1. I BEG YOUR PARDON, MA'AMSELLE   ORCHESTRA

BENNY	George, that was swell! And you look so important directing that orchestra, with the baton in your hand. I don't know—there's something about all you fellows when you stand there with that stick in the air—you demand attention. The thing I'd like to know, George, if the band didn't show up, what would you do with that stick?
GEORGE OLSEN	I'd throw it away and do what you're doing.
BENNY	(LAUGH) Always kidding. And now ladies and gentlemen, may I present a young lady, who is a star of many New York productions—Miss Ethel Shutta—you will remember Miss Shutta best in "Whoopee", playing opposite Eddie Cantor. Is that all right to mention Cantor's name here? Of course, I don't know. This is a new business with me. Ethel, come on over and say "hello."
MISS SHUTTA	Hello.
BENNY	Wasn't that clever? Miss Shutta is going to sing for us. She has a beautiful voice, too. She has a sort of nervous soprano. In fact, last week she had her nose lifted, so she could be heard in Philadelphia—and by the way, here is a little news for you. Miss Shutta is really Mrs. George Olsen, although I wouldn't go as far as to say that that's the reason she happens to be on this program; nevertheless, she's Mrs. George Olsen. And she's such a nice girl—I'm surprised that she's married to Olsen. And now, Miss Shutta will sing. What is that number?
MISS SHUTTA	I FOUND A MILLION DOLLAR BABY.

BENNY	I still feel very frenchy tonight, so Mon Dieux, Mon Dieux.

2. I FOUND A MILLION DOLLAR BABY   MISS SHUTTA

BENNY	Thanks, Ethel. You know, folks, I wish you could all be right here in the studio to see how sweet Miss Shutta looks. And all the time she was singing, I kept thinking of my girl. You know I get so sentimental. I really have a girl – she lives in Newark, New Jersey. You know the girl I go with when I'm in Newark. She's not what you'd call a good-looking girl. In fact she's quite homely, but then she can't stay in the house all the time. I imagine you folks have seen her picture in different magazines. She poses for the beauty 'ads', entitled "Before Taking". And she comes from a very fine family, although her father very often partakes of the forbidden beverage. It's all right for me to mention that, as they have no radio. In fact, her father drank everything in the United States, and then went up north to drink Canada Dry. (Whistle) Gee. I'm glad I thought of that joke – you know – the one about Canada Dry. I'm really supposed to mention it occasionally. After all, I owe it to my sponsors, and they might be listening in. Seriously though, do you realize, folks, that if you want a drink of Canada Dry, – we'll say just a glass—you don't have to buy it by the bottle. You can walk into any drug store or soda fountain, that has that big sign, "Canada Dry Made To Order", ask for a glass, and get it. I know you always have it in your home in bottles, but isn't it nice to know that you don't have to wait until you get home to drink it? Gee, I thought I did that pretty well for a new salesman. I suppose nobody will drink it now.
	And I could tell you a lot more about my girl, but I think we should have another selection by George Olsen and his boys. This time a very stirring number, called, "I Love A Parade", with a vocal refrain by the Messrs. Fran Frey, Bobby Borger and Bob Rice.

3. I LOVE A PARADE

BENNY	That was "I Love A Parade", ladies and gentlemen. The kind of a number that grips and thrills you—gives you that great feeling of patriotism, and makes you glad that you're an American. Personally, it didn't bother me very much, because I took a nap while the boys were playing it.
	Now, folks, in case you have forgotten, this is Jack Benny again. You know, the Canada Dry humorist. Say, I thought that was good—the Canada Dry humorist. I made that up myself.
OLSEN	It sounds like it.
BENNY	That witty retort was by George Olsen, ladies and gentlemen, proving again that he is still an orchestra leader. At that George has a great sense of humor—he told me a story the other day—do you mind if I tell it, George. It's really supposed to be true.

It's about George's uncle, who had been ill for a long time. He had what you would call "Labor Poisoning". You know what I mean, he just couldn't stand working, so his Doctor finally told him that he would have to get a lot of fresh air, do outside work, but not lift anything heavy. He told him that at no time was he to lift anything heavy, so his uncle got a job as garbage man in Scotland. I never heard that before, but the thing that kills me is Olsen telling a Scotch story, because Olsen himself is no spendthrift. In fact, he invited me to dinner the other night, much to his own surprise, and he paid the check with a $5.00 bill that was in his pocket so long, that Lincoln's eyes were blood-shot: however, he will now favor us with that very popular song hit, called, "Paradise." Why should his orchestra be an exception?

4. PARADISE   ORCHESTRA

OLSEN   This is George Olsen speaking. By this time, I know you are thoroughly bored listening to Jack, our Master of Ceremonies, and his Canada Dry humor, and telling you about made-to-order Canada Dry. We have a product that we also sell. That's music. So may we show you "How To Make Music".

5. HOW TO MAKE MUSIC   ORCHESTRA

BENNY   And that, ladies and gentlemen, is the way these boys "Make Music." Now if they could only play it. Mr. Olsen will now play "Come West Little Girl Come West" and I'm supposed to sing a chorus of this little number. And do you know, folks, that six months ago I couldn't sing a note? Really, I could not sing a note, but after taking three glasses every day of Canada Dry Made-To-Order Ginger Ale, I still am unable to sing, and can't even sign a note. The moral of this is drink that champagne of ginger ale—Canada Dry—and don't worry about signing notes. So for want of a better soloist, Miss Shutta will sing, "Come West Little Girl Come West".

6. COME WEST LITTLE GIRL COME WEST   ORCHESTRA & MISS SHUTTA

BENNY   Hello everybody, this is Kate Smith or—er—Jack Benny. See how nervous I am? I hope you'll forgive me, but I have a peculiar name to remember—Jack Benny. Sounds like two first names, doesn't it? But then you take that big operatic star—John Charles Thomas. There's a man with three first names. Maybe he was triplets—although I don't know why I bring that up, it really has nothing to do with made-to-order Canada Dry. I keep getting entirely off the subject. Don't forget folks, that you can walk into your neighborhood drugstore, or any drugstore after all, I don't care what drugstore—I'm only the Master of Ceremonies here. If I'm going to have to worry which drugstore you go into, I'll have my hands full—but go into any drugstore and order a glass—mind you—not a bottle—a glass of made-to-order

Canada Dry Ginger Ale and stagger out. Isn't it marvelous to think you can go into a drugstore and stagger out? Isn't it funny the things you can buy in a drugstore. I went in for an aspirin the other day, and come out with a new hat. I imagine the next number will be George Olsen… He is about to make his first appearance on this program. In fact, I am lucky to get in here at all. This is called, "Drums in my Heart", with Miss Shutta and Fran Frey.

George, now start this number and try to finish all together if you can.

7. DRUMS IN MY HEART   ORCHESTRA

BENNY   That, ladies and gentlemen, was the last number of our first program, on the 2nd of May. Are you sleeping? Hope you'll be with us again Wednesday! In fact, I hope I'll be here Wednesday. Well, good night then.

OLSEN   All aboard! All aboard! (RINGS BELL—BEGIN SIGNATURE)

ANNOUNCER (OVER SIGNATURE)

Ladies and gentlemen, we are concluding the first program in a new series sponsored by Canada Dry, the ginger ale now available Made-To-Order at drug stores and soda fountains as well as in bottles. Canada Dry has presented Jack Benny, Ethel Shutta and George Olsen and his music. This same group of artists will be with you at the same time Wednesday Evening.

May 4, 1932

STATION	WJZ	PROGRAM	CANADA DRY GINGER ALE, INC.
	AND	DATE	WEDNESDAY, MAY 4th, 1932
	BLUE NETWORK	TIME	TIME 9:30-10:00 P.M. (E.D.T.) |оборо
			(REVISED 5/4/32)

[Ed note: cover page missing from original script]

SIGNATURE:

ANNOUNCER Tonight Canada Dry, the champagne of ginger ales, presents the second in a series of programs to advertise the new Canada Dry Made-To-Order, which you can now buy by the glass at drug stores and soda fountains. This series features George Olsen and his music, Miss Ethel Shutta, the star of many Broadway successes, and that suave comedian, and famous master of Ceremonies and Canada Dry Humorist — Jack Benny.

BENNY Greetings, old friends, and welcome to our program, new friends. This is Jack Benny, folks—Benny, B like in Broke, E like in Ego, N like in Pneumonia and the other N, line in Double Pneumonia and Y line in Yolin. Anyway, to make a long story short, this is Jack Benny.

This is the second program of the new made-to-order Canada Dry series, proposed by Canada Dry, sponsored by Canada Dry and paid for by Canada Dry, of the people, by the people and for the people. Thought it would be a good idea to mention Canada Dry as often as possible right now and have it over with. I hope there is no doubt in your mind now, that this is the Canada Dry Program.

Miss Ethel Shutta and George Olsen have graciously consented to reappear for this program. I also have been hanging around the microphone since Monday. I'm no fool. Mr. Olsen, who owns the orchestra and part of his tuxedo, will start his part of the program with a very merry, optimistic number, called, "Jolly Good Company", which he dedicates to the boys in his band and what a jolly crowd they are. Heigh-ho, not three of them talk to each other. (Boys, smile a little bit, please.) They did that much better at rehearsal. Now, folks, their music may sound a little softer to you than usual to-night, but after all, this is a soft drink program. Wasn't that awful? — Suave Comedian. Of course, the boys could play louder, but right now, their instruments happen to be in the hands of the receivers. Let's go George.

1. JOLLY GOOD COMPANY   ORCHESTRA

BENNY Say, George, would you like to say "hello" to the folks?

OLSEN	"Hello", ladies and gentlemen, I'm very happy to be with you again.
BENNY	I'm not only happy but surprised. By the way, George, do you know what I think would be a good idea—now that you have met the folks, personally, maybe they would like to know a few things about you, sort of an impromptu interview—remember your lines? You don't mind being interviewed, do you, George? I know you're so modest.
OLSEN	No, I would rather like it.
BENNY	How about getting Ethel in it? Oh Mrs. Olsen.
MISS SHUTTA	Yes, Jack.
BENNY	George, remember your wife, Mrs. Olsen?
OLSEN	Oh yes, how do you do?
BENNY	Ethel, I'm going to ask you and George a few personal questions. This might be interesting to our audience. George, how old are you?
OLSEN	I'm forty-two.
MISS SHUTTA	He's thirty-nine.
BENNY	Well, everything is being reduced now-a-days. where were you born, George.
OLSEN	Portland, Oregon.
MISS SHUTTA	He was born in Seattle.
BENNY	Well, that's Close. You know it's unusual – as a rule a person is just born in one town at a time. You must have had a hard time running between Portland and Seattle. What's your favorite pastime?
OLSEN	Golf.
MISS SHUTTA	Pinochle.
BENNY	Mine is ringing door bells. I would like to ask you one more question—try and answer it without the echo. How long have you been connected with music?
MISS SHUTTA	He's been a drummer for six years.
BENNY	Well, Ethel, as long as we can't keep you out of this, how about asking—you a few?
MISS SHUTTA	All right.
BENNY	How old are you?
MISS SHUTTA	Twenty-four.
BENNY	(ORCHESTRA LAUGHS) Boys, a little professional courtesy, please. So you're twenty-four—remember, I'm supposed to be the comedian. After all, the best ten years of a woman's life is between twenty-four and twenty-five. Where were you born?

MISS SHUTTA	Pittsburgh, thank you.
BENNY	Don't thank me—I'm just here doing my work. When did you arrive in this country?
MISS SHUTTA	I said I was born in Pittsburgh.
BENNY	Oh, yes, my error, I happened to be looking at George. Have You any Children?
MISS SHUTTA	No, I'm sorry—we have no children.
BENNY	Oh, that's all right—nobody's complaining. Well, Ethel, we can't keep this up all night—how about singing a little song now?
MISS SHUTTA	All right.
BENNY	You know she was going to sing anyway, but I'm supposed to ask her.

2. HUMMING TO MYSELF   MISS SHUTTA

BENNY	I just received a telegram from one of our in-listeners, asking me what is meant by Canada Dry Made-To-Order at soda fountains. I imagine a lot of you folks might be interested in the explanation—in fact, I would like to know something about it myself. However, with what little I know, I shall try to make it as clear as possible. If you walk into a drug store and ask for a glass of Canada Dry Made-To-Order at the fountain, here's exactly what happens:—If you're fortunate enough to find the soda clerk available; that is not too busy making sandwiches, polishing the glasses or, if you can get him to talk to you at all, ask him for a glass of Canada Dry Made-To-Order, then he will put the right amount of the Canada Dry Ginger Ale syrup in the bottom of the glass and add carbonated water from the fountain into it—just the way you make a soda—that is Canada Dry Made-to-order. You see how easy it is. The most difficult part will be to get in touch with the soda clerk, but once you do, the rest is simple.
BENNY	And now another selection by George Olsen and his Public Enemies. Mr. Olsen will lead the number and the boys will follow him—out of the studio. Now take it easy, George, you know one thing about these programs, you don't have to exert yourself playing the numbers. You know what I mean, don't take yourself too seriously, because I bet there are a lot of bridge games going on tonight that we haven't even disturbed. The title of this number is "Sing A New Song" and it's a request. Someone just sent in a telegram—it says, "Mr. Olsen – please play Sing A new Song Wednesday Night and I will be listening in Friday afternoon." George, can you make this last until Friday?

3. SING A NEW SONG   ORCHESTRA

OLSEN	This is George Olsen. Oh, Jack, do you mind if I introduce this number—it's kind of a novel thing and I'd like to announce it myself. You don't mind, do you?

BENNY	All right, it's O.K. with me, George – but I would suggest that you try to make the announcement in English, if possible. But just before you start this, I would like to tell you something confidential. I don't know whether I ought to bring it up here or not, but there has been some complaint about your cornet player. You know the one with big nose. You know, George, that's the largest awning I've ever seen on a man.
OLSEN	Well, he can't help that, Jack.
BENNY	I know, George, but he doesn't have to go around frightening the boys. My, what a nose—I'll bet he can smoke a cigar under a shower.
OLSEN	Makes announcement

4. I'LL MISS YOU IN THE EVENING   ORCHISTRA

BENNY	That Was "I'll Miss You In The Evening", folks, and Canada Dry has spared no expense in giving the boys a real atmosphere for this number—in fact, right now in the studio there's a full moon smiling down at Olsen; there are hundreds of trees with millions of leaves and birds singing in the tree-tops. I Know birds as a rule do not sing in the evening, but I can't help that. I'm only the Master of Ceremonies. You know with the depression even the birds didn't go south this winter—although a few of them went as far as Washington to find out what's the big idea. And now, another number by Mr. Olsen, folks, Olsen—O like in he owes me money, L like he lied when he borrowed it, S like what a sap I was, E like in what an Easy Mark, N like in Never Again. But before they play this number, I'm supposed to say something for the benefit of my sponsors. All I can think of right now is Canada Dry—isn't that funny? I wonder if that can be it? Well, anyway, sometimes your eyes deceive you, often your ears deceive you, but your taste, never—it knows Canada Dry. Oh, well, go ahead boys—and by the way the number is "I Know You're Lying", with the assistance of Fran Frey and Miss Shutta and the Four Marx Brothers.

5. I KNOW YOU'RE LYING   ORCH., MISS SHUTTA, FRAN FREY

BENNY	Say George, I'd like to try out something tonight, if I may. You know, I don't know whether you know this or not, but I used to be in pictures. Of course, I've been away from the screen now for a couple of years, but I am still indirectly connected with it. I'm a sort of scenario writer. I have one that I wrote about a year ago. I still have it, and I'd like to have your approval on it before I send it in to the different studios. I have a nucleus of it here.
GEORGE	WHAT?
BENNY	A nucleus. We'll both look that up later. You see, George, I happen to be very fond of California, and this story is all about the wonderful California climate and air that we hear so much about in the East. You know, we always hear about how wonderful

	the weather is in California. I spent two weeks there last winter and they had fourteen unusual days. Although one thing I like about Los Angeles—no matter how hot it is in the daytime it's always cool in Alaska. Well, anyway, the opening scene takes place in southern California—Los Angeles where a boy and his sister have been living for about ten or fifteen years, and the sister decided to take a trip to New York City, which she does. Well, on the train she becomes a classical dancer. She becomes a dancer. This she learns from trying to get into her clothes in an upper berth. Get the continuity? Well, anyway, she arrives in New York and after two or three days becomes very ill due to the change of climate, so she wires her brother to join her at once, and her brother jumps on a bicycle in Los Angeles and rides all the way into New York, and upon his arrival he finds his sister seriously ill. In fact, she's on her deathbed, and the boy realizes her condition, and he punctures the tire of his bicycle and the wonderful California air immediately cures his sister. I don't know whether to send that in or not. What do you think, George?
GEORGE	WELL, Jack, to tell you the truth, I wasn't listening.
BENNY	Well, that was sweet of you, George. The next selection will be by George Olsen and his Australian Woodchoppers. They will play "Rose Room".

6. ROSE ROOM   ORCHESTRA

BENNY	That, ladies and gentlemen, was the last number of our second program on the fourth of May, and this is Jack Benny talking. Are you restless, hum? Hope to see you next Monday, and don't forget folks, "When the ginger ale comes over the fountain—Well—goodnight then—

ANNOUNCER (Over signature)

    Ladies and gentlemen, we are concluding the second program of a series, sponsored by Canada Dry, the ginger ale now available, made-to-order at drug stores and soda fountains, as well as in bottles. Canada Dry has presented Jack Benny, Ethel Shutta and George Olsen and his music. This same group of artists will be with you at the same time Monday evening.

May 9, 1932

STATION	WJZ	PROGRAM	CANADA DRY GINGER ALE, INC.
	AND	DATE	MONDAY, MAY 9, 1932
	BLUE NETWORK	TIME	9.30 - 10:00 P.M. (E.D.T.)

SIGNATURE—JOLLY GOOD COMPANY

1.	HOW CAN YOU SAY YOU LOVE ME	DoS B & H	ORCHESTRA & GARDNER
2.	IS I IN LOVE	DOs B & H	ORCHESTRA AND MISS SHUTTA
3.	THREE GUESSES	SANTLY	ORCHESTRA & FRAN FREY
4.	AUF WIEDERSEHN, MY DEAR	DoS B & H	ORCHESTRA & JERRY BAKER
5.	SAY from "HOT-CHA"	DoS B & H	ORCHESTRA & CHORUS
6.	HELLO GORGEOUS	D D & G	ORCHESTRA, MISS SHUTTA &FRAN FREY
7.	SOMEBODY LOVES YOU	MORRIS	ORCHESTRA

SIGNATURE -- ROCKABYE MOON

SIGNATURE — ROCKABYE MOON

SIGNATURE: JOLLY GOOD COMPANY

ANNOUNCER	Again Canada Dry, the champagne of ginger ales, presents a program to advertise the new Canada Dry made-to-order by the glass, which is now available at soda fountains. This program features George Olsen and his music, Miss Ethel Shutta, the star of many Broadway successes, and that Canada Dry humorist, Jack Benny. Just to vary things a little, Mr. Olsen and the boys start the program tonight with "HOW CAN YOU SAY YOU LOVE ME?" The vocal chorus is by Dick "Hot-cha" Gardner.

1. HOW CAN YOU SAY YOU LOVE ME   ORCHESTRA & GARDNER

ANNOUNCER	All right, Jack Benny, it's your turn.
BENNY	Thanks, Eddie. That's some introduction. You know, Eddie, this is our third program, and you and I haven't even spoken to each other.
ANNOUNCER	Oh, that's all right, Jack. I know you're busy.
BENNY	I know, but you've been so nice to me – giving me those lovely eulogies and everything, and I haven't even introduced you. Now, friends, I want you to meet Mr. Eddie Thorgerson.
THORGERSON	Good evening, everybody.
BENNY	That was our announcer, folks. An announcer is really a master of ceremonies who doesn't take as many chances. I'd like to describe Mr. Thorgerson to you. He's a tall, handsome fellow, blue eyes, nice sleek Hollywood hair, and he has the cutest little mustache that I've ever seen. And he has it trained. Did you ever see a trained mustache? When he's happy and gay it curls upwards, and when he's sad and gloomy it curls down. Right now his mustache happens to be down, so I'd better be careful what I say. (Announcer laughs). He's laughing now. There it goes up again. Of

	course, there are all kinds of mustaches, but he looks to me like he swallowed Mickey Mouse and left the tail hanging out. You don't mind these little things I say about you, do you Eddie?
THORGERSON	No, that's all right.
BENNY	Now, ladies and gentlemen, a real cute number called "IS I IN LOVE," with a vocal refrain by Miss Ethel Shutta, and played by George Olsen and his Tearful Troubadours. Let's away.
2. IS I IN LOVE	ORCHESTRA & MISS SHUTTA
BENNY	That was Miss Ethel Shutta singing. Oh Ethel.
MISS SHUTTA	What is it, Jack?
BENNY	Do you like broadcasting better than the stage?
MISS SHUTTA	Yes, Jack. But don't you think I am as good here as I was on the stage?

[page 3 of the script in the Library of Congress collection is missing, and there is no copy of this episode in Benny's UCLA papers.]

BENNY	(monologue in progress about latest contest)… Or a handful of Canada Dry with your initials on it. All we ask you to do is to write us a letter of twenty thousand words, no more, no less, twenty thousand words, briefly explaining why you like Canada Dry Made-To-Order at the fountain. First, you must go to your favorite fountain, order twelve glasses of Canada Dry Made-To-Order one at a time, and give us a trial. All you have to do is send us twelve affidavits – one for each drink – witnessed by the soda clerk, the proprietor and the mayor of your city. We will pick the three best letters telling why you like Canada Dry for the prizes. The winner of the first prize will get the second prize and the winner of the second prize will receive the first prize if he's not careful. We will have four judges selected by four other judges who will select the four judges. This contest can be closed without notice, to make room for the new Canada Dry contest which will start Wednesday at 9:30 Eastern Daylight Saving Time, and anytime at all in the West. If anybody knows what I am talking about, please add that to your letter and enlighten me. And now, the next selection will be that famous German selection, "Auf Wiedersehn," which translated into English means, "River Stay Way from My Door." Go ahead, George.
4. AUF WIEDERSEHN	ORCHESTRA
BENNY	That is to me a beautiful number – Auf Wiedersehn. I always liked those hot tunes. Isn't it funny? Here we are in America listening to "Auf Wiedersehn," while right now in Germany the biggest hit is "Minnie the Moocher." Say George, what does "Auf Wiedersehn" really mean?

OLSEN	Well, I don't know how to explain it, Jack. Well, for instance, you ask me to lend you ten dollars.
BENNY	You want me to ask you for ten dollars. All right, George, let me have ten dollars.
GEORGE	Auf Wiedersehn!
BENNY	I see. Well, you see, folks, what Auf Wiedersehn really means. It means that if you happen to be playing poker with Olsen, and he opens the pot, you could throw away four kings. And now, another number called "Say," from that big Broadway extravaganza – "Hot – Cha." Mr. Olsen will direct, the boys will sing, and I will relax.

5. SAY from HOT-CHA   ORCHESTRA & CHORUS

BENNY	That was three broken down boys imitating a phonograph record – or – er- rather three boys imitating a broken down phonograph record. Say George, I just noticed that during the last number one of your saxophone players was sound asleep.
OLSEN	That's all right, Jack, we weren't playing very loud.
BENNY	I know, George, but he kept snoring all through the number. I think he should either play the saxophone or snore in the right key.
OLSEN	Well now Jack, do me a favor, will you?
BENNY	Just a minute George – remember what you were going to say. This is the Canada Dry Made-to-Order-Ginger-Ale-Sold-By-The-Glass-At-All-Fountains-program. Now George, what did you say?
OLSEN	Well, what I started to say was you just attend to your jokes and I'll take care of the orchestra.
BENNY	I'm sorry, George. It just happens that I have a good ear for music. I don't know whether or not you know it, but I'm a very good violinist myself. When I was a kid I worked under Kreisler for years.
OLSEN	The coupe or the sedan? (ORCHESTRA LAUGHS)
BENNY	Now folks, don't forget. This is the Canada Dry ginger ale program.
OLSEN	(LAUGHS) All right Jack. By the way, that's a new suit you have on tonight, isn't it?
JACK	Yes. I was hoping you'd notice it. I bought it yesterday. Paid ninety dollars for it.
OLSEN	That's a lot of money.
BENNY	Yes, but I got nine pairs of pants with the suit. Of course, I haven't got them all on. I guess they gave me more than one pair of pants to take my mind off the coat. Of course, the coat is a little roomy, but then it was made that way.
OLSEN	Isn't that a ready-made suit?

BENNY	Oh, no. It was made to order – That is, it was really made for somebody else, but I bought the ticket.
OLSEN	I think the ticket would fit you better than the suit. (ORCHESTRA LAUGHS)
BENNY	Did you hear that laugh? What a fool I am trying to buck the union. Well, the studio is packed with Olsen's relatives, and they request him to play another number called "Hello Gorgeous." This will be sung by Miss Shutta and Fran Frey. They'll make merry and I'll make up some new jokes.

6. HELLO GORGEOUS   ORCH., MISS SHUTTA & FRAN FREY

BENNY	That was "Hello Gorgeous," played by George Olsen and his Cornfed Cuties. Before I introduce our next number, I want to remind you of the Canada Dry contest which was started ten minutes ago and will end abruptly Wednesday night. In fact, we have already received a wire regarding the contest, by someone who suspected it, and I'd like to read you the wire. "Dear Canada Dry Sold by the Glass at All Fountains": We wish you success in your new contest. Of course, we have been trying to win contests for years, but so far we have lost our home…

[Final pages of May 9, 1932 script are also missing.]

May 11, 1932

STATION	WJZ AND BLUE NETWORK	PROGRAM	CANADA DRY GINGER ALE, INC.
		DATE	WEDNESDAY, MAY 11TH, 1932
		TIME	9:30-10:00 P.M. (E.D.T.)

SIGNATURE

1.	OOH, THAT KISS	HARMS	ORCHESTRA & FRAN FREY
2.	THERE I GO DREAMIMG AGAIN	DeS.B.& H	ORCHESTRA & MISS SHUTTA
3.	CPAZY PEOPLE	FEIST	ORCHESTRA & FRAN FREY
4.	WHEN THE SUN KISSES THE WORLD GOODBYE	DeS.B.& H	ORCHESTRA & MISS SHUTTA
5.	I'M PINS AID NEEDLES IN LOVE WITH YOU	SANTLY	ORCHESTRA, FRAN FREY AID MISS SEUTTA
6.	THEN THE LIGHTS ARE SOFT AND LOW	KEIT-ENGEL	ORCHESTRA & MISS SHUTTA
7.	GOT A DATE WITH AN ANGEL	HARMS	ORCHESTRA & JERRY BAKER

SIGNATURE – JOLLY GOOD COMPANY

ANNOUNCER   Again Canada Dry, the champagne of ginger ales, presents a program to advertise the new Canada Dry made-to-order by the glass, which is now available at soda fountains. This program features George Olsen and his music, Miss Ethel Shutta, the star of many Broadway successes, and their Canada Dry humorist, Jack Benny.

The first number on the program "Ooh That Kiss." Fran Frey sings the vocal chorus.

1. OOH THAT KISS   ORCHESTRA & FRAN FREY

ANNOUNCER   Okay, Jack Benny. You're next.

BENNY   Hello somebody. This is Jack Benny talking. There will be a slight pause while you say "What of it." After all, I know your feelings, folks, I used to listen in myself. Well now that we understand each other, this is the fourth program of the Canada-Dry-Ginger-Ale-Made-To-Order-By-The-Glass-at- all-Soda Fountains-Series. That's my recitation this week. Next Week, I will recite the "Shooting of Dan McGrew" … You remember that one. "A bunch of the boys were whooping it up at the Malumet saloon, when in walked a guy for some Canada Dry with a great big toy balloon." James Finecomb Reilly. I am going to recite that next week by special omission of the copyright owners. Of course, I am not much at poetry, but after all, what is a program without a poem or two? It generally much better. Mr. Olsen and his orchestra will now play a very soothing number called "THERE I GO DREAMING AGAIN," which will be sung by Ethel Shutta while Olsen and his boys do the dreaming. You know that reminds me of something I told you last week. Remember my telling you how wealthy Olsen is? Well, I just found out something very funny. Of course, I don't know how it will strike you. Olsen owns four automobiles, three yachts, two aero planes and six motorcycles, and yet he walks in his sleep. Isn't that funny? Well, maybe I'm wrong. Go ahead, George.

2. THERE I GO DREAMING AGAIN   ORCHESTRA & ETHEL SHUTTA

BENNY   That was "There I Go Dreaming Again," by special permission of two veronal tablets. Say Ethel!

MISS SHUTTA	Yes, Jack.
BENNY	Do you know, Ethel, your voice is improving with each program.
MISS SHUTTA	Do you really think so, Jack?
BENNY	Well, nevermind what I think. I'm just saying what we rehearsed. You remember – we rehearsed this morning. Now let's start it all over. Ethel, I think your voice is improving with each program.
ETHEL	Thanks.
BENNY	Yes, I think it has a much finer quality and you're putting more soul into it.
ETHEL	Well, that's nice to hear it from you.
BENNY	Well, to what do you owe this improvement?
BENNY & SHUTTA	I drink Made-To-Order Canada Dry sold by the glass at all soda fountains.
BENNY	You just heard what Miss Shutta, late of the Follies, said and it was entirely unsolicited. Thank you, Ethel. Here's your check. Don't worry about dropping it. It'll bounce back. You know, silly or not, this is only our fourth broadcast, and I'd like to read you some of the wires and fan mail we received. Eddie, let me have a few of those wires, will you? Thanks. Here's one that I received from Louisville, Kentucky. From Miss Constantine Syriococapopulous. That must be an old established family. It couldn't be a new name. Anyway, it says:

> "DEAR MR. BENNY: I UNDERSTAND YOU ARE MASTER OF CEREMONIES ON THE CANADA DRY PROGRAM TONIGHT. HOPE YOU ARE BETTER THAN THE FELLOW WHO WAS THERE MONDAY NIGHT."

Here's a wire from my favorite uncle in Waukegan, Illinois:

> "MR. JACK BENNY, c/o WJZ, NEW YORK: MY DEAR NEPHEW: LIKE YOU BETTER THAN ANYONE ON THE AIR. YOUR PROGRAMS ARE ABSOLUTELY MARVELOUS AND I WILL BE LOOKING FORWARD TO HEARING YOU EVERY MONDAY AND WEDNESDAY. PLEASE SEND ME FIFTY DOLLARS."

That was my uncle, all right. Now he has something else to look forward to. Here's a letter from Chicago, Illinois. It says "Dear Colonel Stoopnagle". Oh, that's a mistake. Thinks I'm Uncle Don. Oh, George, here's a letter for you. It's signed John MacTavish.

GEORGE	Go ahead, read it, Jack.
BENNY	By the way, there's money in it. It says:

> "DEAR MR. OLSEN: ENCLOSED FIND A ONE DOLLAR BILL. PLEASE PLAY "GOOD NIGHT SWEET HEART" AND SEND ME THE FIFTY CENTS CHANGE. " (Olsen laughs)

	Imagine offering Olsen half a dollar to play a song. Well, he took it. Oh, here's a very sweet wire from a hospital in Philadelphia.
	"DEAR MR. BENNY: I AM A PATIENT IN THIS HOSPITAL AND AT THE PRESENT TIME HAVE THE USE OF ONLY ONE ARM AND ONE LEG. I HEARD YOUR BROADCAST MONDAY NIGHT AND AS SOON AS I CAN USE BOTH ARMS AND BOTH LEGS HEAVEN HELP YOU."
	Now, isn't that sweet?
OLSEN (WHISPERS)	Jack, that's all the mail.
BENNY	Well folks, lack of time prevents us from reading the thousands of letters that are here in the studio. And now, Fran Frey sings a crazy tune called "CRAZY PEOPLE." Of course, I'm all right.

3. CRAZY PEOPLE

BENNY	That gives you a rough idea of what the Canada Dry sponsors are paying for. Say, George, where do you get all those crazy tunes?
OLSEN	Oh, I dig them up, I have a lot of tunes like that.
BENNY	Well George, I think you deserve a lot of credit for the way you arrange those numbers. You know, you're one of the most resourceful leaders I've ever known.
OLSEN	<u>Thanks, Jack</u>. Now I want to tell you something. I think you're one of the best masters of ceremonies I've ever been associated with.
BENNY	<u>Thanks, George</u>. You certainly know your business.
OLSEN	<u>Thanks, Jack</u>. And you certainly know yours.
BENNY	George, between you and me, two finer liars never met. You know, folks, we are two awful liars, with or without a microphone. But to show you what a liar Olsen is, when he wants to feed his own dog he has to get someone else to call him.
OLSEN	Well Jack, last time I whistled to feed my dog, you turned around.
BENNY	Well, you know how tough times are. The next number, ladies and gentlemen—
OLSEN	Say Jack. What about that contest you started on Monday night?
BENNY	What contest?
OLSEN	What contest? Why that thing you started Monday night, asking everybody to send in letters and you'd tell them the results tonight.
BENNY	I don't remember anything about that.

OLSEN	Well that's a fine one. You get everybody sending in thousands of letters and here you don't even remember it.
BENNY	Oh that contest. Oh yes. I forgot all about it. Certainly we have thousands of letters here. Ladies and gentlemen. You remember that tournament we started Monday night asking you to send in a letter of twenty thousand words, briefly explaining why you liked Canada Dry Made To Order At The Fountain? Well, we have already received 94,308 letters (WHISTLE). Oh wait a minute. Here's the letter carrier. That makes it 94,309 letters trying for the valuable prizes offered by Canada Dry. While Miss Shutta sings the next number I'll go through each and every letter very carefully. She's going to sing "WHEN THE SUN KISSES THE WORLD GOODBYE" and goes tabloid. Played by George Olson and his Bearded Ladies.

4. WHEN THE SUN KISSES THE WORLD GOODBYE   **ORCHESTRA & MISS SHUTTA**

OLSEN	Ladies and gentlemen. This is George Olsen. I will have to introduce our next number as Mr. Benny is still busy looking through the contest letters. So with his permission we will play "I'M PINS AND NEEDLES IN LOVE WITH YOU", with the assistance of Miss Shutta and Fran Frey.

5. I'M PINS AND NEEDLES IN LOVE   **ORCHESTRA, MISS SHUTTA & FRAN FREY**

BENNY	George, George, a terrible thing has happened. In looking through some of the letters, ladies and gentlemen I find that we forgot to mention a very important detail last night, which means that you will have to send us in another letter. I will explain this immediately. Of course, your old letters will not be wasted, as we have to paper the walls of our studio. Please disregard the rules we gave you last Monday for this contest, we have changed our mind, and will have to simplify it. We notice that all our letters come from grown-ups. We have none from the children. In fact, one of our letters had gray hair and was postmarked 1864 B.C. – Before Contest. Now, in order for the babies to get in on this, — Hello Babies (RATTLE) (ORCHESTRA ga-gas) here are the new rules. Walk up to your favorite soda fountain, order a glass of Canada Dry Ginger Ale Made To Order By The Glass and sip it through a straw — Of course, this is optional. You can either sip it through a straw or drink it right out loud. But if you _do_ happen to sip it through a straw, save It! Don't go a-losin' it. Why? Send it to your Canada Dry cleaners to be pressed. Then, on one side of the straw write us why you like Canada Dry Made To Order by The Glass, and on the other side, write the Star Spangled Banner. Mail your straws to us at your earliest convenience, as the straw hat season opens next week. We will not tell you what the prize is yet, but keep a scallion in mind. And now, to get on with our program. Miss Shutta will sing "WHILE LIGHTS ARE SOFT AND LOW," accompanied by George Olsen and his Unmounted Police.

6. WHILE LIGHTS ARE SOFT AND LOW   ORCHESTRA & SHUTTA

BENNY	Say, George, would you repeat that last number you just played, I would like to play a chorus on the violin.
OLSEN	You don't play the violin, do you Jack? I thought you were kidding me the other day.
BENNY	Oh yes, I play a little – I'm not a Galli Curci, but I do fairly well. I used to play in vaudeville and there was one number of mine, which was a favorite. It's a little French song called, La Mo To Jour, La Mo. You know, that, don't you, George?
OLSEN	Yes, I think we can play that.
BENNY	Well, wait a minute, I want to explain this number. Ladies and gentlemen, I'm going to play a little French song and as I play it in its native tongue, I think a word of explanation might not be amiss. Years ago, during an Algerian uprising, an Arab Chieftain stole the daughter of a French merchant and carried her away to his camp in the desert. And although he held her a captive, he treated her with utmost kindness and as a matter of fact, fell desperately in love with her. Now, during the period of her incarceration — this is Jack Benny speaking — she reciprocated his love and as he held her madly in his arms, she took the dagger from his belt and stabbed him with a fatal thrust – and made good her escape. And this song, ladies and gentlemen, is the dying wail of the Arab. Now, that I've explained that, there will be no use playing the song. I'll save it for some other time, so now, another number called "GOT A DATE WITH AN ANGEL", sung by Jerry Baker and played by George Olsen and his Ginger-Alians.

7. GOT A DATE WITH AN ANGEL   JERRY BAKER AND ORCHESTRA

BENNY	That was our last number of our fourth program on the eleventh of May. Are you still conscious? Hmm? …Remember the new rules for the contest and we are anxious to get your letters. And by the way, if you happen to have any old clothes or shoes that you're about to throw away, we would appreciate it very much if you would send then to the boys in Olsen's Orchestra. By that I mean instead of throwing your old shoes at the cats in the back yard, send them in here to the boys. They make the same noises and wear the shoes besides.
	GONG
	Goodnight then.

SIGNATURE — ROCK A BYE MOON

ANNOUNCER	Ladies and gentlemen. Canada Dry is saying goodnight until next Monday at this same time, when the champagne of ginger ales will again present Jack Benny, Ethel

Shutta, and George Olsen and his music. Canada Dry is now on sale, Made-To-Order by the glass, at soda fountains, as well as in bottles. This is the National Broadcasting Company.

May 16, 1932

STATION	WJZ AND BLUE NETWORK	PROGRAM	CANADA DRY GINGER ALE, INC.
		DATE	MONDAY, MAY 16TH, 1932
		TIME	9:30-10:00 P.M.

A. SIGNATURE

1. WHO — ORCHESTRA & TRIO

2. MY MOM — DONALDSON, DOUGLAS & GUMBLE — ORCHESTRA AND BADLER

3. SHE DIDN'T SAY YES
   from "Cat and the Fiddle" — HARMS — ORCHESTRA, MISS SHUTTA, FRAK FREY

4. THAT'S HOW WE MAKE MUSIC — ORCHESTRA

5. WHEN WE'RE ONE — FAMOUS MUSIC — ORCHESTRA AND SHUTTA

6. GETTING ALONG WITH YOUR GAL — ORCHESTRA, SHUTTA AND FREY

Z. SIGNATURE

SIGNATURE – JOLLY GOOD COMPANY

ANNOUNCER　　Again Canada Dry, the champagne of Ginger Ales, presents a program to advertise the new Canada Dry made-to-order by the glass, now available at soda fountains. This program features George Olsen and his music, Miss Ethel Shutta, the star of many Broadway successes, and the Canada Dry humorist, Jack Benny.

The first number on the program is "WHO". Fran Frey, Bobby Borger, and Bob Rice sing the vocal chorus.

1. WHO　　　　　　　　ORCHESTRA & TRIO

ANNOUNCER　　And now I take great pleasure in introducing that effervescent comedian – Jack Benny.

BENNY　　Hello anybody. Remember me? I'm the fellow that's been annoying you every Monday and Wednesday. Did you notice the way Mr. Thorgerson introduced me tonight? He called me the effervescent comedian. I kind of like that. Of course, I've been called everything, but never that. Funny thing, but at rehearsal I asked him what effervescent means, and he said, "Well, effervescent for you we would have a very nice program." And that, ladies and gentlemen, is Canada Dry humor. Well, anyway, this is Jack Benny talking. – B as in Canada Dry, E as in Made-to-order, N as in Sold by the Glass, another N as in At All Soda Fountains, and Y because it's good. Now, we're not going to bore you with good entertainment like other programs. Our aim is to give the public what it wants, but the question is, "What does the public want?" One hundred and twenty million people have been trying to find out, and you're asking me. Well, all right, I'll tell you. Nobody knows what the public wants. But I do know that a glass of Canada Dry Made To Order never hurt anybody. And you can buy it at your favorite soda fountain made to order, – for a coin that rhymes with pickle. Or a larger glass for twice that hint. Get it? Well, that's enough of that, even though it is sold in a glass at all fountains. And now, to continue with our program – a very popular song called "MY MOM" played by George Olsen and his Symfunny Orchestra.

2. MY MOM	ORCHESTRA

BENNY   That was My Mom, ladies and gentlemen. My Mom. What a beautiful thought. It takes us back just two weeks ago to Mother's Day. Remember how we sent little remembrances to our mothers? Miss Shutta sent flowers to her mother. The boys in the orchestra sent candy and checks. And Olsen sent his laundry. George, I was only kidding.

OLSEN   It's all right, Jack. Everything's all right – I'll meet you outside.

BENNY   You know, folks, I never saw anyone work as hard as Olsen does on these programs. He's busy every minute. He's either rehearsing his band, or arranging the music, and in his spare time he polishes the instruments. I tell you, a fellow like that deserves a lot of credit. In fact, the only time he sleeps is when he's working. What a Trojan! And to think, years ago he was just a drummer in an orchestra. Then he lost one of his sticks and became a director.

And now, may I present Miss Ethel Shutta and Fran Frey, who will sing "SHE DIDN'T SAY YES", from "The Cat and The Fiddle." Are you all set, Ethel?

ETHEL   Yes, Jack, but before I sing I'd like to tell a joke I heard today. Do you mind?

BENNY   Oh, you want to tell a story first. Well, it's all right with me, but are you sure it's all right? I mean, is it something I've heard?

ETHEL   No, I don't think you've ever heard this one.

BENNY   Well, I'll tell you what. You see, we have to be very careful what we say on the radio, so I think you'd better whisper the story to me first, and then if it's all right you can tell it.

ETHEL   All right Jack.

BENNY   Pardon us a moment, please.

(WHISPERS)

Is that the story?

ETHEL   Yes.

BENNY   Ladies and gentlemen. Miss Shutta and Fran Frey will sing "SHE DIDN'T SAY YES," from "The Cat and The Fiddle."

3. SHE DIDN'T SAY YES	MISS SHUTTA AND FRAN FREY

BENNY   Say Ethel, you've been looking very well lately. Better than ever. How much do you weigh?

ETHEL   118 pounds.

BENNY	You weigh 118 pounds. That's without your lip rouge, of course.
ETHEL	Yes.
BENNY	118 pounds. Ethel, how old were you when you first started to drink Canada Dry?
ETHEL	Twenty-four.
BENNY	There you are, ladies and gentlemen – a gain of ninety-four pounds. You just heard what this young lady said – entirely unsolicited. What Canada Dry did for her will never happen to you. And. here's a letter we just received from a drinker of our beverage. This comes from a lady in Prosperity Corners, Iowa, – and how we've been looking for those corners! Well, here's the letter.

> *"Dear Slur: When I first started to drink Canada Dry Made To Order Ginger Ale By The Glass I weighed three hundred pounds. But since drinking I have lost one hundred pounds, but I have found a husband who weighs 110 pounds, which gives me a net gain of ten pounds. We now have two bouncing baby boys, and Owe it all to Canada Dry. We named the younger boy Olsen, because he plays on the linoleum, and we called the older boy Benny, because he's been talking for three years and we still can't understand him. Hoping this finds you and Olsen, I remain, Yours sincerely,*
>
> *Mrs. Veronica Twilt.*
>
> *P.S. Have seen your picture in our local paper and think you have an ideal face for broadcasting."*

Those are the kind of letters we like to get. And now, ladies and gentlemen, there has been a request for Mr. Olsen to repeat a number that was done on the opening program. And of course, Mr. Olsen and his boys play anything by request, as well as by ear. In fact, since we have started these broadcasts, some of them have even taken up music. George, would you like to announce this yourself? I know how you hate to do it, but come on over.

TERRIBLE CRASH

That's Olsen rushing to the microphone.

OLSEN	Introduces next number.

4. THAT'S' HOW WE MAKE MUSIC   ORCHESTRA

BENNY	Wasn't that cute? That number must have been requested by the lovers of Micky Mouse. And while the boys were playing, we gave our visitors in the studio lollipops and rattles. Olsen himself will be eight years old next Tuesday. Look at him. Right now he's got a great big smile on his face that's fading into a silly grin. And now, ladies and gentleman, what you have all been waiting for, — the progress of our contest.

DRUM ROLL AND FANFARE.

On account of the popularity of our contest that was started last Monday night, the Board of Directors got together and decided to continue it for at least another year, to give the children a chance to grow up and enter it. In picking the winners of this contest, we have already decided what the prizes might be. Now listen to this. How would you like to go to Siam for a three days vacation at our expense? Imagine spending three days with Uncle Siam without any cost to you except the boat fare. Siam – with its beautiful Eiffel Tower, Yangtse River, the pyramids, a trip down the Nile – a trip up the Hudson if you're not careful. Just think of it! Siam – with its sunken mountains and bone dry lakes; it Riviera and its castles in Spain. And at whose expense, ladies and gentlemen? Ah, that's the only thing that worries us. And remember, that is only the first prize. The second surprise – or – er – prize, will be just the reverse – there will be a trip from Siam right to the U.S.A. Our United States, with its beautiful Panama Canal – the Hawaiian Islands – and the 12-mile limit. Our third prize will be a hunting trip – hunting for the first two prizes. Of course, we have new rules governing this contest, which we will give you immediately following the next number. And now, Mr. Olsen and his Disconnected Yankees will play that very beautiful song "WHEN WE'RE ONE." I am very happy to state there will be no vocal chorus, by special permission of our sponsors – Canada Dry Ginger Ale Made To Order …(Music starts)

5. WHEN WE'RE ONE   **ORCHESTRA**

BENNY   Sold by the glass at any soda fountain. I announced there was to be no vocal chorus in that last number, but try and get out of it. And now, for the rules for our contest.

(WEAK FANFARE)

We have been receiving letters every day – some written in pencil, some in ink, and some in Pittsburgh. Of course, they really weren't all letters – some of them were warnings. We also have – now listen to those – (TELEPHONE BELLS RINGING) There are over eight hundred phone calls that we haven't even answered yet, asking about the contest. As per our request last Monday night, many straws were sent in with thoughts regarding Canada Dry written on them, but it turned out to be a straw vote. This is Jack Benny talking. And now for the new rules. Have the male member of your family – either father or brother – put on his stiff bosom dress shirt and stand perfectly still facing the radio. Then take a blue or red crayon and write clearly just twenty-five reasons why you think Canada Dry is the best beverage on the market. This must be written clearly across the bosom of the shirt – between the second button and the fifth rib. When you have finished this simple task, remove your father from the shirt and send us the shirt by parcel post – not the father, mind you, because in a recent contest over six hundred fathers were sent in by mistake, and they're still in the dead letter office. As a final warning, don't tell us you lost your shirt in this contest. I hope this is as clear to you as it is to us. Now go ahead, folks. Good luck, and I'll be a'rootin' for you. George, I think we're on the right track now.

GEORGE	Yes, and I certainly like the way you're handling this contest, and thanks for mentioning my name so many times during this program.
BENNY	That's all right, George. Anytime I can give you a plug I'll be glad to do it.
OLSEN	I know, Jack, and anytime I can give you a plug I'll give you one.
BENNY	Yes, but I hope it's not like the plug you gave me yesterday in the second race. What a horse that was.
OLSEN	Well, he came in, didn't he?
BENNY	Yes, but he took the Lincoln Highway.
OLSEN	How much did you lose on him?
BENNY	That horse cost me twelve dollars.
OLSEN	Well, you shouldn't bet so much.
BENNY	Bet nothing, I bought him. And now, a brand new song called "When You're Getting Along With Your Gal." Played by George Olsen and his Ex-Glass Blowers.

6. WHEN YOU'RE GETTING ALONG WITH YOUR GAL   ORCHESTRA

BENNY	That was the last number of the fifth program on the sixteenth of May. Are you sleeping? Hmm? And don't forget, folks, there's only two weeks until the first of June. The weather will be getting warmer, beverages will be in demand, so first of all I'll ask you what is thirst? Thirst, my friends, is just a mouthful of nonsense which can easily be cured at any soda fountain by asking the clerk for a glass of Canada Dry Made To Order Ginger Ale.
	We have to leave you now, and remember, we'll be back Wednesday night with some new tunes, new rules for the contest, new jokes, and puzzling riddles. And so to bed. Goodnight, then.

SIGNATURE – ROCKABYE MOON

ANNOUNCER	Canada Dry is saying goodnight until next Wednesday at this same time, when the champagne of ginger ales will again present Jack Benny, Ethel Shutta, and George Olsen and his music. Canada Dry is now on sale, made-to-order by the glass, at soda fountains, as well as in bottles. This is the National Broadcasting Company.

May 18, 1932

STATION	WJZ AND BLUE NETWORK	PROGRAM	CANADA DRY GINGER ALE, INC.
		DATE	WEDNESDAY, MAY 18, 1932
		TIME	9.30 - 10:00 P.M. (E.D.T.)

SIGNATURE—JOLLY GOOD COMPANY   CAMPBELL, DONNELLY

1.	WEDDING OF THE PAINTED DOLL from "HOLLYWOOD REVUE"	SHERMAN CLAY	ORCHESTRA & ETHEL SHUTTA
2.	THE TARTAR'S DAUGHTER	Unpublished L616	ORCHESTRA & FRAN FREY
3.	HUMMING TO MYSELF	DeS B & H	ORCHESTRA & ETHEL SHUTTA
4.	COLORS: (A) I'M BRINGING A RED RED ROSE (DONALDSON) (B) WHEN THE BLUE OF THE NIGHT (DeS B&H) (C) YES WE HAVE NO BANANAS (SHAPRIO) (D) LITTLE WHITE LIES (DONALDSON) (E) STARS AND STRIPES FOREVER (SOUSA)		ORCHESTRA
5.	LOVE MAKING WEATHER	TEAM AT WLW (?)	ORCHESTRA
6.	GOOFUS	FEIST	ORCHESTRA
7.	SOMEBODY LOVES YOU	MORRIS	ORCHESTRA

SIGNATURE – JOLLY GOOD MOON [sic] CAMPBELL, DONNELLY

N. DE VORE ADDS: Items queried (?) are inadequately identified and may be performed only on the sole responsibility of the sponsor of the program.

SIGNATURE – JOLLY GOOD MOON [sic] CAMPBELL, DONNELLY

N. DE VORE ADDS: Items queried (?) are inadequately identified and may be performed only on the sole responsibility of the sponsor of the program.

SIGNATURE: JOLLY GOOD COMPANY

ANNOUNCER   Again Canada Dry, the champagne of ginger ales, presents a program to advertise the new Canada Dry made-to-order by the glass, which is now available at soda fountains. This program features George Olsen and his music, Miss Ethel Shutta, the star of many Broadway successes, and that Canada Dry humorist, Jack Benny. Our program opens with an old favorite, "WEDDING OF THE PAINTED DOLL."

1. WEDDING OF THE PAINTED DOLL   ORCHESTRA

THORGERSEN   And now we will hear from our messer of ceremonies – Jack Benny.

BENNY   Hello nearly everybody, this is little Jack Benny talking. Benny – B as in Hive, E as in irritate, N as in alphabet soup another N as in the same soup and Y as in Vice President. We all know this is a rather late hour – at least here in the East—and that at this time mothers are usually singing their children to sleep. <u>But</u> who sings the mothers and fathers to sleep? That is the object of our programs, ladies and gentlemen. That is our aim – to sing and talk you to sleep, and to those of you who have already gone to bed, let me say this – several glasses of Canada Dry will not only pep you up, but will keep you awake, at least until our program is over. And that's something in times like this. And now, on with our entertainment. The next number will be a very novel number called "The Tarter's Darter," and will be sung as usual by Mr. Fran Frey, our vocalist. And by the way, ladies and gentlemen – I have introduced nearly everyone on this program but Mr. Frey. I must apologize. Say Fran, say something to our customers.

FREY   Hello everybody, I have been waiting for this chance to talk to you, and you don't know how glad I am to be here…

BENNY	All right, Fran. Never mind. I just wanted you to say hello. Mr. Frey is – er—what you would call a – er—reformed crooner, and he comes to us directly from the Metropolitan Opera House, where he was an usher for five years. Of course, that wasn't meant to be funny, ladies and gentlemen, because an usher at the Metropolitan Opera House is by no means a small position. I might say it is equivalent to a one-club bid in bridge. Are you tuned in, dummies? Hmm? For the benefit of those of you who do not play bridge, the dummies are the people who sit around and play while the fourth one goes out for a drink. Incidentally, this is the Canada Dry Program. However, to get back, Mr. Frey, who is still standing here, I might add that he has a very distinctive personality, and resembles three movie stars. He has Jimmy Durante's nose, Garbo's feet, and Gable's ears. In fact, he's a sort of a cross between the devil and the deep blue sea. And he's the kind of a fellow that <u>sips</u> Canada Dry Ginger Ale. You know what I mean – he's a sipper. I treated him to a glass last night and he made an evening of it. You can't make any money out of a guy like that. I could tell you more, but Mr. Frey is anxious to sing. He will be accompanied, of course, by George Olsen and his Hungry Hungarians.

2. THE TARTAR'S DAUGHTER   ORCHESTRA & FREY

BENNY	That's the silliest thing I've ever heard in my life – "The Tartar's Darter." What titles they're getting nowadays. I don't know where Olsen digs them up. And now, my followers…
OLSEN (interrupts)	Just a minute Jack. What do you mean – "my followers." You know I'm on this program too.
BENNY	I know, George, but whenever I mention myself, I always mean both of us. You and I are pals – fifty-fifty on everything.
OLSEN	Well, that's all right, then.
BENNY	For instance, you know that hundred dollars I owe you?
OLSEN	Yes.
BENNY	Well, I'm willing to split it.
OLSEN	Thanks, Jack. And to show you that I'm a regular fellow, I'll forget fifty of it.
BENNY	Okay, George, and I'll forget the other fifty.
(BOTH LAUGH)	
OLSEN	That was very funny, Jack, but you've told that before.
BENNY	What's the difference? You've been wearing that same suit for three years.
OLSEN	Well, it's a good looking suit, isn't it?
BENNY	You and it remind me of that popular song – "SHINE ON, HARVEST MOON."

OLSEN	Of course, Jack. You're the Beau Brummel of this outfit. How do you keep your clothes in such good shape?
BENNY	Well, George, I have a Japanese valet who keeps everything in tip-top shape. Yogi, come here. Yogi, this is Mr. Olsen. George, this is Yogi.
OLSEN	I'm glad to meet you. How do you like working for Jack Benny?
VALET (with Jewish accent)	Well, I'll tell you. It's dis vay.
BENNY	Get out of here.
OLSEN	I thought he was a Japanese.
BENNY	He is, but don't forget he's worked two years for Benny Rubin. And if Benny is listening in, I mean Georgie Jessel. The next number is "HUMMING TO MYSELF" and Ethel Shutta sings the vocal chorus.

3. HUMMING TO MYSELF   SHUTTA

BENNY	THAT was 'Humming to Myself," sung by that sweet and charming Ethel Shutta. What a sense of humor she has. Say Ethel, I'd like to tell that story you told me about George and your brother Frank. Do you mind?
ETHEL	No, Jack. Go ahead. It's all right with me.
BENNY	Well, it's the funniest thing I ever heard. I must tell them. You know, folks, this is really a true story. I'm going to tell it, Ethel.
ETHEL	Go ahead.
BENNY	Well, anyway, Ethel Shutta and George Olsen have been married for six years. Isn't that right, Ethel?
ETHEL	Six years and a week.
BENNY	Six years and a week. Gee, and it only seems like six years to George. Well, anyway, the second year they were married, Ethel's brother Frank came to visit them. He came for lunch one day and stayed six months. You know – one of those hanger – arounders? Of course, to appreciate this story you should know Ethel's brother. I mean he's one of those fellows when you first meet him you don't like him at all, and after you know him a while you hate him. Well anyway, George finally got tired of Frank hanging around, so he asked his wife how long her brother was going to stay, and Ethel said that she didn't know. They just couldn't get rid of him. So George said, "I've got a great idea! Tonight at dinner I'll start a big argument over the soup. You see, I'll say the soup is bad and you say it's good, and finally I'll ask your brother Frank what he thinks of it, and if he sides with either one of us we will tell him that he cannot agree with one or the other in the family and he'll have to leave." So that

night at dinner – this'll kill you – that night at dinner when the soup was served, George started the argument, and he said, "Ethel, this soup is awful tonight!" And Ethel said, "I think it's better than usual." So George – you'll scream at this – George said, "I think it's terrible," and he turned to her brother and he said, "Frank, what do you think of the soup?" And Frank said. "I don't know anything about it. I'm staying for four more weeks." From last reports, he's still with them, and Olsen is wearing his clothes.

OLSEN Say Jack, I'd like to introduce our next number.

OLSEN Introduces Color Tune.

BENNY Heliotrope routine.

4. COLOR TUNE

BENNY Is that the finish of that number, George?

OLSEN Yes.

BENNY Oh you should have kept that up two or three days. It's a shame to drop a high class thing like that. Now, let's play "Ring Around the Rosy." And now, ladies and gentlemen, the highlight of our program – the continuation of our Canada Dry contest.

(FANFARE)

I know you will all be glad to hear that our contest is coming along great. We have had returns from all points on the map. Some people have returned their radios, others have returned to their phonographs and our sponsors have returned to billboard advertising. In fact, the progress is phenomenal. Remember folks, on Monday night we told you that the first prize <u>might</u> be a trip to Siam? But remember this, anyone who is not a winner of this contest and takes the trip to Siam does so at his own risk. We have already received a postcard from the King of Siam congratulating us on our idea. Here's the card, which reads:

> Our natives are tickled black over the prospect of taking your winners to lunch. They will be the lunch. Seventy-five years ago we had a group of contest winners here for dinner. They were put in the pot and were they mad? Huh! They were boiling!

You just heard what the King of Siam said about Canada Dry Made To Order Ginger Ale Sold At All Fountains. Now we have also found that on account of the excellent results we are getting we are able to offer a fourth, fifth and sixth prize. Listen carefully. How would you like to own your own tooth brush? Think of it! Your own tooth brush, and each and every bristle yours.

(TELEPHONE BELL)

Hello. Hello. Yes, this is Jack Benny. Yes lady, your radio is okay. I said a tooth brush. What? What? No no. I'm sorry, we cannot make it a shoe horn. No no, you'll have to try some other contest. Good bye. And now folks, I'll tell you how to win our shoe horn – or – er—tooth brush. In the first place, we just want your spare time and your weekends. Now in order to give us an even break, we have several new rules governing this contest, which will be announced immediately after the next number, which is "LOVE-MAKING WEATHER," played by George Olsen and his Disappointed Maestros.

5. LOVEMAKING WEATHER

BENNY   Now folks, take out your papers and pencils and follow the new rules closely. First, you must forget all the other rules, and prepare for another brand new idea – the first time on the air – a limerick contest. What an idea! I will now give you the first limerick, but you will have to follow closely an remember each and every word and rhyme.

(CYMBAL CRASH)

> There once was a girlie named Henry
> Who helped her mother on Thursday
> She heard Olsen's band on her radio
> And now she is living in Newark.

Now all you have to do is write four new lines in place of our four lines, using the words "Canada Dry Made To Order By The Glass" in each sentence. Now, to be sure that you have the limerick correct, I will repeat it. Listen closely.

> There once was a girlie named Olsen
> Who helped her mother in Newark
> She heard Thursday's band on Saturday night
> Hickory, dickory, dock.

You have been hearing limericks, — not static. Please send in immediately your four lines on a piece of cheese in sandwich form, with mustard. This must be placed between two slices of rye bread.

OLSEN   Make mine ham.

BENNY   One ham – toast. Imagine how these answers will go with a glass of Canada Dry Made to Order at your soda fountain. And now, another crazy tune called "Goofus," sung be Dick "Hot-Cha" Gardner, and played by George Olsen and his Ginger-Alians.

6. GOOFUS   ORCHESTRA & GARDNER

BENNY   That was the last number of the sixth program on the nineteenth [sic] of May. And this was the Canada Dry Ginger Ale Program. Are you drinking, hmm? Do you remember, there was a request made last week for you to send old shoes to Olsen's boys in the orchestra? There was a slight mistake made, and we would like to have the names and addresses of the two people who did send in shoes, as they forgot to take their feet out. Next week we are going to show you how Canada Dry Ginger Ale is really made to order at the fountain. We hate to leave you now, but we must go. Goodnight then.

SIGNATURE – ROCKABYE MOON

THORGERSON   Canada Dry is saying goodnight until Monday at this same time, when the champagne of ginger ales will again present Jack Benny, Ethel Shutta, and George Olsen and his music. Canada Dry is now on sale, made-to-order by the glass, at soda fountains, as well as in bottles. This is the National Broadcasting Company.

May 23, 1932

STATION	WJZ	PROGRAM	CANADA DRY GINGER ALE, INC.
	AND	DATE	MONDAY, MAY 23, 1932
	BLUE NETWORK	TIME	9:30-10:00 P.M. (E.D.T.)

A. SIGNATURE

1. BLUE DANUBE	SPEC. ARR.	ORCHESTRA
2. ROMANCING WITH ROMANCE	UNPUBLISHED	ORCHESTRA & SHUTTA
3. SILENT LOVE	FAMOUS MUSIC	ORCHESTRA & SMALL
4. I'VE GOT THE POTATOES	UNPUBLISHED	ORCHESTRA & SMALL
5. TENDER CHILD	BERLIN	ORCH. SHUTTA & FREY
6. YEAH MAN	DeS. B. & H.	ORCHESTRA & GARDNER

7. SIGNATURE

SIGNATURE – JOLLY GOOD COMPANY

ANNOUNCER   Again Canada Dry, the champagne of ginger ales, presents a program to advertise the new Canada Dry made-to-order by the glass, which is now available at soda fountains. This program features George Olsen and his music, Miss Ethel Shutta, the star of many Broadway successes, and the Canada Dry humorist, Jack Benny.

Our program opens with a special fox trot arrangement of the "BLUE DANUBE" waltz.

1. BLUE DANUBE   ORCHESTRA

ANNOUNCER   Go ahead, Jack, you're on.

BENNY   Good evening, Easterners — good afternoon, Westerners – and good morning, Siam! This is Jack Benny talking — Jack Benny with new jokes, new contest rules, new shoes and a haircut. Are you looking, hmmm? Nothing small on this program.

You know, folks, I came pretty near not getting here tonight. All right, all right, I know you don't care … But I had to make it. You see, I happen to be playing in a theatre here in town. Of course I'm not allowed to advertise the name of the theatre while broadcasting. You couldn't blame my sponsors, however, because, after all, what's the Paramount Theatre got to do with Canada Dry Ginger Ale?

Well, anyway, we're all here — I came over in one taxi and Olsen's band in another — and Ethel Shutta walked and got here first and — of course the reason I was late — my taxi missed a pedestrian and chased him up an alley. Seems to me I've heard <u>that</u> one before.

You know, I wonder if everyone who has been listening in on our programs knows that I'm talking about — because here's a letter I received this morning from a lady in Boston Annex, Ohio. She says —

"Dear You:
I took your word for Canada Dry and tried to dry my dishes with it. But they are still wet. Why do you fool us?
(Signed) Mrs. Iona Poodle.

Isn't that awful? I'll have to answer her letter right away … Oh, Miss Jones!

FRAN	Yes, Mr. Benny.
BENNY	Ah, a little horse this morning, eh? — Take a sip of this Canada Dry — Feel better?
ETHEL	Yes, thank you.
BENNY	Well, take a letter.
ETHEL	In shorthand?
BENNY	Either hand —

"Dear Madame:
I deny having said anything about Canada Dry drying dishes. You could not have been tuned in on our program. You probably turned the doorknob and got the janitor. Why do you fool us?"

ETHEL	Is that all?
BENNY	Wait a minute, Miss Jones. We'll have to get even with her in some way — Enclose a picture of George Olsen. And now to get even with me, Mr. Olsen and his orchestra will play "Roaming for Romance." It will be sung by Ethel Shutta.

2. ROAMING FOR ROMANCE   ETHEL SHUTTA

BENNY	Say, Ethel, how did you happen to walk over to the Studio tonight? You usually ride over with us.
ETHEL	I know, Jack – but I'm tired of paying those taxi bills.
BENNY	You will have your little joke — Anyway, that's a beautiful gown you're wearing — From Paris?
ETHEL	No, I got it here.
BENNY	Nobody can see it, Ethel. Didn't that gown come from Paris?
ETHEL	Oh yes, Jack.
BENNY	Gee, I'll bet it cost a lot of money — didn't It?
ETHEL	No, it's just a cheap knock about Jersey and stop kicking me in the shins.
BENNY	Ethel, I wish you would help us a little bit — Were you ever in Hollywood?

ETHEL	No, Jack.
BENNY	Two years in pictures, eh? … And what was your biggest success.
ETHEL	What success?
BENNY	Grand Hotel! Isn't wonderful! … And to what do you owe all of it?
ETHEL	I don't think I owe anything to anyone.
BENNY	There you are, ladies and gentlemen — another great victory for Canada Dry, made-to-order by the glass. And let me say this, ladies and gentlemen — I do not claim that Canada Dry will cure falling arches, dandruff or baggy knees. But I will say this — I <u>know</u> it is a refreshing drink because — believe it or not — I tried a glass of it at the fountain. And It wasn't bad … it was <u>not</u> bad … in fact, it was good … I liked it … Gee, I thought it was swell … Ladies and gentlemen, it was <u>excellent</u>!… Are you paying attention, sponsors, hmmmm? And now a familiar radio personality, making his first appearance on our program, Mr. Paul Small who will sing "Silent Love", accompanied by George Olsen and his Alimony Club Orchestra.

3. SILENT LOVE   **PAUL SMALL**

BENNY	Say, George, do you really play golf or do you just wear those knickers to lead the orchestra? I noticed that the saxophone player was in the rough all during the last number.
OLSEN	Of course I play golf. I played with you two weeks ago, didn't I?
BENNY	Oh yes, and there is one thing I distinctly remember — we started out with five golf balls apiece. I came back with three and you came back with seven.
OLSEN	You don't think I picked up any of your golf balls, do you?
BENNY	No, George, I wouldn't say that. But I think that if we hadn't played together I'd still have my five.
OLSEN	That's fine appreciation after taking you to my Club.
BENNY	On the level, George, was that really a club? That's the worst golf course I ever played on. You know, I lost one ball on the green.
OLSEN	Aw, you did not.
BENNY	Yes, I did — and then I laid down the bag to look for the ball and lost the bag. One thing about your Club House, George — they serve great food there — and so reasonable, too. That's what I like about it. You can sit down and order an anchovy for two dollars!
OLSEN	But don't forget you get ketchup with it.

BENNY	And don't you forget we're working for Canada Dry. Ladies and gentlemen, the same Mr. Olsen and his Glorified Caddies will now play, "I've Got The Potatoes" which is more than we got at the Club. Paul Small will sing the vocal chorus.

4. I'VE GOT THE POTATOES   PAUL SMALL

ANNOUNCER	Where's Jack Benny?
RICE	He just went down to the soda fountain for a drink.
ANNOUNCER	But who's going to take charge of the program?
RICE	I don't know.
ANNOUNCER	I think I'll tune in the soda fountain and see what's going on there… (AD LIB AND FADE OUT)

(FADE IN: SCENE AT SODA FOUNTAIN. SOUND EFFECTS: CLINK OF GLASSES, FIZZES OF CHARGED WATER, BABBLE OF VOICES REQUESTING DRINKS, ETC.)

ALLEN	And I'll have a chocolate malted milk.
ETHEL	Make mine a made-to-order Canada Dry.
FREY	There you are — – and what will you have, sir?
BENNY	Give me two nickels — I want to telephone.
FREY	Say, this is a soda fountain.
BENNY	I'll have a glass of Canada Dry Ginger Ale, made-to-order, by the glass at all soda fountains.
FREY	Do you know the chorus, Mister?
BENNY	Oh, I see — – Now just give me a glass of Canada Dry.
FREY	Would you like a little flavor in it, sir? Say, a little cherry?
BENNY	No — No — just plain Canada Dry.
FREY	How about putting some ice cream in it? It's swell with ice cream.
BENNY	Yes, I imagine it is very good. But if you don't mind, I'll have just the plain Canada Dry — see?
FREY	Would you like toast with it?
BENNY	<u>No</u>!! — Say, were you ever a barber?
FREY	Who wants to know?
BENNY	Jack Benny.

FREY	Are you Jack Benny?
BENNY	Yes — yes.
FREY	The Jack Benny who broadcasts for Canada Dry?
BENNY	Yes.
FREY	Every Monday and Wednesday?
BENNY	Yes
FREY	And you ask me if I was ever a barber! Gee, that's hot.
BENNY	Will you please give me a glass of — — — (ETHEL ENTERS AND INTERRUPTS)
ETHEL	Oh, Jack — -
BENNY	Hello, Ethel.
ETHEL	You'd better hurry back. George is getting ready to play a number.
BENNY	Come on, let's have a drink first.
ETHEL	No, thanks — I don't want …
BENNY	Come on, Ethel — - I'll pay for mine. (ETHEL LAUGHS AT THIS)
BENNY	Aw, I'm only kidding'. Come on, Ethel, I'll buy them. Hey! Give us two Canada Dry's. And make mine large.
FREY	Okay… say, do you want a piece of cake with it?
BENNY	Come here — Lean over a minute.

(SOUND EFFECT: CRASH OF PLATE)

And now give us two glasses of Canada Dry.

(SOUND EFFECT: FIZZES OF CHARGED WATER)

What's he doing?

BENNY	That's the way you make it — first put just the right amount of syrup in — then add the charged water — and there you are! Well, here it is, Ethel … Good Luck!
ETHEL & BENNY (SINGING)	How Canada Dry I am… how Canada Dry I am … (BOTH START TO LAUGH) (FADE IN: PIANO MUSIC – OPENING BARS OF "TENDER CHILD")
ETHEL	What's that?
BENNY	Say, that's George beginning to play the next number.
ETHEL	Gee, I'd better run back — I have to sing it with Fran.

5. TENDER CHILD   ETHEL SHUTTA and FRAN FREY

BENNY   Well, folks, this is Jack Benny back at the Studio. Well, to tell you the truth, we never even left here. Olsen's bass drum was the counter. And the fizz you heard was one of the boys sneezing. And the crowd at the fountain was Phil Cook.

Now, ladies and gentlemen, we are very glad to tell you that our contest has just hit its stride.

(WEAK FANFARE)

We have received so many millions of letters that we finally had to get a secretary. With so many people after our prizes, we realized how valuable they really were, so we sold them. We're no fools... But don't let that worry you as with the same money we went out and purchased entirely new prizes and still had ten dollars left over.

We have also received thousands of answers to the limerick I read to you last Wednesday night, some of them containing only three words telling us what to do. But an unfortunate thing happened. You remember we asked you to send in your limerick in sandwich form between two slices of rye bread. Well unfortunately, we have to abandon the whole idea as too many of the sandwiches came in <u>without mustard</u>. And from way out West we received nothing but Western sandwiches which, ladies and gentlemen, consist of two pieces of white bread filled with wide open spaces. This is Jack Benny talking —

So you can see what a fix we are in. Therefore, we will again have to give you other rules for all contestants in this battle of wits.

Now this time do not write with pen or pencil as the other answers came in too clearly — too clearly what you think of our contest. So now try it this way —

Take a cone-full of whipped cream and write plainly by squeezing the whipped cream thru the cone across a chocolate birthday cake, using hazel nuts for periods and Brazil nuts for commas, exactly what you think of Canada Dry, made-to-order, by the glass at all soda fountains.

And say, you don't have to follow our rules if you don't want to — – you can make up your own rules. If you feel like it, write your answers with hot tar across a sidewalk. But how are you going to mail us a sidewalk? After all, common sense must prevail in this contest of the century.

NOW for the new prizes which we have substituted for the old ones.

(TRUMPET CALL — TA-DA-DA)

Well, here it goes again — do you know that in trying to please everyone, we have gotten ourselves so mixed up that we are sorry we ever started this contest. But Canada Dry <u>never</u> quits.

(DRUM ROLL)

And now here are the prizes — a little less valuable, perhaps, but much more useful.

How would you like to own a hairless St. Bernard dog — a watch dog that minds his own business, sees all and won't talk. That, ladies and gentlemen, is our first prize.

Now for our second prize — a real German police dog, including the uniform and nightstick.

And for the third and last prize, if you are still in town — something for the ear — a genuine Swiss echo — an echo imported from the yodels of Switzerland.

These prizes will surely come to you Wednesday night. However, in the event of rain Wednesday, you will receive rain checks good for the following Monday night.

And now "Hotcha" Gardner will sing "Yeah Man", accompanied by George Olsen and his afore mentioned Gingeralians.

6. YEAH MAN   **"HOTCHA" GARDNER**

BENNY   That was the last of the seventh program on the twenty-third of May. Are you still with us, hmm? And don't forget to listen in Wednesday night for the results of the Canada Dry Contest. And this was Jack — Canada Dry, made-to-order, by the glass at all soda fountains — Benny talking. See you Wednesday. Good night, then.

SIGNATURE—ROCKABYE MOON

ANNOUNCER   Canada Dry is saying goodnight until Wednesday at this same time, when the champagne of ginger ales will again present Jack Benny, Ethel Shutta, and George Olsen and his music. Canada Dry is now on sale, mad-to-order by the glass, at soda fountains, as well as in bottles. This is the National Broadcasting Company.

⇒ May 25, 1932 ⇐

STATION	WJZ	PROGRAM	CANADA DRY GINGER ALE, INC.
	AND	DATE	WEDNESDAY, MAY 25, 1932
	BLUE NETWORK	TIME	9.30 - 10:00 P.M. (E.D.T.)

A. SIGNATURE

1.	ASK YOURSELF WHO LOVES YOU	FEIST	SHUTTA & FREY
2.	MOONLIGHT BRINGS ME YOU	SANYLEY	PAUL SMALL
3.	OH, SAY, CAN'T YOU SEE	BERLIN	SHUTTA
4.	YOU CAN MAKE MY LIFE A BED OF ROSES	DE S. B. H.	FRAN FREY
5.	THE NIGHT SHALL BE FILLED WITH MUSIC	SANTLEY	SHUTTA
6.	OF THEE I SING	HARMS	FRAN FREY

SIGNATURE – JOLLY GOOD COMPANY

ANNOUNCER Again Canada Dry, the champagne of ginger ales, presents a program to advertise the new Canada Dry made-to-order by the glass, which is now available at soda fountains. This program features George Olsen and his music, Miss Ethel Shutta, the star of many Broadway successes, and the Canada Dry humorist, Jack Benny.

      Our program opens with "Ask Yourself Who Loves you".

1. ASK YOURSELF WHO LOVES YOU   SHUTTA & FREY

ANNOUNCER Here's Jack Benny.

BENNY   Hello, anybody. This is Jack Benny telling … Are you asking, Hmmm? This is Jack Benny — "B" as in fish – bluefish… "E" as in esparagus … "when it comes to the 'n' of a perfect day… Another "N" as in when it comes "knock"… And "Y" as in Alban – Y, New York. In fact, this is Jack Benny.

      And now, ladies and gentlemen, starting with tonight's program we are going to introduce the various celebrities who have helped make these broadcasts possible. I think It is no more than fair. Tonight we want to pre-sent to you the janitor of this building, Mr. Philander Kvetch! who has done so much to aid our programs by dusting off the boys in the orchestra and keeping everything spick and span. Philander, say something to the folks.

BOBBY MOORE Umph – gloop – bla, bla, etc.

BENNY   Uh, uh, a little risqué, Philander … Folks, he said it's a shame that he works so hard for the money he gets while Olsen does nothing but wave a stick at his men. Philander, he's not waving at them – he's threatening them. So don't let that worry you.

      Now, girls, I want to give you a description of this man. First, close your eyes and think of Clark Gable. Now forget Gable and think of Dracula — think of Dracula after a bad night. And <u>that's</u> Philander. In fact, Philander met Dracula on the street the other day and scared him out of town. You know the type. He has a moustache, something like Ed Thorgerson's – our announcer — only larger. I mean, he looks as

	though he had swallowed a bicycle and left the handlebars sticking out. Well, to give you a clearer description: if he had no arms or legs, he'd look like a sea lion.
BOBBY MOORE	Umph – gloop – bla, bla, bla, etc,
BENNY	All right, all right Kvetch, I'll tell them. It's a good thing I spent a year in Paris… Mr. Kvetch has to leave now. He has a date with the waste basket on the third floor.
	On each of our succeeding programs we will try to present to you only those celebrities in whom you are interested. Next Monday we will introduce a friend of George Olsen's chauffeur!
	At this time a number called, "Moonlight Brings Me You". Paul Small will sing — Olsen will direct — and I will read the want ads.

2. MOONLIGHT BRINGS ME YOU   PAUL SMALL

BENNY	That, ladies and gentlemen, was Paul Small singing. Paul is the newest member of our little stranded road show, and seems to be quite happy being associated with us. But we'll stop that …
	Paul, we're all glad to have you with us. Have you met the boys?
SMALL	No.
BENNY	Boys, meet Paul Small.
ORCHESTRA (with sarcasm)	Hello…
BENNY	Just one big happy family … Paul, you're going to love this gang. Now go over in the corner and sit down until we need you.
	And now get ready, music-lovers. Miss Ethel Shutta is going to sing "Auf Wiedersehn", dedicated to Amelia Earhart who landed in Ireland. Remember, folks, dedicated to Amelia Earhart who crossed the ocean… and played by George Olsen who double-crossed his cornet-player.
Shutta	No, Jack, I'm going to sing, "Oh Say, Can't You See."
BENNY	Double-crossed again. Oh Ethel, what are you and George going to do tonight after the broadcast.
SHUTTA	Oh, we're going out to see a movie. Would you like to join us?
BENNY	Sure, what are you going to see?
SHUTTA	We're going to see James Cagney. I was crazy about James Cagney in "Taxi" … weren't you?
BENNY	No, I prefer Garbo in the same taxi.

SHUTTA	Say, Jack, how does it happen that you didn't keep on in the talkies? I thought you were awfully good in them.
BENNY	Oh, I don't know. I used to play lover parts … you know, I was an assistant lover. Ramon Navarro was first lover and I was his assistant. But he always showed up and I got sick of it.
SHUTTA	But I thought you were great, Jack. And particularly in that picture you made celled "The Medicine Man."
BENNY	Oh, did you see that?
SHUTTA	Uh-huh.
BENNY	Oh, you're the one who saw it.
SHUTTA	Really, Jack, I thought you were swell.
BENNY	No, I wasn't myself in that picture… I was in love … you know, heartsick. And you can't work very well under those conditions.
SHUTTA	Who were you in love with, Jack?
BENNY	Oh, I don't want to bring it up here.
SHUTTA	Aw, come on … please!
BENNY	Well, you know that movie star, Zasu Pitts?
SEUTTA	Yes.
BENNY	I went around with her sister, Peach Pitts. This is Jack Benny apologizing … hmmm?
SHUTTA	You know, Jack, I like to talk to you. You're so… so interesting … You know about everything.
BENNY	Do you know what kills me, Ethel! Everybody thinks we're here to talk about Canada Dry, made-to-order… (Music starts opening bars) by the glass … at all fountains

3. OH SAY CAN'T YOU SEE   **ETHEL SHUTTA**

BENNY	How many of you people are aware of the real value of Canada Dry Ginger Ale? How many of you think it is merely a good drink, Hmmm?
	Now we received a letter from a man out West – I'm not going to bore you by reading it — But this man claims that he has, for years, been troubled with neuritis. In fact, he had the oldest neuritis in the West, left to him in a will by a relative — which included one cattle. Well, to make a long story monotonous, this fellow states in his letter that for two years he has been unable to walk. And what did he do? Only last week, after hearing us on the air, he bought a glass of Canada Dry … and is now

able to walk with the aid of two crutches. So, folks, you see that besides being a great drink, Canada Dry also has the heart of a mother.

I expect another testimonial tomorrow — which we mailed at five o'clock today.

And let me tell you just one little thing that happened to me this afternoon … this is not because I am advertising this product …

While walking down the street, I turned a corner looking for prosperity, and ran into a severe headache. So what did I do? You can't tell me, eh? Just as I thought … well, I'll tell you.

I walked to the nearest soda fountain, ordered a glass of made-to-order Canada Dry, and drank it. And have I still got my headache, ladies and gentlemen? You said it!

And now to make it worse, Fran Frey will sing, "You Can Make My Life A Bed of Roses."

4. YOU CAN MAKE MY LIFE A BED OF ROSES   FRAN FREY

BENNY   George, I think that number you just played cured my headache. I know it couldn't have been those four aspirins I took.

And now, ladies and gentlemen, just relax and prepare for more news of our contest. Are you prepared, hmmm?

(WEAK FANFARE)

But first of all folks, I'd like to read what some of the greatest men in the world have said about our contest.

A few of the eulogies…

Here's what Arthur Brisbane, the famous cartoonist, says, "I never heard of it." One from Herbert Hoover, vice-president of the United States.

He says: "It is contests like yours that will bring back prosperity – to England."

And here's one from Paul Revere. He says: "I'd like to ride in your next contest."

Ah! One from ex-Kaiser Wilhelm. Here's what he says: "Vot contest?" We say: "Dot contest!"

Here's one from John D. Rockefeller … the golf player … He says: "Your contest is oil-right." Remember, ladies and gentlemen, I only read these … I don't write them.

Ah! Here's one from Calvin Coolidge. He says … "Humph!"

And now that I've read you these lovely eulogies, it is with the greatest of sorrow that I must tell you that our contest dropped 16-1/4 points and is now in the hands of the receivers. Our liabilities are three valuable prizes including a round-trip ticket to Siam, two dogs and an echo. Our assets are three million and one fan letters, one toothbrush and six pictures of Olsen. The sheriff has attached the three prizes which would have gone to the following unlucky winners…

(SOUR CORNET)

The first prize was won by Sven Olsen … who happens to be George Olsen's brother… Congratulations, George!

The second prize was won by Robert L. Jennings. And what a coincidence! He happens to be the second violinist in Olsen's Band … Congratulations, George!

And the third prize, strange to say, would have gone to Ethel Shutta's sister who sent in her answers two weeks before the contest started.

This amazing paradox has never been equaled. However, three people out West deserve honorable mention … one from Idaho … one from South Dakota … and one from Nebraska … Congratulations, Wyoming!

And now, folks, this contest will be resumed just as soon as we can talk things over with the sheriff, who, I understand, is a <u>pretty tough</u> <u>mug</u>.

Next number, ladies and gentlemen, is called "The Night Shall Be Filled with Music," played by George Olsen, sung by Ethel Shutta and watched by the sheriff.

5. THE NIGHT SHALL BE FILLED WITH MUSIC   ETHEL SHUTTA

BENNY   I have just talked to the sheriff and we may be able to get our prizes, after all. So do not leave your homes until further notice!

And now, folks, a very important detail that I forgot to mention. Last week we made several tests of this priceless beverage, Canada Dry. Static proves … I mean, statistics prove that there are 254,763 products in this country… perhaps more. And out of this huge, amazing number, only Canada Dry, made-to-order, has stood the test. Now how – why – and where? First, we will take "how". Or, let's take "why". No, let's take "where" …

Last week we visited a big industrial plant in the hills of Kentucky where thirty-six thousand man were employed making something or other. Mind you, ladies and gentlemen, thirty-six thousand men in one plant! We took each and every man, blindfolded him securely with clear cellophane, then gave to each of them a glass of made-to-order Canada Dry. They drank it thoroly. And what was the result? Out of the thirty-six thousand men, only <u>THREE</u> said it was Russ Columbo!

And not being satisfied with this, tomorrow afternoon we are going to subject Canada Dry <u>to the acid test</u> – an endurance test which will startle the world.

And now George Olsen will startle all of us by playing "Of Thee I Sing" in the proper key. Go ahead … startle us, George.

6. OF THEE I SING**ORCHESTRA**

BENNY   That was the last number of the eighth program on the twenty-fifth of May. And don't forget to listen in next Monday night when we come to you with the new tests including a mental one for this program, and tell you more serious facts about Canada Dry, made-to-order, by the glass at all soda fountains.

This is Jack Benny talking. See you Monday … Are you suspicious, hmmm? Good—night, then.

SIGNATURE – ROCK A BYE MOON

ANNOUNCER   Canada Dry is saying good night until Monday at this same time, when the champagne of ginger ales will again present Jack Benny, Ethel Shutta, and George Olsen and his music. Canada Dry is now on sale, made- to-order by the glass, at soda fountains, as well as in bottles. This is the National Broadcasting Company.

May 30, 1932

STATION	WJZ	PROGRAM	CANADA DRY GINGER ALE, INC.
	AND	DATE	MONDAY, MAY 30, 1932
	BLUE NETWORK	TIME	9.30 - 10:00 P.M. (E.D.T.)

[song credits are missing from this script copy]

SIGNATURE: JOLLY GOOD COMPANY

ANNOUNCER　　Ladies and gentlemen, another half hour of entertainment about Canada Dry Ginger Ale, now available made-to-order, by the glass at soda fountains. George Olsen, Ethel Shutta and Jack Benny, the Canada Dry humorist, again perform for your enjoyment. First George Olsen and the Boys in a medley, including "Home," "Good-Night, Moon" and "Dream, Sweetheart."

1. MEDLEY OF INSTRUMENTAL NUMBERS　　　　ORCHESTRA

ANNOUNCER　　Here he is, ladies and gentlemen… Jack Benny.

BENNY　　Hello, victims! This is Public Enemy Number 2 speaking. Jack Benny…"B" as in Little Boy Blue…"E" as in eeny-meeny-miny-mo…"N" as in anything at all…another "N"… and "Y" … I don't know. Am I wasting my time? Well, aren't we all? Hmmmm?

And now, ladies and gentlemen, after four weeks or eight broadcasts, we have just found out that Canada Dry is without a theme song. Can you imagine that? How can you drink Canada Dry without a theme song? Well, we have overcome this situation, and tonight, for the first time, you will hear the Canada Dry theme. We have with us tonight the gentleman who wrote it and who is going to sing it. He holds a diploma from the Short Circuit School of Broadcasting in Germantown, Pennsylvania, where he spent seven years as a freshman and graduated very abruptly. May I present Mr. E. Livermore Dunk, from Tyronner, West Virginia. Mr. Dunk has never broadcast before and this song has never been sung. Therefore, they will both start in together from scratch. You, of course, want music with this, Mr. Dunk.

DUNK　　If you please.

BENNY　　All right, boys　(PICK-UP FOR ORCHESTRA)

DUNK　　Dunk a doughnut in your Canada Dry!
Why, oh why, oh why?
It is made-to-order, sold at every fountain.
From the Mexican border to the new-mown hay.

> Hey! Hey!
> Dunk a doughnut in your Canada Dry!
> Still, we wonder why…
> It is the best drink …and good with ice cream…
> But your mother is your best friend after all.
> (SOUND EFFECT: Pistol shot)

BENNY: Ladies and gentlemen, we have just shot the copyright owners. We also wish to state that Victor Herbert had nothing whatever to do with the writing of this number.

DUNK: Didn't you like that, Mr. Benny?

BENNY: Well, I'll tell you, Mr. Dunk…you plugged your name a good deal more than you did our product. As a matter of fact, you only mentioned once that Canada Dry could be bought by the glass, made-to-order, at all soda fountains.

DUNK: Well, I'm sorry, Mr. Benny, but you sent for me. And besides, this isn't my regular work.

BENNY: Oh, you're telling me… Well, what do you do?

DUNK: I work in a doughnut factory.

BENNY: Oh, I get it… Dunk a doughnut, hey?

DUNK: Yes.

BENNY: Tell me, do you make the entire doughnut?

DUNK: No, just the inner tubes.

BENNY: My next trick, ladies and gentlemen, will be sawing a man in half. Well, so long Dunkey, see you again… we will have a new theme song next Wednesday night. I will see to that, personally. Or your money will be refunded. And now George Olsen will play "Sharing," sung by Paul Small whose right name is …Paul Small. Okay, Fran!

2. SHARING   PAUL SMALL

BENNY: We received a letter yesterday from a lady, asking us to desert to the interior of a broadcasting studio during one of our programs. I have an idea that some of you folks who have not had an opportunity to visit one, imagine it is like a theatre…with the orchestra on the stage, and footlights, scenery, and all of us in evening clothes… Well, let me give you the real low-down. If you should be here right now, you would see Olsen's orchestra sitting here, half asleep. In fact, the whole place looks like Ellis Island, with four of the musicians waiting to be deported. This is just a rough idea… Olsen himself is wearing pajamas because he is going to bed right after the broadcast. Ethel is over in one corner, ironing Olsen's other shirt. Fran Frey is standing at the window, keeping the flies out of the studio. There are fifty or sixty people sitting around on uncomfortable chairs, really waiting for the Fifth Avenue bus which stops at the door here every three or four minutes.

	And the only drape we have here is our janitor's mustache. You remember our janitor…Philander Kvetch? Since we spoke of it last Wednesday, he had his mustache trimmed. Now he looks like our announcer, Ed Thorgerson. The only way we tell them apart is that Philander carries a pail.
OLSEN	Say, Jack, what's the idea of misleading the public? You know you're not telling the truth…telling people that I'm wearing pajamas. This is a light summer suit I have on.
BENNY	Yes, and if you had a number on it, you could enter the Olympic Games.
OLSEN	Jack, nobody is interested in how we look. All they want to do is listen in.
BENNY	Who's listening in?…On nights like this, people are out at soda fountains, drinking Canada Dry, made-to-order…
OLSEN (joining in with Benny)	Made-to-order…by the glass…sold at all fountains…
BENNY	Yes, and not bad with ice cream. Now let's stop arguing, George… People want entertainment.
OLSEN	Okay.
BENNY	And now, Ethel Shutta, who has just finished her ironing, will sing "I'm that Way about Broadway"… Oh, by the way, Ethel, I'm crazy about that song. In fact, I'm singing it at the Paramount Theatre in Brooklyn this week.
ETHEL	Why, Jack, I didn't know you sing.
BENNY	Oh, yes, yes… I've been singing for quite a few years. I studied three years with Paderewski.
ETHEL	Why, Paderewski is a pianist.
BENNY	He is?
ETHEL	Yes.
BENNY	So that's what's the matter with my voice! I was wondering why I sing so badly.
ETHEL	Say, Jack, what are you doing at the Paramount this week?
BENNY	Oh, I'm singing and telling jokes. But I'm doing very well at the Paramount. And Olsen sent me the nicest telegram. I thought it was sweet. Here it is…

"Jack Benny, Paramount Theatre, Brooklyn, New York

Dear Jack—
I passed the Paramount and saw your name out front so I passed the Paramount."

Now wasn't that sweet, Ethel? |
ETHEL	I'd love to see you on the stage, Jack. What do you do?
BENNY	Oh, I sing and tell jokes.
ETHEL	Oh, you tell jokes, eh? I'd like to hear one of your stage jokes.

BENNY	Well, here's one that will kill you. Come here, Ethel… I don't want anyone else to hear it because it's new. Now get this for a joke… I say to the orchestra leader… we have a goat over at our house that hasn't any nose…see?
ETHEL	Well, where does the poor thing hang his eye-glasses?
BENNY	Ladies and gentlemen, the next number is called "Holding My Honey's Hand." It will be played by George Olsen's stockholders and sung by Ethel Shutta.

3. I'M THAT WAY ABOUT BROADWAY (other song was substituted)   ETHEL SHUTTA & TRIO

BENNY	I forgot to mention the trio that accompanied Ethel in that last number. A trio, ladies and gentlemen, is a Scotch quartet. And now, folks, and those of you children who are sacrificing good sleep, let me tell you what is in this precious beverage, namely …Canada Dry Ginger Ale, made-to-order, by the glass. First, how is glass made? It is made of sand, by a process of heating and blowing. Not me, folks… The glass! I know what you're thinking of, you little public, you… I own a radio… that is, two more payments and then its mine.
	Anyway, that is how <u>glass</u> is made. Now… how is Canada Dry Ginger Ale made? You don't have to take my word for it… Ha! Ha! I'm telling <u>you</u>… but you can't fool a dictionary. Here it is, page 148, in the Standard Walter Winchell Dictionary. Now first, let us take the words "ginger ale"… Let me see…ginger ale…ginger… GINGER SNAPS… No, no, we don't want that… Ah! GINGER ROGERS… Telephone, Bryant 6-8003…No, we don't want that… THAT's the word, "GINGER".. meaning "lacka-daisical…tired…or lazy." Well, there's "GINGER."
	Now the word "ALE,"… What does "ALE" mean? Ale…ale…wait a minute, here it is .."Ale"… a college in New Haven, Connecticut… No, we don't want that… Let me see.. "ALE," … here we are … A…L…E…"ALE" meaning indisposed or not feeling right… So what does "GINGER ALE" mean, folks?… If you are tired or indisposed and don't feel like going to college or don't care to see Ginger Rogers, throw away your dictionary and have a drink of made-to-order Canada Dry… Am I ,making myself clear, hmmmm?
	So now when you drink a glass of it, you know what you are getting. Canada Dry does not have to be sipped from a water glass. No, you can drink it out of a shaving mug, a goldfish bowl…or your hat. I mean, folks, we are not going to worry about HOW you drink it…just drink it… Personally, I take mine home in a paper bag.

[PENCIL MARKING ON THE SCRIPT SAYS THIS ROUTINE WAS CUT]

HOLDING MY HONEY'S HAND   ETHEL SHUTTA [this is also added in pencil]

BENNY	<u>That's</u> what I've been trying to tell you for the last ten minutes.

4. YOU'RE BLASÉ   PAUL SMALL

BENNY | And now for more of our contest (SOUR FANFARE)

You remember our telling you last Wednesday that our three prizes were in the hands of the sheriff? Well they are STILL in the sheriff's office…In fact, he was seen eating the third prize yesterday. But we didn't bother him as he washed it down with a glass of Canada Dry Ginger Ale, made-to-order, and so forth. He did it entirely and irrevocably unsolicited by us.

While waiting for the receivers to release this contest, take a glass of Canada Dry and feel the material in it. Then put your forefinger and right thumb into a glue-pot, rub thoroughly and feel the difference. Ladies and gentlemen, there *is* a difference!… Of course, this is not a request. Do so only if you feel like it. Aha, I'm telling *you*.

However, Decoration Day is not a day in which to discuss business, and contests. So we will not get to the Sheriff until tomorrow. This is a day when soldiers parade – a day on which the people remember the brave heroes of the past. And what a grand parade we had today, with George Olsen leading a band of 300 men and two musicians. They were all out of step but George. But there he was marching, with head up, his chest out, spinning a baton. I'm telling you it was a sight never to be forgotten. But try and forget it.

Say, George, that was a nice uniform you wore in the parade today. The coat was so long I couldn't tell whether you had any trousers on.

OLSEN | That was my war uniform.

BENNY | Oh, I know… Your father wore it.. your uncle wore it…your grandfather wore it…So you were in the war, hey?

OLSEN | YES SIR!

BENNY | Well, tell me… what kind of a fellow was General Grant?

OLSEN | You mean Pershing… Don't you know a uniform when you see one?

BENNY | Well, I was looking at the wear and tear.

OLSEN | What are you talking about? Were *you* in the war?

BENNY | Certainly I was in the war… I was a cavalry man.

OLSEN | Yeah? Well, where were you stationed?

BENNY | On the merry-go-round in Coney Island.

OLSEN | Ladies and gentlemen, the next number will be "Gosh Darn" sung by Ethel Shutta and Fran Frey.

5.	GOSH DARN	ETHEL SHUTTA and FRAN FREY

BENNY How many people have asked me whether or not Canada Dry Ginger Ale has endurance. Why not ask me whether there is strength in the Rock of Gibraltar? I don't know… I never tasted Gibraltar.

For instance, take the traveling salesman, the farmer and the farmer's daughter… Or, take three other people… Or take a walk around your own home town… And what do you see? … Or, let's go back to 1851, when… No, let's go back to 1841. No, let's go back to where we started. Well, what happened then? Who knows? All we can go by is what history tells us. And the answer is you can't cheat facts. And, therefore, I… I… Say, George, what am I talking about?

OLSEN The endurance of Canada Dry.

BENNY Are you sure?

OLSEN Yes, that's how you started.

BENNY Has Canada Dry endurance? Ha! Ha! That makes me form a laugh. Right now, in this studio, ladies and gentlemen…before your very eyes… we are going to subject Canada Dry to a <u>test of endurance</u>. You will see a cross-studio race, including a hurdle over Olsen's feet, in which the following contestants will participate…

Number 1… a glass of Canada Dry (CHEERS AND APPLAUSE)

Number 2… a bottle of ketchup (CHEERS AND APPLAUSE)

Number 3…a can of beans (CHEERS AND APPLAUSE)

Number 4…a jar of maple syrup (CHEERS AND APPLAUSE) (applause very light on this one)

And now let me give you a round-by-round description of this contest of endurance…   (BUGLE CALL)

They are marching to the post…   (MUMBLING OF THE CROWD)

Now they are lining up… Ketchup looks worried… But Canada Dry is full of spark and rarin' to go… (GONG RINGS)

They're off!!! (HURRY MUSIC BEGINS – something very pianissimo)

There they go…<u>Beans</u> takes the lead…with <u>ketchup</u> in close pursuit…<u>Canada</u> <u>Dry</u> taking it easy at the rail… While <u>maple syrup</u> seems to be stuck at the post.

Now they're at the first quarter… <u>Beans</u> still in the lead…What a race! What a race!… <u>Ketchup</u> ketching-up with <u>Beans</u>…This is Floyd MacNamee announcing from the steam room of the Turkish Bath…

There they go! <u>Canada Dry</u> still third in the race while <u>Maple Syrup</u> is slower than molasses.

	Now they're at the half… <u>Beans</u> still in the lead…with <u>Ketchup</u> on top… Ah! Look at <u>Old Made-to-Order</u> go…gaining inch by inch.

Aha! What's that? A CRASH! <u>Maple Syrup</u> bumps into a Waffle, and is disqualified.

They are now at the third quarter…Look at 'em go! They're crowding each other… <u>Beans</u> and <u>Ketchup</u> blocking <u>Canada Dry</u>… <u>Canada Dry</u> looking for an opening… <u>Beans</u> now weakening, but as game as they make 'em. And don't forget, folks, this is an <u>endurance</u> test…

There go <u>Ketchup</u> and <u>Canada Dry</u>, neck and glass. What a race! <u>What a race</u>… now they're coming down the home stretch. COME ON, CANADA DRY!… <u>Ketchup</u> ahead by half a length. Here they come… what's this? WHAT'S THIS?… They're nearing the finish line, and again, they are neck and glass.

Hooray! Hooray! Canada Dry JUMPS out of the glass and <u>wins by a splash</u>! HOORAY! HOORAY! (CROWD BREAKS INTO LOUD CHEERS AND APPLAUSE)

Come here, Canada Dry, say something over the microphone.

BENNY (in high, falsetto voice) Hello, mom… I had a tough struggle, but I'm glad I won… I'll be right home, mom… (CROWD MUMBLING, CHEERING, OFFERING CONGRATULATIONS, etc.)

6. THERE'S OCEANS OF LOVE BY THE BEAUTIFUL SEA   PAUL SMALL

BENNY That was the last number on the ninth program on Decoration Day. Are you away over the weekend… or were you tuned in? And now we have a little treat for the ladies on Wednesday Night. Wednesday will be Ladies Night…that is, only ladies accompanied by their escorts will be admitted. So choose your nearest escort now. Must leave you now, folks. Hope you had a very pleasant holiday. See you Wednesday…Good-night, please.

THORGERSON The next time you visit a soda fountain, ask for a Canada Dry Ice Cream Soda. You will find it a delicious drink — a real pick-me-up on a hot day. Canada Dry is also available in bottles, as well as made-to-order by the glass. You are invited to listen in again at the same time Wednesday night when Jack Benny, Ethel Shutta and George Olsen will entertain. This is the National Broadcasting Company.

June 1, 1932

STATION	WJZ	PROGRAM	CANADA DRY GINGER ALE, INC.
	AND	DATE	WEDNESDAY, JUNE 1, 1932
	BLUE NETWORK	TIME	9:30-10:00 P.M. (E.D.T.)

SIGNATURE - JOLLY GOOD COMPANY

1. WHEN GABRIEL BLOWS HIS HORN — FRAN FREY

2. LULLABY OF THE LEAVES — PAUL SMALL

3. UNDER THE OLD CROW'S NEST — SHUTTA

4. SOMEBODY LOVES YOU — PAUL SMALL

5. TENDER CHILD — FREY & SHUTTA

6. DRUMS IN MY HEART

SIGNATURE - ROCKABYE MOON

CANADA DRY GINGER ALE PROGRAM   WEDNESDAY, JUNE 1, 1932

SIGNATURE — JOLLY GOOD COMPANY

ANNOUNCER   Ladies and gentlemen. Another half hour of entertainment about Canada Dry Ginger Ale now available Made-To-Order by the Glass at soda fountains. George Olsen, Ethel Shutta and Jack Benny, the Canada Dry humorist, again perform for your enjoyment.

                           First we are going to hear "WHEN GABRIEL BLOWS HIS HORN" by George Olsen and his Music. [ed — this is the actual name of Olsen's band]

1. WHEN GABRIEL BLOWS HIS HORN   ORCHESTRA & GREY

ANNOUNCER   You remember last Monday Jack Benny promised that tonight would be Ladies Night? Well he's kept his promise and here he is.

BENNY   Hello, every lady …   You remember we told you on Monday that this would be Ladies' Night? Well, we've kept our promise … This is Jack Benny giving — are you receiving?

                           This is Jackie Benny… "B" as in your bonnet… "E" as in engagement ring… "N" as in Niagara Falls … another "N" as in now's the time to fall in love … And "Y" – AS in wye-o-lets.

                           I have been told that even though this is <u>Ladies' Night</u>, there are several men listening in while some others are peeping thru the radio. Uh-uh, we can't have that. Well, anyway, you should see the gang here in the studio for this occasion. The orchestra boys are dressed in Little Lord Fauntleroy suits… with blue ribbons neatly tied on their instruments. The saxophone players smell from perfume which they made themselves … and didn't allow to age. Our announcer, Ed Thorgersen, has a finger wave in his mustache and can't get his finger out … Ethel is wearing a corsage which Olsen found on Decoration Day. And Olsen himself is manicured… that is, only the two fingers with which he holds the baton.

                           I might also add that ninety percent of our audience in the studio is comprised of women … while the other ten percent, did not show up. Well anyway, to make a long story short, this is Ladies' Night! On the Canada Dry made-to-order and sold by the glass program.

Our janitor, Philander Kvetch … you all remember Philander … has graciously allowed his wife to tidy up the building and help out on our program. Mrs. Kvetch is right here with us … She has beautiful yellow and black hair, done up in a permanent … towel. The yellow is sort of crowding the black a little … And her teeth are like pearls … in fact, you should see Pearl's teeth … they're no bargain, either. She has a perfect 42 waist, and her limbs suggest that she might have been a model in an ice-tong factory.

Well, anyway, here's Mrs. Marmalade Kvetch! Mrs. Kvetch, say something to the ladies…

MRS. KVETCH (IN HEAVY GERMANIC ACCENT)

    Hello, everybody… I'm so much obliged to be here. Mr. Benny, I'd like to act on the radio.

BENNY	Well, what can you do?
MRS. KVETCH	I sink.
BENNY	You… what ?
MRS. KVETCH	I sink.
BENNY	Can't you swim?
MRS. KVETCH	No, I sink like eis …Yen de cow yumps over the mountings… di-do-di-de-de (finishing with a whistle). And I can do imidations, too… (routine)
BENNY	All right, that will do, Mrs. Kvetch. Now if you'll come back later, we might let you do something.
MRS. KVETCH	When will I come?
BENNY	Oh, in about 1947.
MRS. KVETCH	Thank you … you can depend on me.
BENNY	Thank you, Mrs. Kvetch … good-bye … Say, Paul, keep that door closed. This is still Ladies' Night, ladies. And George Olsen will play, "Lullaby of the Leaves." It will be sung by Paul Small… whom we will have to call Pauline for tonight only.

2. LULLABY OF THE LEAVES   PAUL SMALL

BENNY	That was Paul Small singing, and he's all dressed up for this festive party. He has on a brown suit, a green hat … and a black eye. You don't mind if I tell it, Paul … if I don't, Ed Sullivan will … You know, Paul got that black eye last night. A bridegroom gave it to him for kissing the bride. That sounds ridiculous … of course, that's an old custom, kissing the bride. But Paul did it two years after the ceremony … You have

	to be a little careful, Paul, about those things. And, say, what are you doing for that eye? It looks black and swollen.
SMALL	I'm not doing anything for it.
BENNY	Well, I'll tell you what to do for it.
SMALL	What ?
BENNY	Go over to a soda fountain, order a nice tall glass of Canada Dry… they'll make it right up for you …and drink about two-thirds of it.
SMALL	Well, will that help my eye?
BENNY	No, but at least you won't be thirsty. And say, Paul, while you're at the fountain, give your shoe a drink … its tongue is hanging out…Uh-uh, I must apologize for that one.
	And now, Ethel Shutta is going to sing, "Under the Old Crow's Nest" which is not far from here …as we are broadcasting from the roof.
	Olsen will play … Ethel will sing …and I'll run home and listen in.

3. UNDER THE OLD CROW'S NEST   ETHEL SHUTTA

BENNY	Say, Ethel, tonight being Ladies' Night, I wish you'd help me out a little bit. I am going to give the ladies a few household hints … also offer a little advice on "How to attract a man who is flirting with you," through the courtesy of Canada Dry … Ethel, you <u>will</u> help me out on this, won't you?
ETHEL	Why, certainly, Jack.
BENNY	And I'll reciprocate on Gentlemen's Night.
ETHEL	Okay.
BENNY	First, let's take "Household hints"… how to prepare dishes that will keep your husband at home.
ETHEL	That's a very good idea, Jack.
BENNY	You know, folks, Ethel is really an excellent cook. I had dinner at her house the other night and, for dessert, she served Cottage Pudding. Isn't that what it was, Ethel… Cottage Pudding?
ETHEL	That's right, Jack.
BENNY	I thought so … I had a piece of the door …
	All right, ladies, are you prepared …Hmmm? Now put on your aprons …I'm going to take you out of the darkness and enlighten you on "How To Fray A Demi-Tasse."

ETHEL	Oh, Jack, a demi-tasse is a small cup of black coffee.
BENNY	You know that and I know that …but do the people in Siam know that?
	First, you take a large demi —whip it thoroly, say for about nine rounds, until it is beaten to a pulp … then you peel it from the inside… that is, from the inside of the house. Are you inside of your house, ladies … hmm? Then you add 110 and divide it by 6. But don't sell short. That is the important thing. And if you own any rubber, hold it for a long pull… Now, when the demi is cooled off …let's see, when the demi is cooled off … don't leave me, Ethel. What's next?
ETHEL	Oh, forget about it, Jack.
BENNY	Then you forget about it …no, wait a minute, that isn't it …then when the demi is thoroly cool, you add a teaspoonful of tasse then serve it with gusto. Or, let Gusto bring it in himself … that's entirely up to you. Of course, it can also be served with a summons. This is only one man's opinion. Now by following these instructions closely, this should make six generous portions of demi good tasse …er, pardon me, good demi-tasse. Doesn't that sound appetizing, Ethel?
ETHEL	Yes, but I still claim that demi-tasse is French for a small cup of coffee … Say, Jack, parlay-vous Francais?
BENNY	What?
ETHEL	Parlay-vous Francais?
BENNY	What did you say?
ETHEL	I said, do you speak French?
BENNY	Certainly, why didn't you ask me that in the first place?
ETHEL	Say, Jack, you didn't mention one thing about Canada Dry, made-to-order, and sold at all fountains.
BENNY	By the glass.
ETHEL	Yes …by the glass.
BENNY	Ethel, this being Ladies' Night, I thought I'd leave that to you. Why don't you say something about Canada Dry?
ETHEL	I don't know how to start it.
BENNY	Well, just start out by saying …Fellow Ladies …
ETHEL (REPEATING)	Fellow ladies …
BENNY	Now just tell them why you like Canada Dry.
ETHEL (VERY ANGRILY)	

	Well, I like Canada Dry because whenever I'm thirsty, I can go up to the soda fountain and order a glass and get it. <u>That's</u> why I like Canada Dry.
BENNY	Ethel, if you're going to get mad about it, just forget the whole thing… Ethel is really a sweet girl. She was just enthused.
	And now, after the next number, we will continue with our little social gathering in which I will give all you single girls advice on "How to attract a man."
	Paul Small is going to sing, "Somebody Loves You," played by George Olsen and his unemployed gigolos.

4. SOMEBODY LOVES YOU   PAUL SMALL

BENNY	Say, George, is that a <u>man</u> sitting over there in your audience? You know there are no men allowed in here tonight.
OLSEN	No, no… that's a lady!
BENNY	Well, tell her to throw away her pipe and go out and get a shave. And now a word to all you lonesome single girls … My subject, as mentioned before, will be: "How to attract a man." Of course, you married ladies can play, too… if you want to.
	To begin with, you <u>must</u> have personality! Of course, some girls are born with it… some acquire it… while others just <u>smear</u> it on… Now, what is personality? It might be just the twitch in your eye… or the dimple in your cheek… or the way you walk… back. Now I go with a girl who lives in Newark, New Jersey. She has nothing to recommend her but her father's money. And <u>still</u> I love her. <u>That</u> is real personality. It's personality like that that will balance the budget in this country.
	The first thing about a girl that attracts a man is the manner in which she eats. How is <u>your</u> table etiquette? When you are invited out to dine … I don't mean this year, I mean when times were good… When a man asks you to dinner, do you combine your three meals in one? Or do you go out with the same man again?… Do you get it? <u>That</u> is a very important item.
	Now, let's take the dinner right from the beginning. Do you order shrimp or are you satisfied with your present escort? And when the soup is served, do you use your noodle … or do you take vegetable? When you eat your soup, do you keep your muffler closed or does it sound like this?
(Cornet suction)	
	I'll bet you've never given those things a thought …have you, girls? When you order <u>filet mignon</u>… or <u>patie de foie gras</u> …do you know what you're talking about? If you do, you're better off than I am. Ah, take my advice, girls …order hash and gamble with your boyfriend. Keep him happy. That's what I mean by personality.
ETHEL	Well, Jack, what kind of girl do you like?

BENNY | The girl I don't like, don't live.

(TELEPHONE RINGS)

Ethel, answer the phone, please.

ETHEL | Yes, yes …one minute, please.

BENNY | Who is it?

ETHEL | It's a lady who's been listening in …claims she has personality and wants to know how she can win Clark Gable.

BENNY | Tell her to listen in on our contest as we are trying to make arrangements to have him as one of our prizes.

And now, there has been a request to repeat a number called "Tender Child." This will be sung by Ethel Shutta and Fran Frey … whom we will have to call Francis for tonight.

5. TENDER CHILD   ETHEL SHUTTA AND FRAN FREY

BENNY | Hello, this is Jack Benny again. And now some more news about our contest.

(HEAVY DISCORDANT FANFARE)

We are in receipt of a letter postmarked Washington, D.C. It is from J. Enchilado Tango, of the Embassy of the Republic of Santo Mongo Fongo. The Island of Santo Mongo Fongo, as you all know, is half way between South America, and its chief industry is chasing flies out of the country. Well, anyway, here is what Senor Tango has to say—

"My dear Olsen-Shutta-Benny-Canada Dry, Made-to-order, By-the-Glass, Sold-at-all-fountains, Ginger Ale:

Things are so bad in our little republic that we are desperate. A good half dollar would balance our budget. Our cows have gone Canada Dry, and our chickens are laying off instead of laying eggs.

Now what we would like you to do is to start a contest in our country like the one you started in your own. And I feel confident that such a contest would help restore prosperity to us. One of your prizes alone would feed our population as we only have twelve people.

This is signed — J. Enchilado Tango

P.S. *"I am the ninth president this month, so please answer immediately or the new president will receive this letter."*

Well, alright, Enchilado, you shall have your contest. Here we go. Get ready, Santo Mongo Fongo. First take seventeen of your native jumping beans, examine them thoroughly and find out what makes them jump. Then take a sharpened banana, write clearly across a cocoanut why you like Canada Dry Ginger Ale, made-to-order, by the glass, sold at all fountains. Now these cocoanuts <u>must not be mailed to us</u>. No… they must be <u>rolled</u> in, and no hitch hiking, mind you. The three cocoanuts arriving here first will receive the following prizes: Our first prize will be I.O.U…and the second prize, F.O.H… and the third prize will come C.O.D. This offer positively expires as soon as we see the first cocoanut. So much for that.

Of course, ladies, you know that was just one of our branch contests. Now to get back to our own… George Olsen is using his influence to get an injunction restraining the sheriff from eating our second and third prizes.

And now, George and his Canada Dry Gingeralians will play, "Drums in My Heart."

6. DRUMS IN MY HEART   ORCHESTRA

BENNY   That was the last number of the tenth program on the first of June. Did you like it, ladies?… I want to thank you for your time. And remember our date next Monday night at nine-thirty. Of course this will be <u>Everybody's</u> Night… Pleasant dreams… Good-night, if I'm not too inquisitive…

SIGNATURE — ROCKABYE MOON

ANNOUNCER   The next time you visit a soda fountain, ask for a Canada Dry ice cream soda. You will find it a delicious drink – a real treat on a hot day. Canada Dry is also available in bottles as well as made to order by the glass. You are invited to listen in again at this same time Monday night, when Jack Benny, Ethel Shutta and George Olsen will entertain. This is the National Broadcasting Company.

June 6, 1932

STATION	WJZ	PROGRAM	CANADA DRY GINGER ALE, INC.
	AND	DATE	MONDAY, JUNE 6TH, 1932
	BLUE NETWORK	TIME	9.30 - 10:00 P.M. (E.D.T.)

SIGNATURE — JOLLY GOOD COMPANY — ORCHESTRA

1. I LOVE A PARADE — ORCHESTRA & CHORUS

2. THE CLOUDS WILL SOON ROLL BY — PAUL SMALL

3. IS I IN LOVE I IS — ETHEL SHUTTA

4. LOVE YOU FUNNY THING — FRAN FREY

5. OH WHAT A THRILL — ETHEL SHUTTA

6. EAT DRINK AND BE MERRY — FRAN FREY

SIGNATURE — ROCKABYE MOON

CANADA DRY GINGER ALE PROGRAM — MONDAY, JUNE 6, 1932.

SIGNATURE — JOLLY GOOD COMPANY

ANNOUNCER Ladies and gentlemen. Another half hour of entertainment about Canada Dry Ginger Ale, now available made-to-order by the glass at soda fountains. George Olsen, Ethel Shutta and Jack Benny, the Canada Dry humorist, again perform for your enjoyment.

By request, George Olsen opens the program with "I Love A Parade".

1. I LOVE A PARADE ORCHESTRA

ANNOUNCER And now it's Jack Benny's turn at the mike. Here you are, Jack.

BENNY Hello, you lovers of the classics. This is Jack Benny raving — Jack Benny — blue eyes, rich wavy hair – both of them — no moustache, not even fuzz — shoes, size ten — collar, the same — hat, size 9 if you laugh at my jokes — if you don't laugh, size 6 — born in Illinois — razzed in Kentucky — and considered very handsome by parents. This is Jack Benny…

I hope all you men-folks are listening in again tonight. You remember last Wednesday we had a night for Ladies' Only? I want to tell you we had a grand time. Of course since then, we have received many congratulations from the men regarding our Ladies' Night — some came by telephone — some by telegram — and some came anyway.

Now here's a letter from a man in Lunch Wagon, Ohio.

"Dear Mr. Benny: -

I thought your Ladies' Night was rotten. I'm in love with my wife and can't stand being away from her for even five minutes. And to think I was forced to go to the Club with the boys and leave my precious little wife home all alone listening to your program. You've a lot of nerve pulling that kind of stuff.

(Signed) Leonard L. Fenchel

P.S.: My wife just left the room. Your Ladies' Night was great. I went out with the boys and had a grand time."

Well, our Ladies' Night was not in vain.

Ah, here's a wire from a ladies bridge circle in Columbus Circle, New York. It reads:

"We thought your Ladies' Night was a complete failure. We sent our husbands out so we could listen in to your program, and we weren't even embarrassed. Stop fooling us!"

Now, ladies, we are <u>not</u> trying to fool you. We were kidding ourselves and you <u>happened</u> to be listening in.

You see, George, we can't please <u>everybody</u>.

Ah, here's a wire from a man in Apple Center, Core—olina.

"Your Ladies' Night was wasted as far as we are concerned, as I could not listen in and my wife doesn't like you either. Received your photograph which we will return to you by next mail, as there was no calendar on it."

You see, George, we can't please <u>anybody</u>.

So now Paul Small will please himself by singing, "The Clouds will Soon Roll By", played by George Olsen and his Empty Hotel Orchestra. Olsen's orchestra has been engaged to play in this hotel until somebody moves in. All right, George!

2. THE CLOUDS WILL SOON ROLL BY   PAUL SMALL & ORCHESTRA

BENNY	Ladies and gentlemen, you have probably noticed on the sporting page of your favorite paper the result of the six-day Bicycle Race in Pedalville, Pennsylvania. Again, Canada Dry made-to-order Ginger Ale finished first, completing the 6-day contest in 3 days, 17 minutes and 2 and 2/5 seconds, lapping the field 65 times, while the people were lapping Canada Dry at the counter. Another great victory for Canada Dry!
OLSEN	Say, Jack what <u>are</u> you talking about?
BENNY	I often wonder.
OLSEN	You know, you talk about Canada Dry as though you'd invented it. Why, I've been drinking it long before this program ever started.
BENNY	You're telling me! I paid for it.
OLSEN	All right, Jack, I'll buy you a drink someday.
BENNY	And that will be <u>some</u> day. Listen, George, if you don't like the way I talk about Canada Dry Ginger Ale, why don't you do it?
OLSEN	I would, but I have my orchestra to worry about.
BENNY	Oh, are you worrying about it, too?

OLSEN	Well, I don't have to worry exactly. I've got a pretty good bunch of fellows in my band. They're all soloists.
BENNY	I know – every man for himself.
OLSEN	Jack, I don't think you know very much about music.
BENNY	I don't, eh? — George, you've never heard me play violin, have you? Why, I can play as well as anybody in your orchestra. I know all the classics.
OLSEN	Now wait a minute, Jack — I'm going to call your bluff. Let me hear you play something.
BENNY	Okay, George, give me a violin — what will I play?

(OLSEN HANDS BENNY VIOLIN WHICH HE STARTS TUNING UP.)

OLSEN	Can you play "Faust?"
BENNY	Faust or slow – any tempo.
OLSEN	Oh, play anything. What is your favorite area?
BENNY	My favorite area is WJZ — I'm no fool! And this is the Canada Dry, made-to-order program. I'll play something popular — boys, do you "Lovable?"
OLSEN	Don't play it, Jack, and keep it popular.
BENNY	Now, boys, follow me on this, but don't get in my way. Better give me an "A".
BOYS (TOGETHER)	"A"…
BENNY	Thanks — and now, folks, I'll bet you don't believe I'm really going to play. But I am, honestly … Give me a chord, Bert.

(PIANO CHORD — BENNY STARTS TO PLAY FIRST FEW BARS OF "LOVEABLE" – THEN STRIKES A BLUE NOTE)

Oh this violin is awful — are you surprised?

(STARTS TO SING LINE OF CHORUS)

BOYS (ABOUT 5 OF THEM) Play, it!… .play it!

(BENNY STOPS PLAYING AND SPEAKS LINE —

BENNY	Canada Dry, made-to-order, can be bought at the fountain …
BOYS	Play it!… play it!…

(BENNY RESUMES PLAYING)

BENNY	I'll bet nobody will believe it's me playing.
OLSEN	I hope they don't think it's one of my boys.

(FINISHES NUMBER. ROUND OF APPLAUSE)

BENNY	That was Jack Benny fiddling, ladies and gentlemen. They laughed when I picked up the violin – but they didn't know I was from the finance company.
	And now George Olsen has just looked in the mirror and requested himself to repeat that very popular number, "Is I In Love? I Is", sung by Ethel Shutta. This is coming to you thru the courtesy of Canada Dry Ginger Ale, made-to-order…

(ORCHESTRA STARTS UP ON THE CUE "TO-ORDER")

3. IS I IN LOVE? I IS.   ETHEL SHUTTA

BENNY	And now, ladies and gentlemen, the next number will be that very popular number, "Is I In Love? I Is.…
ETHEL	Jack, I just sang that.
BENNY	Oh, pardon me – I fell asleep for a couple of minutes. How was it – all right? Well, I'll talk a while now, Ethel, and <u>you</u> can go to sleep. By the way, better wake up Fran Frey – he's on next. Isn't it nice the way we relieve each other? Say, Ethel, you're looking rather tired tonight. You're not the same Ethel.
ETHEL	Well, I was up late last night. I gave a birthday party to George.
BENNY	Oh, you did… Was it George's birthday yesterday?
ETHEL	No, it's in August, but I thought I'd get it over with.
BENNY	Oh, in August — well, Ethel, if you meet me tomorrow, I'll give you your Christmas present and get that over with. Why didn't you invite me to the party?
ETHEL	Oh, it was just for people we know.
BENNY	Thanks – I'd like to meet you and George sometime.
(ETHEL LAUGHS)	
ETHEL	Don't you know George?
BENNY	Yes, I gave him a party the night before last at a soda fountain.
ETHEL	And what happened?
BENNY	<u>Again</u> I picked up a check for two glasses of Canada Dry Ginger Ale, made-to-order, at all soda fountains, with the right amount of syrup.
ETHEL	Now, Jack, do you mean to tell me that George <u>never</u> picks up a check?
BENNY	Yes he picks them up. — Ethel, I'm going to tell you something. I like George personally — he's a nice fellow. But he's the most conservative man I've ever met. Many times I've heard him say that he'd give a thousand dollars to be a millionaire.
ETHEL	Aw, you're kidding.

BENNY	No, I'm not. But I fooled him last Wednesday night after our broadcast. We went to a soda fountain to have a drink of Canada Dry, and I accidently left my money at home — on <u>purpose</u> — so George had to pay the check. Which is another victory for Canada Dry Ginger Ale, made-to-order, and so forth.
OLSEN	Yes, I remember that, Jack. And you still owe me a dime.
BENNY	Oh, no, George — I had a small glass. … Great guy, Olsen — I took him to the dog races one day and he bet fifty dollars on the rabbit — to show.
	Well, anyway, ladies and gentlemen, George is now going to play "Love, You Funny Thing," which will be sung by Fran Frey — who is also a funny thing — I mean a nice fellow.

4. LOVE, YOU FUNNY THING   FRAN FREY

BENNY	Ladies and gentlemen, starting tonight, we are going to introduce to you each week a new guest star — that is, we get the <u>star</u> and you <u>guest</u> who it is. We will bring to you only those people whom you all know — names like Albert EinSTEIN - FrankenSTEIN - and the STEIN song.
	Tonight, our guest star will be — -
(HEAVY APPLAUSE)	
	Tonight, we have with us <u>in the flesh</u> - Mr. J. Nottingham Leeke — - who happened to be on the beach, picking up a pebble from a spot right near the place where Amelia Earhart started her marvelous flight across the Atlantic. What a flight that was — and here <u>he</u> is in person!
	It is with the greatest pleasure that I present to you this evening the Honorable and Distinguished J. Nottingham Leeke!
(MORE APPLAUSE)	
	Where is he?
ETHEL	There he is — under the sink.
BENNY	Tell him to put down his wrench and come here … Oh, Mr. Leeke, tell us how you stood on the beach while Amelia Earhart took off.
LEEKE	It was a balmy summer's evening. And a goodly crowd was there, That well-nigh filled Frank's fountain On the corner of the square. The songs and witty sayings flowed thru the summer breeze When just then — in walked a girl — The lady that's known as Petrolia.

BENNY	That's very interesting… Now tell us, Mr. Leeke, did Miss Earhart have any difficulty getting started?
LEEKE	A bunch of boys were whooping it up in the Malumet soda fountain. A boy stood there at the music-box, playing a ragtime tune. The songs and witty sayings floated thru the air, When in walked a boy for a Canada Dry - With a lady that's known as Petrolia.
BENNY	Tell me — did the plane run into any air pockets?
LEEKE	Under a spreading stop-go tree, the village copper stands. The smith, a mighty man was he And in walked —
BENNY	I know – I know — and in walked a lady that's known as Petrolia … Well, Mr. Leeke, it was very nice of you to come here, as these little intellectual discourses by a mug like you are very enlightening.
LEEKE	Thank you.
BENNY	And, Mr. Leeke — will you forget everything that happened tonight — <u>including</u> our <u>address</u>?
LEEKE	I'll be glad to. How do I get out of here?
BENNY	Do you see that window over there?
LEEKE	Yes.
BENNY	Well, jump out and turn to your left … This leads into our next number called, "Oh, What A Thrill"! George Olsen and his Malumet Cafe Orchestra will now whoop it up — and it will be sung by the lady known as Ethel Shutta.

5.   OH, WHAT A THRILL!   ETHEL SHUTTA

BENNY	Hello! This is Jack again. And now for more news of our contest — – –
(SOUR FANFARE)	
	Of course you all know the trouble we had recently in trying to run a hundred percent contest. You remember it finally went into the hands of the receivers? Well, we are now very happy to announce that the sheriff has returned our prizes, realizing the situation and how times are — thousands of people walking around without first, second or even a third prize. Mighty square of the sheriff…

	We have been receiving so much fan mail lately, asking us what has become of our Limerick Contest — why did we drop it — or <u>did</u> we drop it?
	Here's a letter from a lady in <u>Junk</u> Junction, N. W.
ETHEL	Where's N.W., Jack?
BENNY	Near Washington — the letter reads:

"Dear, oh dear — what became of your Limerick Contest? You told us to write five new lines for a four-line verse, and the following week you sing a theme song. What do you expect us to do with our limericks?"

Well, ladies and gentlemen, this is all Greek to us, as we do not even remember the incident. We had absolutely nothing to do with limericks – unless my memory has failed me — which has often happened. However, it is a corking idea and an excellent suggestion.

So tonight we will <u>give</u> you a limerick… All right now, fellows, put down your girls and pick up your paper and a pencil. Prepare for the limerick — and listen carefully. Here it is:

There was a young girl from Czecho-Slovakia, who had all her jewels in Hock-ia…

She married a man from Kro-dents-ko-vitch, Russheea.

JOCKIA…SOCKIA…MOCKIA

Very clever, isn't it? That poem, folks, received the Kibitzer Prize in New York City as the best limerick of the year, and was given 24 hours to leave town.

Now listen very carefully — all you have to do is fill in the period at the finish of this limerick – with a little plug for Canada Dry. THE BEST PERIOD WINS A PRIZE! Don't send in commas or quotation marks – we have enough of these — just a neatly written PERIOD. Penmanship and neatness <u>will count</u>. Write your period on one side of the paper only, using a capital period — <u>not a small period</u>. PERIOD!

Our first prize will be a baby safety razor — making it safe to raise the little shaver… This is J.B. talking.

The second prize will be a complimentary ticket to the Sahara Desert, good for the month of August only. This ticket is not transferable.

The third prize will be three cheers – and a table, making a lovely set for your dining-room.

Each and every one of these prizes will come to you, fully equipped with freewheeling and balloon tires.

No employee or relative of Canada Dry and, more important, of George Olsen – will be allowed to enter this contest. Of course if they do, it's just low—down politics. That's all I can say.

And now a happy, optimistic little number called, "Eat, Drink and Be Merry," played by George Olsen who can certainly do the first two. Fran Frey will sing, accompanied by the Canada Dry Ginger-Alians.

6. EAT DRINK AND BE MERRY   FRAN FREY

BENNY   That was the last number of the eleventh program on the sixth of June. Hope you will all be with us next Wednesday night – as we are going to have a lot of fun. The sheriff has left for a two weeks' vacation.

Have to leave you now. Are you yawning? — hmmm?   Well, good-night, if you feel that way…

SIGNATURE—ROCKABYE MOON

ANNOUNCER   The next time you visit a soda fountain, ask for a Canada Dry ice cream soda. You will find it a delicious drink – a real treat on a hot day. Canada Dry is also available in bottles as well as made to order by the glass. You are invited to listen in again at this same time Wednesday night, whom Jack Benny, Ethel Shutta and George Olsen will entertain. This is the National Broadcasting Company.

June 8, 1932

STATION	WJZ	PROGRAM	CANADA DRY GINGER ALE, INC.
	AND	DATE	WEDNESDAY, JUNE 8, 1932
	BLUE NETWORK	TIME	9:30-10:00 P.M. (E.D.T.)

SIGNATURE - JOLLY GOOD COMPANY ORCHESTRA

1. EAT DRINK AND BE MERRY STEPT & POWERS ORCHESTRA & FREY

2. IF I WERE ONLY SURE OF YOU BERLIN ORCHESTRA & SMALL

3. PICNIC FOR TWO AGER, YELLEN & BORN. ORCH. SHUTTA & FREY

4. THE NIGHT SHALL BE FILLED WITH MUSIC SANTLY ORCHESTRA & SHUTTA

5. SHE'S A CORNFED INDIANA GAL FEIST ORCHESTRA & FREY

6. I BEG YOUR PARDON MADEMOISELLE STEPT & POWERS ORCHESTRA

SIGNATURE - ROCKABYE MOON

		PROGRAM	CANADA DRY GINGER ALE, INC.
		DATE	WEDNESDAY, JUNE 8, 1932
STATION	WJZ	TIME	9:30-10:00 P.M. (E.D.T.)
	AND		
	BLUE NETWORK		

SIGNATURE – JOLLY GOOD COMPANY   ORCHESTRA

ANNOUNCER	Ladies and gentlemen. Another half-hour of entertainment about Canada Dry Ginger Ale, now available made-to-order by the glass at soda fountains. George Olsen, Ethel Shutta and Jack Benny, the Canada Dry humorist, again perform for your enjoyment.
	By request, George Olsen opens the program with "Eat, Drink and Be Merry."

1. EAT DRINK AND BE MERRY   **ORCHESTRA & FREY**

ANNOUNCER	And now Jack, the American people are clamoring for you. Here he is, folks, Jack Benny.
BENNY	Hello, if you're not too busy. This is Jack Benny talking — Jack Benny —height, 5 foot, 9 — complexion, fair — jokes, the same — despises work — fond of good food — hobby, golf — very bad at hobby — weight, 155 pounds – I mean, 153.
VOICE	Jack, 151.
BENNY	Sold at 151 — well, to make a long story uninteresting, this is Jack Benny … "B" as in Bye, Bye Blackbird — "E" as in —
OLSEN	Say, Jack, you're not going to start that again.
BENNY	All right, George, any time you've heard it, stop me. Did you hear the one about the two Irishmen —
OLSEN	Stop, Jack, Stop.
BENNY	Okay, George. You know, a lot of people have been complaining that we do not answer their fan letters promptly. So before going any further, I want to dispose of our fan mail immediately. BOY, hand me those letters.
VOICE	<u>Here it is</u>, Jack.

BENNY	Your English is awful. You should say, "Here they are."
VOICE	No, here <u>it is</u>.
BENNY	All right, give me that letter. It reads: "We heard you play the violin Monday night and enjoyed it very much. All our neighbors moved — even the wolf left our door.
	(Signed) Francis H. Glum.
	Hmmm, <u>Francis</u>, eh? Well, we'll have to answer that.
	"Dear Sir — or Madame, as the Francis might be. I did not take up the violin to keep the wolf from your door.
	And now there has been a request for Paul Small to sing: "If I Were Only Sure of You". Okay, Paul —

2. IF I WERE ONLY SURE OF YOU   ORCHESTRA & PAUL SMALL

BENNY	That was "Minnie, the Moocher", sung by Paul Small. I'd like to tell you Paul's right name, but we are only allowed 30 minutes on the air. Say, I don't believe I ever described Paul to you. Well, he's a dreamy, romantic type of fellow, — a cross between Robert Montgomery and Wallace Beery-more — or less. He's quiet, unassuming — almost monotonous. In fact, he's an ex-service man. Only this morning he asked me if I'd take a walk with him to Washington. Can you imagine that? One night he got into a fight in a poolroom, and now he wants a bonus. Well, <u>that's</u> Paul Small.
	And now, before introducing the next number, I just want to say that a lot of people have asked us what <u>is</u> Canada Dry, made at the fountain, and all the details. So to make it clear, we have brought Canada Dry down to the studio by-the-glass IN PERSON, and we are going to interview him. CANADA DRY, meet the ladies and gentlemen!
HIGH-PITCHED VOICE	Hello, everybody.
BENNY	Now, CANADA DRY, tell me where you were born?
HIGH-PITCHED VOICE	Canada.
BENNY	That's strange — how were you brought up?
HIGH-PITCHED VOICE	By the bottle — but they tell me I'm just as good by-the-glass.
BENNY	What's your full name? (SPEAKING IN DEEP-SET VOICE) CANADA DRY GINGER ALE.
(Changing quickly to…)	
HIGH-PITCHED VOICE	Canada Dry Ginger Ale,

BENNY	(In high-pitched voice) How you like

(changing quickly to heavy voice)

	How do you like living at the fountain?
HIGH-PITCHED VOICE	Everything is all right – until the clerk puts me in the glass and squirts charged water in my eye.
BENNY	Well, remember you're just <u>the flavor</u>.
HIGH-PITCHED VOICE	I'm very popular, though. Lots of people ask for me.
BENNY	You're a pretty good-sized fellow, aren't you?
HIGH-PITCHED VOICE	Yes, but I want you to meet my big brother, LARGE GLASS.
BENNY	(In high voice)
	Where is he?

(Changing quickly to heavy voice)

	Where is he?
HIGH-PITCHED VOICE	Here he is.
BENNY	Large Glass, say something to the people.
TOUGH VOICE	Hello, everybody.
BENNY	I'll bet you folks think I'm a ventriloquist… Say, your big-brother looks like quite a husky fellow.
HIGH-PITCHED VOICE	He's the champion of ginger ales.
BENNY	You mean, <u>the champagne</u>.
HIGH-PITCHED VOICE	Oh, is that the way you say it?
BENNY	All right, boys – thanks. You can go now. That was a great boost. Where are you going now?
HIGH-PITCHED VOICE	Back to the fountain. This is a busy day. They need us.
BENNY	Well – goodbye.
HIGH-PITCHED VOICE	Good-bye.
BENNY	Two swell fellows.

(Changing to high-pitched voice)

          And now, ladies and gentlemen —

(Into normal voice)

	The next number on our program is called, "A Picnic for Two", which will be sung by Ethel Shutta and Fran Frey…
(changing into high voice)	
	And played by George Olsen
(Back to normal voice)	
	I'll kill those two guys.

3. A PICNIC FOR TWO   ORCHESTRA, SHUTTA & FREY

BENNY	That was "I Love A Parade", sung by Ethel Shutta and Fran Frey. Say, Ethel. I'm going away for the week-end — a little vacation. Would you and George like to go along?
ETHEL	Well, George and I were planning to go away, too. Where do you generally go, Jack?
BENNY	Oh, I go to a place in the country called Hay Fever Falls — gee, it's swell up there, Ethel — so nice and quiet, and healthful, too. As soon as you get there, the mosquitoes come over and vaccinate you.
ETHEL (LAUGHS)	No, I wouldn't care for that.
BENNY	Oh, you'd like to, Ethel. It's so quiet and restful — the idea of a place where you go to bed with the chickens and get up full of feathers.
	But, Ethel, speaking about vacations — I want to tell you what I think is the finest rest in the world.
ETHEL	What's that, Jack?
BENNY	A boat trip to Europe.
ETHEL	You know, Jack, I've never been, to Europe.
BENNY	Well, I went last summer on my first trip, and it was a great thrill. Ethel, if you ever go abroad, do as I did – take a sixteen-day boat — you know, one of those small cabin steamers … I want to tell you, Ethel. it's the most soothing trip in the world.
ETHEL	Is it really, Jack?
BENNY	<u>Yes, ma'am</u>. All you do is lean over the railing and relax.
ETHEL	Were you sick, Jack?
BENNY	Sick? Why, the third day out I commenced to look like my passport picture.
ETHEL	You must have had rough weather.
BENNY	Rough? See this ring around my neck, Ethel?

ETHEL	Yes, I often wondered what that was.
BENNY	Well, that's where I wore a port hole for sixteen days. But, Ethel there was one fellow on that boat for whom I felt really sorry. I mean I never saw a man that ill. For four days he just sat in a deck-chair without moving. He was as pale as a ghost.
ETHEL	Poor fellow.
BENNY	Ethel, I felt so sorry for him that I walked over and spoke to him. I said — "Mister, this boat doesn't seem to agree with you, either. Have you ever made an ocean trip before?" And he said, "Have I? I'm the CAPTAIN!" Say, Ethel, you're going to sing the next number, aren't you?
ETHEL	Yes, Jack.
BENNY	And now, George Olsen and his Deckhands will sail into a number called "The Night Shall be Filled with Music," piloted by Olsen, while Ethel will semaphore the lyrics. Ahoy there, Mates!

4. THE NIGHT SHALL BE FILLED WITH MUSIC   ORCHESTRA & ETHEL SHUTTA

BENNY	That was "The Saint Louis Blues", sung by Ethel Shutta. This is Jack Benny again, the traveling sailor.
	Say, do you know when I was telling you about my boat trip to Europe, I left out the funniest incident of all?
THORGERSEN	Say, Jack…
BENNY	You'll scream, at this … this'll kill you …
THORGERSEN	But, Jack …
BENNY	All right, Ed, I'll be with you in a minute. When we landed at Cherbourg — a port in Ireland —
THORGERSEN	Say, Jack, the sponsors want you to devote a few minutes to telling the audience about the product.
BENNY	What product?
THORGERSEN	Canada Dry Ginger Ale, made-to-order.
BENNY	By-the glass?
THORGERSEN	Yes, by-the-glass.
BENNY	Are the sponsors listening in tonight?
THORGERSEN	Certainly.

BENNY	Funny – I never get any fan mail from them.
THORGERSEN	Jack, just say a few words about Canada Dry.
JACK	All right, Ed — get me that soap box. I'll make a speech tonight that will go down in history.
	Ladies and gentlemen — Toastmaster — Guest of Honor — Friends, Romans and Countrymen … step up closer while I say a few words to you about the champagne of ginger ales. Now <u>you</u> drink Canada Dry and <u>I</u> drink Canada Dry. WHY? Step up a little closer, folks, and I'll tell you why. BECAUSE — it's an economical, thirst-quenching, thoroly satisfying effervescent beverage. (WHISTLES)

(ROUND OF APPLAUSE)

> I thank you!
>
> And furthermore, we are not merely satisfied with the fact that you order a glass of Canada Dry. We are also interested in the <u>spirit</u> in which you order it. That's the thing! When you go to a soda fountain, do you walk in with vim and vigor — or do you come in alone? There's only one man I know of who hesitates about drinking Canada Dry by-the-glass — and that man is — George Olsen! Why? Because – one glass of Canada Dry makes him feel like a new man, and how he hates to buy the new man a drink.

(MORE APPLAUSE)

> Now you take conditions in Nicaragua fifteen years ago — the year they had peace. Was there ever a happier, healthier race of people in the world than in Puerto Rico —

THORGERSEN (CORRECTING HIM)	Nicaragua, Jack.
BENNY	I mean, in Nicaragua. Sugar was plentiful that year. So were pineapples. And, if you're still listening in, so were bananas. That is why they were so healthy, folks — bananas never hurt anyone — they're yellow! … Of course, I personally like bananas because there are no bones in them.
	And in conclusion, all I can say, fellow-citizens and voters, is that if I am elected, I will do just as I promised. I want to thank you all for your kind consideration and careful attention.

(APPLAUSE – CHEERS, ETC)

(BREATHLESSLY)	Hello, everybody, this is Jack Benny, talking from a horizontal position on the floor of the NBC Studios. <u>Am I tired</u>?
	So now, Fran Frey will sing a little novelty number which he wrote himself, called "I'm A Cornfed Indiana Girl." Fran will sing – George will direct — and I will catch my breath.

5. I'M A CORNFED INDIANA GIRL   ORCHESTRA & FRAN FREY

BENNY   Fran, I must compliment you. Did you really write that song?

FRAN   Yes, Sir — what do you think of it?

BENNY   Well, Fran, don't get discouraged. Rome wasn't built in a day. (LAUGHS) Lovely fellow, Fran. And now, ladies and gentlemen, more news of our contest.

(CORNET SOLO — "HUNT" MUSIC)

                Say, George, this is a CONTEST — not a fox hunt.

(SOUR FANFARE)

                Since Monday night we have received bundles of limericks filled in with periods, as we requested. We have looked each and every one over carefully — that is, <u>each bundle</u> — and the periods came in swell, although some jumped out of the envelopes. People who could not write periods sent in poppy seeds, while others sent in ball bearings. These, of course, were immediately disqualified.

                Now we're not going to beat around the bush or stall with our prizes — we will give them out immediately. Here are the winners — 34,765 people were tied for first place. <u>Great work</u>. And 65,012 were tied for second place. Congratulations, second placers. While 13,876 were tied for third place. In fact, we only found one loser who happened to be out of town and knew nothing about our contest. So we will immediately send him the three prizes. His name is … J. Fitzhugh Quick, of Apple Dumpling, Indiana. Congratulations, Fitzhugh, and I hope the prizes fits-you, Fitzhugh. Gee, I wish I had picked out a guy by the name of Smith.

                And now, ladies and gentlemen, I wish to announce that on next Monday night on this Canada Dry program, we are going to have a world-wide hook-up — a network hooking up New York – China – Alaska – the South Pole – and Jimmy Durante's schnozzle in Hollywood, California. DON'T FORGET TO LISTEN IN. We will not hook YOU.

                While you are making a note of this announcement, we will hear a snappy little number called "I Beg Your Pardon, Mademoiselle," sung by our trio, and played by George Olsen and his champagne of Ginger-Alians.

6. I BEG YOUR PARDON, MADEMOISELLE   ORCHESTRA & TRIO

BENNY   That was the last number of our twelfth program on the 8th of June.

SIGNATURE – ROCKABYE MOON

ANNOUNCER   The next time you visit a soda fountain, ask for a Canada Dry ice cream soda. You will find it a delicious drink – a real treat on a hot day. Canada Dry is also available in bottles as well as made-to-order by the glass. You are invited to listen in again at this same time Monday night, when Jack Benny, Ethel Shutta and George Olsen will entertain. This is the National Broadcasting Company.

June 13, 1932

STATION	WJZ AND BLUE NETWORK	PROGRAM	CANADA DRY GINGER ALE, INC.
		DATE	MONDAY, JUNE 13, 1932
		TIME	9:30-10:00 P.M. (E.D.T.)

SIGNATURE — JOLLY GOOD COMPANY ORCHESTRA

1. BLUE DANUBE   STRAUSS   SPECIAL ARR. ORCHESTRA

2. ROCK A BYE MOON   ROBBINS   ORCHESTRA & SHUTTA

3. SCAT SONG   MILLS   ORCHESTRA & GARDNER

4. LULLABY OF THE LEAVES   BERLIN   ORCHESTRA & SMALL

5. BANKING ON THE WEATHER   WITMANN   ORCH. SHUTTA & FREY

6. I'VE GOT THE POTATOES   DES. BROWN & HEN.   ORCHESTRA & FREY

SIGNATURE -- ROCKABYE MOON

STATION	WJZ AND BLUE NETWORK	PROGRAM	CANADA DRY GINGER ALE, INC.
		DATE	MONDAY, JUNE 13, 1932
		TIME	9:30-10:00 P.M. (E.D.T.)

SIGNATURE – JOLLY GOOD COMPANY ORCHESTRA

ANNOUNCER   Ladies and gentlemen. Another half-hour of entertainment about Canada Dry Ginger Ale, now available made-to-order by the glass at soda fountains. George Olsen, Ethel Shutta and Jack Benny, the Canada Dry humorist, again perform for your enjoyment.

By request, George Olsen opens the program with a special arrangement of "Blue Danube."

1. BLUE DANUBE   ORCHESTRA

ANNOUNCER   And now, folks, here's Jack Benny. Okay, Jack.

BENNY   Are you ready – hmmm? As they say in the stock market. … high – low, everybody. This is Jack Benny…the masseur of ceremonies, coming to you direct from the Canada Dry Room. Am I steamed up?

Tonight, folks, is our big night… the coast-to-coast-to-coast hookup between Alaska and New York … coasting us a Pretty Penny. Do I know what I'm talking about? Of coast!

This hookup will come to you at exactly ten minutes of ten … Eastern Standard Daylight Saving Time… or ten o'clock If your watch is fast… or any time if it stopped.

This being the sixth successive week of our serious …er, series … I have been requested to say a few words regarding our product … Canada Dry Ginger Ale which is now sold by-the-glass at all fountains. How many …

(PHONE STARTS RINGING)

of you are still unfamiliar with the method of making Canada Dry at the fountain?

(VOICE HEARD ANSWERING PHONE: Hello! yes, yes, etc…)

How many of you are still in doubt as to how to order it? Well, I'd like to tell you that —

COULTER	Call for you, Jack.
BENNY	Pardon me just a moment…

Hello! … Who? … Oh, Molly … Hello, Molly … Please don't call me here … I'm busy… Yes, yes … I've got the tickets … huh-huh, two tickets for Central Park, right on the aisle … All right … all right … call me later… Yeah, next winter … I'm going to be busy all summer … Good-bye.

(SOUND EFFECT: HANGING UP RECEIVER)

Now when you are thirsty and step up to the fountain and ask for a glass …

(PHONE RINGS AGAIN. VOICE HEARD ANSWERING IT)

of Canada Dry, here is exactly what will happen … the Soda clerk will put the right amount of syrup in the glass …

COULTER	For you again, Jack.
BENNY	Pardon me a moment, folks …

Hello … hello … Molly? … For heaven's sake, Molly, certainly I love you … of course I do, but there's a time and place for everything… This is not the <u>place</u> and it isn't <u>time</u> yet … Good-bye …

(BLOWS KISS INTO PHONE)

Good-bye …

(SOUND EFFECT: HANGING UP RECEIVER)

That was <u>not</u> static folks… those were kisses.

Now as I said before, the soda clerk will put the right amount of Syrup in the glass … then he will add charged water…

(PHONE RINGS AGAIN)

Stir it up and then … it's Molly! … Never mind, Doug, I'll answer that.

Hello! … Who is this? … Yes, this is Jack … WRONG NUMBER!

(SOUND EFFECT: HANGING UP RECEIVER)

That was Molly's sister, Hotta …You know… .Hotta-Molly … Am I hotta to-night-a?

Well, anyway, that's how Canada Dry Ginger Ale is made-to-order at the fountain. It's also good with ice cream…and <u>still better without phone calls</u>.

And now Ethel Shutta will sing, "Rockabye Moon." It will be played by George Olsen and his Panama Hat Band. Hmm!

2. ROCK A BYE MOON   ETHEL SHUTTA

BENNY	That was "Rock a Bye Moon", sung by the sweet and charming Ethel… Say, Ethel, where did you get that wonderful coat of tan?
ETHEL	I told you I was going to the beach for the weekend… Where did you go, Jack?
BENNY	I spent four days at Lake Chip-a-munga-chakwa-chobee.
ETHEL	Where?
BENNY	Lake Chopee-Chippee…Ethel, do I have to go thru <u>that</u> again?
ETHEL	Is it nice up there?
BENNY	It's a lovely place, Ethel. But it's the smallest lake you've ever seen. In fact, it reminds me of a glass of Canada Dry without the glass.
ETHEL	Aw, a lake can't be that small.
BENNY	It can't, eh?… I'd hate to drop a blotter in it.
ETHEL	Is it hard to get fish up there?
BENNY	No, all the grocery stores have them.
ETHEL	That must be <u>some</u> place.
BENNY	Oh, I had a lot of fun. I lived in one of those small country hotels where you get real good meals. You know, for breakfast, we had scrambled eggs…one egg on the table and everybody scrambled for it…And the best coffee you ever drank. And I liked the way they served it, too … half-and-half… half in the cup and half in the saucer… You don't lose any of it that way. But I never tasted such fruit. They had a bowl of fruit on the table…plums, peaches, and grapes…and it all tasted alike… tasted like <u>wax</u> to me.
ETHEL	Jack, maybe it was <u>ornament</u> fruit.
BENNY	No, just plums, peaches and grapes… I liked the plums, tho… they looked like prunes with a face massage.
ETHEL	My favorite fruit is bananas.
BENNY	I like Bananas, too… no Bones in them. Of course, that was just for breakfast. Then at dinner, they served the wolf at the door…I was afraid to come down for supper because my police dog was missing.
ETHEL	Didn't they have any sports up there at all?
BENNY	Oh yes… we played tennis on Sunday… without tennis balls.
ETHEL	Well, Jack, how could you play?
BENNY	We swatted flies at each other… And what do you suppose happened the last day, Ethel?

ETHEL	I don't know, Jack.
BENNY	The hotel burned down…and 80,000 insects were homeless.
ETHEL	Jack, I don't believe a word you say.
BENNY	Neither do I… Are you singing the next number, Ethel?
ETHEL	No, Hotcha Gardner will sing "The Scat Song." It will be played by George Olsen and—
BENNY	…and his Musical Kindergarten…Come, Ethel, let's away…

3. SCAT SONG   HOTCHA GARDNER

BENNY	As you all know, we try on nearly every one of our programs to bring a celebrity to you as our Guest Star— someone who has accomplished something outstanding. Tonight we have with us the famous orator, Theodolphus…T… Snick…Professor of Pig Latin in the University of Notre-Public.
(APPLAUSE)	
	You have, perhaps, read some of the learned professor's books, including "The Outline of History" by H. G. Wells…If you haven't, it's your loss… Snick's. His last famous speech took place while walking down Broadway, talking to himself. He will continue it on the air at this time and place.
	And now may I present the eminent professor Theodolphus… T… Snick! Who will speak to you on the subject: "Alphabet Soup and how to Read It."
(MORE APPLAUSE)	
	He comes to you through the courtesy of Canada Dry Ginger Ale, made-to-order by the glass at all soda fountains.
	Why is Canada Dry Ginger Ale the finest drink on the market today?
COULTER	Jack, the professor is waiting.
BENNY	I beg your pardon… Go ahead, Professor.
SNICK (stuttering)	Hello… every b-b-b-b-b-body.
BENNY	Guess I'll take a nap for a while.
SNICK	Ladies and g-g-g-g-g-g Ladies and g-g-g-g-g-
BENNY	Ladies and gentlemen! … go ahead…
SNICK	It b- b – b – b – b – b— be—hooooooo—
BENNY	It behooves me to say…You know, Snick, we're only on the air for half an hour. You'll have to do something about it.

SNICK (hurriedly)	Well, all I want to s-s-s-say is that I g-g-g-g-g-g-got—I got—I got— I got — (whistles)
BENNY	Are you Snick or Ray Perkins? Now listen, Professor, President Hoover only talks fifteen minutes. Who do you think you are?
SNICK	w-w-w—well—I'll t-t-t-t- tell you.
BENNY	Now wait a minute…do you stutter like that all the time?
STICK (straight)	No, only when I t-t-t—t—t—talk.
BENNY	I see. Go ahead with your speech.
SNICK	In order to read alfa-alfa-alfa-alfa…
BENNY	Say, Snick, I'm afraid we'll have to call the whole thing off. You remind me of the travelling salesman…the farmer…and the farmer's stutter. Well, to be honest with you, Snick, <u>our time is limited</u>. So if you'll just announce the next number on our program, we'll call it square.
SNICK	Aw-aw-aw-aw-aw-all right… the next number will b.b.b.b.b…

(SOUND EFFECT: GLASS CRASH)

BENNY	Ladies and gentlemen, the next number will be a request to repeat, "The Lullaby of the Leaves," played by George Olsen and sung by p-p-p-p-p-p- (whistles)…Paul Small

4. LULLABY OF THE LEAVES   PAUL SMALL

BENNY	And now, ladies and gentlemen, for the biggest event in our Canada Dry series… the greatest accomplishment since the history of the radio…our hookup with Station W-O-O-F, Alaskal!…
	We will take you right to the Ice Palace, Where you will hear Eski-Mo Bimberg and his Igloo Syncopators. Moe from Alaska…do you NOME?
	There will be a slight delay, folks, sometimes it takes three or four days to get this hookup. So please stand by…or sit by… or go to sleep and we'll call you.
	HERE WE GO!

(BEGIN STATIC NOW)

B.K. ALASKA!

(START TRAIN EFFECT)

We are passing Florida!…the playground of America…with apologies to Atlantic City…

(BOAT WHISTLE)

        Now we're passing over Havana. Hello, there, you peanut vendors… get a load of that rhumba

(SECOND BOAT WHISTLE)

        Ah, now we're nearing Sweden! George, say hello to the folks.

OLSEN   Jack, this isn't the way to Alaska.

BENNY   It's all right. I've got a tourist ticket … it doesn't cost any more.

(AEROPLANE EFFECT)

        Is that an aeroplane … or Uncle Don?

(COW BELLS)

        Ah! at last, <u>Alaska</u>!… hear those sleigh bells…HELLOOOOOOOOO, ALASKA!

DISTANT VOICE   You've got the wrong station…this is BROOKLYN!

BENNY   After all that travelling…Hello, hello… Operator… Operator…

(STOP ALL STATIC EFFECT HERE)

        Ladies and gentlemen, something has gone wrong with our hookup. While we're investigating, George Olsen and his Stand-by Orchestra will entertain us with "Banking on The Weather." It will be sung by Ethel Shutta and Fran Frey.

6. BANKING ON THE WEATHER   ETHEL SHUTTA AND FRAN FREY

BENNY   We have finally succeeded in getting Alaska. You see, we had a small map before and didn't realize how far away Alaska really is…DO you Saskatche-wan?

(START STATIC AGAIN)

        In just a moment you will hear the voice of Eski-Mo Bimberg, formerly of St. Louis, MO. And mo' popular than ever.

        Here we are … HELLOOOOOO, ALASKA!

MOE (from distance)   HELLOOOOOOO!

BENNY   Is this Alaska…or Chile?

MOE   It's Alaska and it's chilly.

BENNY   How's the weather up there?

MOE   It's 40 below zero, and we're having our Indian Summer.

This is Station W—O—O—F, Alaska … Moe Bimberg and his Igloo Syncopators… We are broadcasting from the Ice Palace, thru the courtesy of Canada Dry Ginger Ale…with ice. We will now play the latest song hit to reach Alaska.

(3-piece brass band go into "HI LEE…HI LOW" while they are playing, Jack Benny ad libs —

BENNY   We had to get Alaska to hear that…

Well, you can't expect any hot numbers from those guys—they're all sitting on cakes of ice.

SNICK   Say, what's g-g-g-go … go-go—going on there?

BENNY   Hey, Snick, get out of Alaska… You're in Moe's way.

(FINISH OF NUMBER "HI LEE HI LOW".)

That's fine, Moe. Now play an <u>old</u> number.

MOE   We don't know any old numbers. Say, Jack, since I got up here, I notice the Alaskans have been crazy about the Canada Dry contest, and they want to know if you'll start one for them.

(FADE DOWN ON STATIC)

BENNY   Why, certainly, Moe…be glad to… We have never failed anybody…So listen carefully, you little Eskimosers… it is very simple and takes just two days of your spare time.

MOE   The days are six months long up here.

BENNY   Well, I can't help that…

Here are the simple rules…never mind using pens or pencils. Since we have started our contests, the pencil companies have sold as many pencils as we have sold Canada Dry Ginger Ale, and we can't have that.

So follow these rules closely…take a dried fish… bite clearly across the back what you think of Canada Dry, made-to-order. Bite on <u>one side</u> of the fish <u>only</u>. In fact, we want you to tell the whole tale at the end of the fish. <u>Words</u> are all we want… don't write music on the scales…

(That may be a bad joke, but somebody will like it.)

And now, Alaskans, it is very essential in your message on the fish that you say something nice about Canada Dry, as we might as well remain friends.

Your entries must be packed tightly in cans and shipped to us prepaid. Try to get these fish to us by Friday…as things are bad here, too. Don't send us any sea lions as our janitor gets very jealous of anything around here that looks like him.

And now for the prizes … the winner of the first prize will receive a photograph of a ten-dollar bill…The second prize will be a large handsome sized box of wrinkles, gathered from the face on the bar-room floor…

	And the third prize—which is always our best prize — will be six assorted icicles… which will be sent to you in time to start your 6-day bicycle race. Is it all clear, Alaska?
MOE	Yes, the weather up here is marvelous.
BENNY	Well, our time is up … Cheerio, Moe!
MOE	Cheerio, Jack!

(CUT OFF ALL STATIC HERE)

BENNY	Ladies and gentlemen, we are back in New York… Turn off the heat, Kvetch.
MOE	Say. Jack, can I go home now?
BENNY	Yes. here's your check.
	And now George Olsen and his Ginger-alians will play another request number, "I've Got the Potatoes," sung by Fran Frey. Say, Fran, is Ethel going to sing it, too?
FREY	Alasker.
BENNY	Oh, Fran!

6. I'VE GOT THE POTATOES　　　　　　　　FRAN FREY

BENNY	That was the last number on our thirteenth program on the 13th of June. Are you superstitious…hmmmm? Be sure to listen in Wednesday night for the announcement of the winners of tonight's contest. I must leave you until Wednesday…And as they say Alaska, YOUkon go to bed now…so goodnight, then.

SIGNATURE – ROCKABYE MOON

ANNOUNCER	The next time you visit a soda fountain, ask for a Canada Dry ice cream soda. You will find it a delicious drink – a real treat on a hot day. Canada Dry is also available in bottles as well as made-to-order by the glass. You are invited to listen in again at this same time Wednesday night, when Jack Benny, Ethel Shutta and George Olsen will entertain. This is the National Broadcasting Company.

June 15, 1932

STATION	WJZ	PROGRAM	CANADA DRY GINGER ALE, INC.
	AND	DATE	WEDNESDAY, JUNE 15, 1932
	BLUE NETWORK	TIME	9.30 - 10:00 P.M. (E.D.T.)

SIGNATURE -- JOLLY GOOD COMPANY

1. BUGLE CALL RAG	SPEC. MATERIAL	ORCHESTRA
2. PARADISE	FEIST	ORCHESTRA & SMALL
3. CRAZY PEOPLE	FEIST	ORCHESTRA & FREY
4. ROAMING FOR ROMANCE	DeS. B. & H.	ORCHESTRA & SHUTTA
5. WHY DON'T YOU GET LOST	JOE DAVIS	ORCHESTRA & GARDNER
6. I'M THAT WAY ABOUT BROADWAY	DeS.B. & H.	ORCHESTRA & SHUTTA

SIGNATURE — ROCKABYE MOON

		PROGRAM	CANADA DRY GINGER ALE, INC.
		DATE	WEDNESDAY, JUNE 15, 1932
STATION	WJZ	TIME	9.30 - 10:00 P.M. (E.D.T.)
	AND		
	BLUE NETWORK		

SIGNATURE — JOLLY GOOD COMPANY

ANNOUNCER   Ladies and gentlemen. Another half-hour of entertainment about Canada Dry Ginger Ale, now available made-to-order by the glass at soda fountains. George Olsen, Ethel Shutta and Jack Benny, the Canada Dry humorist, again perform for your enjoyment.

George Olsen opens the program with "BUGLE CALL RAG."

1. BUGLE CALL RAG   ORCHESTRA

ANNOUNCER   Jack Benny is ambling over now, folks, so I'll have to make way.

BENNY   Hello, cash customers … this is Jack Benny … Jack as in MULE and Benny as in BENNY FRANKLIN … the man that put a wisecrack in the Liberty Bell.

Everything's fine in the Studio tonight. I think we're all here. Let's call the roll…

Fran Frey

FREY   Here!

BENNY   Ethel Shutta…

ETHEL   Here I am, Jack.

BENNY   George Olsen

OLSEN   Present.

BENNY   I was afraid of that   Where's that handsome boy in the orchestra?

ORCHESTRA (TOGETHER) Here!

BENNY   Dick "Hotcha" Gardner…

GARDNER   Here.

BENNY   Paul Small. …

SMALL	I couldn't come tonight … I'm home with a headache.
BENNY	Well, be here Monday…Philander Kvetch, our janitor…
KVETCH (HARRY CONN)	HERE!
BENNY	Well, you should be downstairs, cleaning up. …I guess we're all set. George Olsen looks particularly well this evening. He has a ruddy complexion from the Beach. … Ethel has one from the drugstore… and the boys in the band are all sun-kissed. How the sun could kiss those faces, I don't know…

(BOYS IN ORCHESTRA LAUGH)

The boys laughed at that. If they understood English, I'd get killed. And now, ladies and gentlemen, I have a little surprise for you … and a shock to me. George Olsen has gone the way of all flesh and will play "PARADISE" again. This number must have been a request, as I am sure Olsen would never have thought of that himself … George, are you really going to play "Paradise"?

OLSEN	Yes, Jack. People have written in, asking for it. They say it's a haunting melody.
BENNY	That's what you get for murdering it the last time you played it … Say, George, did you ever go haunting?
OLSEN	No, did you?
BENNY	Oh yes, I used to haunt big game in Africa.
OLSEN	Did you find any?
BENNY	Well, a two-bit limit was the best I could find… Say, folks, are we wasting our time?

George Olsen will now play "PARADISE", sung by Paul Small…by special permission of Canada Dry, made-to-order, by the glass…

(ORCHESTRA STARTS PLAYING OPENING BARS OF "PARADISE" OVER THIS SPEECH) at all fountains   …

2. PARADISE   PAUL SMALL

BENNY (YAWNING) That was "Paradise," ladies and gentlemen… this is Jack Benny yawning…

And now, just a few words regarding our contest …

(WEAK SOUR FANFARE)

We didn't need that, George… We have been getting so much undesirable mail lately regarding our contest and prizes… people who received the first prize claim that they really won the third, and vice versa… who also entered our contest. Others claim that they received no prizes at all. In fact, we have one letter from a man signing himself, <u>Ed Cetera</u>… who claims he has been waiting weeks for his prize, and wants to know what's the big idea. Therefore, on account of the tremendous amount of detail work on program like this … you know, there's a lot of work mailing out fifty or sixty prizes <u>every day</u>, besides keeping Olsen's white shoes cleaned. So I put an ad in the paper today for a secretary…

ANNOUNCER   Say, Jack, there's a young lady out here to see you.

BENNY   That's what I call service! … How do you do, Miss?

GARBO (MISS STEWART)   Is this Mr. Jack-Olsen-Shutta-Benny?

BENNY   Oh, I'm part of it…What can I do for you?

GARBO   Did you advertise for a secter-ary?

BENNY   A what?

GARBO   A secter-ary…you know, a woman to be your right-hand man.

BENNY   You mean a <u>secretary</u>.

GARBO   Yes… I think so.

BENNY   I want a girl to help me with the details of this program…answering the fan mail, and so forth.

GARBO   Oh, that should be <u>easy</u>… I've answered <u>as many as three</u> letters a day.

BENNY   Hm, I see…Have you had any experience?

GARBO   <u>Have I</u>? Why, I was up in an aeroplane once, and when we were flying back we ran into a big mountain and it hit us and…

BENNY   All right… experience OKAY… Now how much money do you want?

GARBO   Well…

BENNY   Well?

GARBO   Well…the money…

BENNY   Yes, the money. …How much salary do you want?

GARBO   Well. … I'm in the habit of getting fifty dollars a week.

BENNY   That's fine … but this job will <u>break</u> you of that <u>habit</u>. Now I'll give you twenty dollars a week…and, as business picks up and things get better, I'll make it eighteen!

GARBO   Thanks, Mr. Benny … that's awfully nice of you, because I've only got five dollars to my name.

BENNY   Here, give me that five and you'll have twenty-three coming to you on pay day…

Oh, by the way, what's your name?

GARBO	Garbo.
BENNY	Garbo…that's a familiar name…you're not <u>Greta</u>.
GARBO	No, Smalla.
BENNY	Oh, Smalla Garbo! … were you ever in the movies?
GARBO	Sure, I just came from there… I had a nice seat in the balcony and…
BENNY	That's two dollars off your salary… Well, Miss Garbo, you're my secretary now. Will you take the duster and do a little shorthand around the furniture. I'll call you later. Mr. Olsen is getting impatient to play another request number called "CRAZY PEOPLE," sung by Fran Frey, played by George Olsen and requested by nobody.

3. CRAZY PEOPLE   FRAN FREY

BENNY	Oh, Miss Garbo…Smalla
GARBO	Yes, Mr. Benny.
BENNY	Come over here, we've got work to do today … Say, Smalla, you're not a very pretty girl. Did you have your face lifted?
GARBO (SLOWLY)	No, I've still got it.
BENNY	That was my fault for asking. …Now, let's get down to work. First, I want you to take a very important letter. We are going to find out <u>right now</u> why the company that manufactures our prizes has not sent them to us. TAKE A LETTER. Fink, Jones, Smith, Watkins, Goldman Brothers and Gillihan… and Sons Company, Incorporated … Better put another Gillihan in so they'll be <u>sure</u> to get it. Dear Frank … We are having a lot of trouble with our Canada Dry Ginger Ale, made-to-order, by the glass contest …
GARBO	What?
BENNY	Canada Dry Contest … you've heard of <u>Canada Dry</u>, haven't you?
GARBO (WITH ASSURANCE)	Oh yes, I was there when it was raining, too.
BENNY	Something tells me you'll be out of work tomorrow … now, let's go ahead. … We have ordered six Grade A Contest Prizes and one dozen Grade B and C for our foreign trade, but so far have not received these shipments, and three of our best states are without prizes. If we do not receive the merchandise by morning, we will have to order our prizes in future from Sink, Schmell, Twunk, Hoomentasch, Wheeler and Woolsey, Brothers and Sons, Incorporated … who have been soliciting our business for some time.
I certainly hope you are not letting that little bill we owe you from last year stand in the way of our friendship. I know we promised to pay you ON time, but what I really meant was that we will pay in IN time. If you are worrying about the money we owe you, <u>stop it immediately</u>. Let <u>us</u> do the worrying. I have worried so much lately that even my toupee is getting gray.

So just forget everything and send us our prizes without further delay. If we do not hear from you by return mail I will not only put the matter in the hands of my attorney, but am seriously thinking of beating you up.

Yours very truly,

Sign it— GEORGE OLSEN

P.S...

Regards to your wives ... Mrs. Fink, Jones, Smith, Watkins, Goldman Brothers and Gillihan...Sons, Company, Incorporated, and whatever new partners you may have added, who have wives... Well, that's that... Now, Miss Garbo, what have you got?

GARBO   Just a little rheumatism.

BENNY   Didn't you take down what I just dictated?

GARBO   Dictated?... Why, I thought you were talking to Olsen.

BENNY   My next trick, ladies and gentlemen will be making a woman disappear ... Miss Garbo, will you please run out and get me some Christmas cards?

GARBO   Sure, but they won't be ready until Christmas.

BENNY   Wait for them. And now, Ethel Shutta will sing another request entitled, "ROAMING FOR ROMANCE." This will be played by King Cole Olsen and his Fiddlers Three... while I gaze out of the window into the silly...stilly night.

4. ROAMING FOR ROMANCE   ETHEL SHUTTA

OLSEN   This is George Olsen, ladies and gentlemen. Jack Benny seems to be busy at the moment, arranging another very important hookup, and has asked me to introduce the next number, "WHY DON'T YOU GET LOST?" It will be sung by Dick Hotcha Gardner. Let's go, boys.

5. WHY DON'T YOU GET LOST?   DICK HOTCHA GARDNER

BENNY   And now, ladies and gentlemen, another big event comes to you tonight thru the courtesy Of Canada Dry Ginger Ale, made-to-order, by the glass — another severe test of endurance ... stamina ...and class.

Tonight, CANADA DRY boxes for the Middle weight Championship of the World, including Siam and Hello, Alaska. His opponent will be the present champion, ONE-ROUND CIRCLE of Roundhouse, Pennsylvania... CIRCLE has a great record...in one hundred and twelve fights he won 12 on fouls and the other hundred were in the bag, but CANADA DRY won all of his fights in the glass.

This fight will be brought to you thru another tremendous hookup … we will now take you direct to the Ring side of MEDICINE CHEST GARDEN …where this battle of the Half Century… everything's coming down … will take place!

(BEGIN STATIC…CROWD MUMBLING, EXCHANGING BETS, BUZZING, ETC.)

Well, here we are … The house is jammed! People are hanging on the grafters … rafters. And what a beautiful sight… the Garden is filled with roses… Harry Rose… Billy Rose… and Sam Rose…

The place is packed with celebrities …Mayor Hoover just walked in and took his customary seat at the ring side … members of the Senate and Congress are here… Ah! here comes E. Livermore Dunk, Secretary of the Navy… Bean Company … followed by the Honorable C. Berry, Secretary of Research… In the third row I see Philander Kvetch, Secretary of the Interior …of our Studio…   Ah! here comes J. Herkimer Twazz, Secretary of Space… and over there's Miss Smalla Garbo, Secretary of Jack Benny… In fact, the whole cabinet is here …they think this fight is going to be a pudding… Get it?…cabinet pudding… I will now turn the mike over to Mike Angelo, the great chiseler … Okay, Mike…take the mike…

MIKE (HARRY CONN)   Thanks, Jack.

BENNY   Thanks, Mike.

MIKE   Dis fight comes to you tru de coitesy of Canada Dry Ginger Ale, which is now sold at all fountains in the glass…it is made to order with the right amount of syrup and charged water. No kiddin', folks, it's A GREAT DRINK, … take it, Jack.

BENNY   Thanks, Mike.

MIKE   Thanks, Jack.

BENNY   They are now in the center of the ring, taking instructions from the referee … who used to be an umpire but couldn't see good. ONE-ROUND CIRCLE is the first to enter the ring…Take it, Mike.

MIKE   Thanks, Jack.

BENNY   Thanks, Mike.

MIKE   Dis fight comes to you tru de coitesy of Canada Dry Ginger Ale…which you can get at the fountain in the glass. Take it, Jack…

BENNY   Thanks, Mike.

MIKE   Thanks, Jack.

BENNY   What a fight!…what a fight!…Oh, Pardon me, it hasn't started yet. They are sitting in their corners awaiting the bell. The betting is furious … George Olsen just bet the carbon from his motor that the fight won't go four years… Mike, take the mike.

MIKE   Thanks, Jack.

BENNY	Thanks, Mike.
MIKE	Dis terrif battle is coming to you tru de coitesy of… You take it, Jack.
BENNY	Thanks, Mike.
MIKE	You're welcome, Jack.

(WARNING WHISTLE)

BENNY That was the 65-minute warning… they are getting ready… ONE-ROUND is removing his robe… he has trained faithfully and looks the picture of health… CANADA DRY removes his glass… making the weight makes him look a little drawn and pale dry… but he's in there to fight for the Champagne-ship… are you following me, sponsors?

(GONG RINGS)

There they go … ROUND ONE! …

ONE-R0UND walks to the center of the ring … CANADA DRY runs …they are now sparring for an opener… er, opening …ONE-ROUND looks worried, but CANADA DRY is very cool … are you at the fight, sponsors?… ONE-ROUND leads a terrific clinch to the jaw, but CANADA DRY can take it …the referee separates them… CANADA DRY misses a left to the referee ONE-ROUND is fainting, but CANADA DRY revives him …

What's this? SCHMELLING walks in to the ring to be introduced, and is knocked out… Ah, well, he came in a week too soon…

CANADA DRY keeps stabbing his left… he's very good with his left but he's also good with ice cream… ONE-ROUND pokes a straw into Canada Dry's eye … THERE THEY GO! … left-right … left-right…left-right …left-right … left-right … what a fight…WHAT A MIX-UP!…left-right … left-right…

(ORCHESTRA GOES INTO "ANVIL CHORUS" – IN TEMPO BUT VERY PIANISSIMO)

The boys are now marching to their corners …WHAT A FIGHT! And the best round since Prosperity went around the corner… Mike Angelo…

MIKE	Thanks, Jack.
BENNY	You're welcome, Mike.
MIKE	Dis slaughter comes to you tru de coitesy of—

(GONG RINGS)

BENNY ROUND TWO!…

They both rush to the center of the ring, but ONE-ROUND detours … CANADA DRY follows him in a taxi …they are back to the center of the ring …ONE-ROUND has a deep cut over his lip …No, he drank water out of a ketchup bottle … CANADA DRY swings thirty-seven hard rights to ONE-ROUND'S jaw and receives 110 in return … each a knockout punch…

(ROAR OF THE CROWD)

The crowd roars … with James Cagney …

WHAT'S THAT?… CANADA DRY is down on one knee and is going to sing "Mammy"… but Olsen can't play it … So he gets up and goes after ONE-ROUND… They go into a clinch… again they go into a clinch – clinch – clinch – clinch…<u>what a fight</u>! I mean, <u>what a clinch</u>!… This clinch comes to you thru the courtesy of Canada Dry…

Look!   Canada Dry is chewing ONE-ROUND'S ear… he likes cauliflower … WHAT A FIGHT, but try to get your money back…CANADA DRY leads a right to the ankle … ONE-ROUND claims a foul, but it was a clean kick in the ankle …he's yellow but CANADA DRY IS amber… he is <u>some</u> amber (HOMBRE) ombray… They're now going into a clinch… hugging each other… Joan Crawford's entering the ring and claims the scene was stolen from her last picture with Clark Gable … But such is <u>not</u> the case…

Again, they are fighting … ONE-ROUND crosses a right to the jaw… Joan Crawford crosses the street …CANADA DRY counters with an uppercut and, incidentally, CANADA DRY is sold at the counter…

THE CROWD IS GOING MAD! I don't blame them. CANADA DRY lunges forward with a hard right to the jaw ONE-ROUND goes down ONE! … TWO… THREE!… FOUR!…

(TERRIFIC ROAR OF CROWD)

FIVE! …SIX! …SEVEN! …EIGHT! …

(NOISE DIES DOWN)

NINE to be continued on Monday night by courtesy of Canada Dry Ginger Ale, sold at all fountains … by the glass.

Follow this closely… <u>who</u> wins this big fight? Who knows… who cares? Order your copies of our next broadcast in advance… DID ONE-ROUND take a dive?… or has CANADA DRY something on him? WHO KNOWS?…WHO CARES? … OR DON'T YOU CARE?…

(WHISPERS INTO MIKE)

I don't know who's going to win, folks … but keep this under your hat… here's a little tip … IF ONE-ROUND CIRCLE doesn't win, then CANADA DRY is a cinch … Even George Olsen bet on him, and you know Olsen. George spent a week in Glasgow and three Scotchmen who hung out with him, went broke… All right, George, let's get back to the Studio.

6. I'M THAT WAY ABOUT BROADWAY   ETHEL SHUTTA

BENNY   That, ladies and gentlemen, was the last number of the fourteenth program on the 15th of June… Were you excited, hmmmm? … Be sure to listen in Wednesday night for the continuation of this terrific battle… Sorry we couldn't finish it tonight. And, as they say in Germany, are you Berlin?… Well, good-night, then…

SIGNATURE – ROCKABYE MOON

ANNOUNCER The next time you visit a soda fountain, ask for a Canada Dry ice cream soda. You will find it a delicious drink – a real treat on a hot day. Canada Dry is also available in bottles as well as made-to-order by the glass. You are invited to listen in again at this same time Monday night, when Jack Benny, Ethel Shutta and George Olsen will entertain. This is the National Broadcasting Company.

June 20, 1932

STATION	WJZ	PROGRAM	CANADA DRY GINGER ALE, INC.
	AND	DATE	MONDAY, JUNE 20, 1932
	BLUE NETWORK	TIME	9.30 - 10:00 P.M. (E.D.T.)

SIGNATURE - JOLLY GOOD COMPANY

1. LORD YOU MADE THE NIGHT TOO LONG	PAUL SMALL
2. MY HEART'S AT EASE	ETHEL SHUTTA
3. SHE DIDN'T SAY YES (CAT AND THE FIDDLE)	FREY & SHUTTA
4. MASQUERADE	PAUL SMALL
5. O.K. AMERICA	ORCHESTRA
6. KEEP AWAY	GARDNER

SIGNATURE - ROCKABYE MOON

SIGNATURE — JOLLY GOOD COMPANY

ANNOUNCER   Ladies and gentlemen. Another half-hour of entertainment about Canada Dry Ginger Ale, now available made-to-order by the glass at soda fountains. George Olsen, Ethel Shutta and Jack Benny, the Canada Dry humorist, again perform for your enjoyment.

George Olsen opens the program with "LORD YOU MADE THE NIGHT TOO LONG."

1. LORD YOU MADE THE NIGHT TOO LONG   ORCHESTRA

ANNOUNCER   Here he is, folks, Jack Benny.

JACK   By special request … hello, anybody! … this is Jack Benny guiding you … are you following? … hmmmmnm? … BENNY … X as in ex-President … V as in Five Dollars … C as in the Latin phrase, Gee Whiz   … I as in Ego … and O as in Bryant 9850.

This program comes to you thru the courtesy of Canada Dry, and has nothing whatever to do with the conventions in Chicago. Any noises you may hear tonight will be real static and nothing to worry about.

And now I have a little surprise for you … our entire company was invited to dinner this evening by George Olsen! It was nobody's farewell party … nobody's birthday … he just felt good. He took us to a beautiful place in the country called Hollywood Gardens, where he and the boys are playing. And a good time was had by all. Yes, sir … George finally opened up his pocket book and <u>Abe Lincoln stepped out of a five-dollar bill and stretched</u>.

Say, George, that's a swell place you have out there … and the food was excellent.

GEORGE   Thanks, Jack.

JACK   That is … what there was of it. I never saw such big holes in Swiss Cheese in my life … And those sardines … <u>four dollars</u> for sardines!

GEORGE	Well, Jack, don't forget they're imported.
JACK	I know, George, but why should I pay their fare over here?… Say, Ethel, what was that special dish we had tonight that was <u>so good</u>?
ETHEL	You mean the broiled mushrooms under glass?
JACK	That's it … broiled mushrooms under glass … wasn't it delicious?
ETHEL	Uh-huh.
JACK	Well, the mushrooms were awfully good, but the glass didn't agree with me very well… Ethel, George <u>really</u> paid that check, didn't he?
ETHEL	Yes, of course he did. It was twenty-three dollars and ninety cents.
JACK	Twenty – three ninety … that must have been twenty-four dollars with the tip.
ETHEL	Well, you had a good time there … didn't you?
JACK	Did I! … I certainly did. And I enjoyed that moonlight dance that you and I had together … you know, when they lowered the lights and George was playing "Paradise."
ETHEL	Was that <u>you</u> I danced with?
JACK	Uh-huh don't you remember when I came over are asked you … all dressed up in my Tuxedo?
ETHEL	Gee, and I thought it was the head waiter.
JACK	All right, Ethel, if you feel like going now, it's okay with me. I'll see you later. Say, George, do me a favor … will you? When you go back to the Gardens tonight, see if you can get my hat back from the check-room girl.
GEORGE	Why, Jack, you could have gotten it yourself.
JACK	I know, but maybe you can get it for me cheaper. She knows you … you work there. Well, the boys are in a huddle now, and from what I can gather they are going to play a song. Ethel Shutta, who ate well tonight, will sing better than usual… Do you feel like singing tonight, Ethel?
ETHEL	No, Jack … I ate too much.
JACK	Nevertheless, Ethel will sing, "My Heart's At Ease," played by George Olsen and his Hollywood-bees.

2. MY HEART'S AT EASE   ETHEL SHUTTA

JACK

Now for the result of our Middleweight Champagne-ship Fight last Wednesday night ... between One-Round Circle of Roundhouse, Pennsylvania and Canada Dry of Soda Fountain, New York.

You remember One-Round Circle was down for the count of fourteen, and they continued that terrific clinch until three o'clock in the morning, only stopping to catch a train for Scranton, Pennsylvania where they fought again the following night. From last reports it is still a fierce battle, Canada Dry being one up and two to play, and One-Round Circle having three men on base, with five yards to goal, and it's Harvard's ball. Tomorrow night they fight in Buffalo.

Now please don't write us, asking any more regarding this fight as we are perfectly willing to drop the whole thing if you are. However, I might mention the fact that Canada Dry also won the American Derby in Chicago last Saturday afternoon. He ran under the name of <u>Gusto</u> ... Remember, we are just giving you the facts, folks!

And now, while we are on the subject, let me read you a dispatch we received from our representative in North Africa ... Sand Done, a Scotchman. He wires us regarding another severe test of Canada Dry Ginger Ale. Incidentally, this representative of ours has the <u>entire</u> territory of the Sahara Desert, including the principal cities of <u>O-Aces</u> ... <u>Grand Salam</u> ... and <u>No-Trumpia</u>.

Now all you people who have walked across the Sahara Desert ... <u>and who hasn't</u>? ... know what a colossal task it is. Well, for the benefit of those who have not been there, let me say it is just like the beach in Atlantic City <u>if they remove the ocean</u> ... thousands and thousands of miles of hot, burning sands, with no relief from the blistering sun and terrific heat ... with nothing in sight but <u>a camel waking a mile for an Arab</u>.

Here's the dispatch that we received from our Sahara representative.

He says,

"On my fourth trip across the Desert yesterday afternoon, I discovered a band of eight European tourists who had wandered away from their caravan. They had been deserted on this desert without <u>food</u> ... <u>drink</u> ... or <u>desert</u>... <u>dessert</u> ... or thirty days, no more ... no less. Imagine that! ... thirty days on the desert <u>without a drink</u> ...their throats parched ... their tongues hanging out ... begging and pleading for <u>any kind</u> of liquid."

"I came to their rescue," says he, "gave each of them a glass of CANADA DRY made-to-order Ginger Ale ... and <u>not one of them</u> said he did not like it!"

ANOTHER GREAT VICTORY FOR CANADA DRY! ... And to commemorate this great victory, George Olsen and his Arabian Knights will play, "HE DIDN'T SAY YES, HE DIDN'T SAY NO," by H. Hoover ... I mean, from "The Cat and The Fiddle."

3. SHE DIDN'T SAY YES, SHE DIDN'T SAY NO   ETHEL SHUTTA AND FRAN FREY

JACK   Say, Ethel, I'm very busy right now preparing the big surprise of the evening. Would you mind introducing the next number?

ETHEL   Not at all, Jack.

JACK   Are you nervous?

ETHEL   No.

JACK   Well, go ahead.

ETHEL   Ladies and gentlemen, the <u>romantic</u> Paul Small will sing the next number which is called, "MASQUERADE," played by <u>handsome</u> George Olsen and his <u>Sweet Boys</u> … thru the courtesy of Canada Dry … Ginger Ale… made-to-order by the glass …

JACK   Oh, Ethel, you spoil everything.

(ORCHESTRA GOES INTO OPENING OF NUMBER ON CUE "BY THE GLASS")

4. MASQUERADE   PAUL SMALL

JACK   Ladies and gentlemen, we have been singing and joking tonight, but we realize our mistake. Your minds are at present concentrated on the political situation. What you want now is <u>politics</u> … not hokum … so <u>politics</u> you'll get.

         You are very fortunate being tuned in on our program tonight, as we are holding our own political convention for the purpose of nominating a candidate for President on the Canada Dry MADE-TO-ORDER ticket. As there is a great deal of jealousy in Washington over our candidate, we had a difficult time arranging a national hookup, so we have arranged a hookup with ourselves <u>right here in the Studi</u>o … with the assistance of our janitor, Philander George Bernard Kvetch.

         And what a hookup we have … Fran Frey is hooked to his saxophone … Kvetch is hooked to his mop … Paul Small is hooked for two dollars playing bridge … Ethel Shutta is hooked to George Olsen and, if you ask me, it's Ethel that's hooked … and I am hooked with our candidate.

         We will now take you to the Canada Dry Convention Hall in the NBC Studios, New York … <u>Hello, ourselves</u>!

(LITTLE STATIC — CROWD TALKING)

         Here we are where we were all the time … and I'm telling you this place is full of candi<u>dates</u> … dele<u>gates</u> … and fig-<u>dates</u>.

(ROUND OF APPLAUSE AND CHEERS)

What <u>date</u> is this?

As I look around the convention Hall, I see five delegates from Hawaii … and eight delegates from <u>How've-you-been</u>? … And, in another section, twelve delegates from <u>Columbo, Russ</u> … the land of Croonia.

(MORE APPLAUSE)

There are twenty delegates here from <u>Turkey</u> … the place where they made the <u>terking</u>-pictures … this is Jack Benny <u>terking</u> … do you get the <u>pernt</u>? Good English gets 'em all the time, George.

Hollywood is highly interested in our Convention. We just got a <u>gable</u> from <u>Clark</u>, saying that everything is <u>Oakie</u> is Hollywood … but we also have another wire from <u>Oakie</u>, saying that everything there is <u>Gable</u> …<u>Oakie</u> … <u>Gable</u>!

Garbo is for us <u>with both feet</u> … Jimmy Durante just opened the door and is <u>nose-ing</u> around our Convention … And we see people here from the wild <u>Wheeler and Woolsey</u> West … all <u>Laurel and Hardy</u> people.

Five delegates just walked in from Siam! They want more contests on our platform … Don't worry, Siam, you'll get them.

Ah! four men just arrived <u>from India</u>, they look like four ombrays from Bombay … headed by Mahatma Gandhi and his three brothers. Ma-coata-Ma-vesta … and Ma … pantsa … Come here, Mahatma, say something to the people.

GANDHI

(Whistles first four bars of "Paradise")

JACK　　Thank you, Mahatma. And who is this lady following him? Ah! it's the landlady … trying to get her bed-sheet back.

And now, to liven up the Convention, George Olsen, of the Not-so-Liberal party, will play "EVERYTHING'S GOING TO BE OKAY, AMERICA!" after which the nomination will take place on the Canada Dry MADE-TO-ORDER ticket.

5. EVERYTHING'S GOING TO BE OKAY, AMERICA!　　ORCHESTRA

JACK　　And now, ladies and gentlemen, let's get down to politics. First, I will introduce to you our dark horse … the Man of the Hour … the man who broke his umbrella and is <u>neither wet or dry</u>. He is a <u>friend of the farmer</u> … and is also a friend of the traveling salesman and the farmer's daughter … He is a soldier, a scholar and a citizen … and has proved his worth at Leavenworth … where, for eight years, he lived in the little gray home in the West, sung by Paul Small and Fran Frey … Pardon me, where am I?…

And it now be<u>hoovers</u> me to say that he is the logical man to nominate for this office … a man who reminds you of George Washington … he also has <u>two</u> arms and <u>two</u> legs.

Now, may I present the Man of the Half-Hour ... a wide-awake fellow full of GINGER and ALE-RIGHT ... the Honorable Trafalgar Bee-Fuddle!

(ROUND OF HEAVY APPLAUSE)

FUDDLE

(COUGHS, HEMS, HAWS)

Ladies and gentlemen ... fellow citizens and ladies and gentlemen ... and Brother Voters, and ladies and gentlemen...

(COUGHS AGAIN)

When you hear three little chimes, it will be exactly four O'clock in Samoa...

JACK	Tell us some-moah!
FUDDLE	If I am nominated at this Convention for the highest honor that can ever be bestowed upon an American Citizen, I will ... er, I will ... that is, er ... er ... I will be FOR the people ... By the people ... OF the people ... WITH the people ... ON the people ... and IN SPITE of the people...

(APPLAUSE – CHEERS – HURRAHS!)

JACK	Now, Mr. Fuddle, What do you think is the matter with our country today?
FUDDLE	FOR the people ... BY the people ... OF the people ... and TO the people.
JACK	Well, how do you think we can remedy those conditions?
FUDDLE	BY the people ... FOR the people ... and OF the people.

(MORE APPLAUSE)

JACK	Say, Traffic, where did you get those bullet marks ... in the war?
FUDDLE	No, I was President <u>of – Mexico</u> for five minutes.
JACK	All of which proves that our candidate <u>can take it</u>! ... Tell me where did you get that medal?
FUDDLE	I jumped in the water after a drowning woman.
JACK	He's also a hero! ... Did you save that woman?
FUDDLE	No.
JACK	Well, who gave you the medal?
FUDDLE	Her husband.
JACK	That's fine ... you should <u>also</u> have an ornament around your neck ... Strangler Lewis' head lock.

(HOORAY! CHEERS!)

	And now, Fuddle, tell us why do you want to be President?
FUDDLE	BECAUSE IF I can't be <u>head man</u>, I don't want to play.

(BEGINS TO CRY)

JACK	It's all right … there, there … don't cry … here's a nice lollipop for you.
FUDDLE	

(CONTINUES TO CRY)

	I wanna be President…
JACK	Don't cry … You'll be President … here's a nickel … put it in your pocket before you're investigated.
FUDDLE	

(CRIES LOUDER THAN EVER)

I wanna be President … I wanna be President…

(PISTOL SHOT FIRED – FOLLOWED BY ABSOLUTE SILENCE)

JACK	Ladies and gentlemen, there is nothing to worry about … The <u>Late</u> Trafalgar Bee-Fuddle will not run for President … But no matter who's elected, Canada Dry Ginger Ale will be sold by-the-glass, at all soda fountains, TO the people … BY the people … and FOR the people. And it's darned good … several people told me.
	And now George Olsen and <u>his own</u> delegates will play, "KEEP AWAY." Dick Hotcha Gardner will sing while I try and revive Mr. Fuddle.

6. KEEP AWAY   **DICK HOTCHA GARDNER**

JACK	That was the last number of the fifteenth program on the twentieth of June. Are you weakening … hmmmmm? … I expect to have some interesting news for you on Wednesday night as I am going to see the Sharkey-Schmelling Fight tomorrow. And I hope it won't <u>Schmell</u> this time! … Well, good-night, please.
ANNOUNCER	The next time you visit a soda fountain, ask for a Canada Dry ice cream soda. You will find it a delicious drink – a real treat on a hot day. Canada Dry is also available in bottles as well as made-to-order by the glass. You are invited to listen in again at this same time Wednesday night, when Jack Benny, Ethel Shutta and George Olsen will entertain. This is the National Broadcasting Company.

June 22, 1932

STATION	WJZ AND BLUE NETWORK	PROGRAM DATE TIME	CANADA DRY GINGER ALE, INC. WEDNESDAY, JUNE 22, 1932 9.30 - 10:00 P.M. (E.D.T.)

SIGNATURE - JOLLY GOOD COMPANY

1. MARIETTA	CORNHEISER	ORCHESTRA & SMALL
2. WHY DID YOU COME ALONG	DeS. B. & H.	ORCHESTRA & SHUTTA
3. YEAH MAN	DeS. B. & H.	ORCHESTRA & GARDNER
4. BRING BACK THOSE DEAR OLD CIRCUS DAYS UNPUB		ORCHESTRA & FREY

SIGNATURE - ROCKABYE MOON

SIGNATURE JOLLY GOOD COMPANY

ANNOUNCER	Ladies and gentlemen, before we take you to the studio where George Olsen, Ethel Shutta, and Jack Benny are waiting to entertain you, I want to introduce Mr. P. D. Saylor, President of Canada Dry Ginger Ale, Inc., who will speak to you for just a few moments. Mr. Saylor.

MR. SAYLOR [His speech was not included in the script]

ANNOUNCER	Thank you, Mr. Saylor! And now we switch you to Olsen, Shutta and Benny – the big three on Canada Dry! George Olsen begins with "MARIETTA," Paul Small singing the vocal.

1. MARIETTA … ORCHESTRA

ANNOUNCER	And here's the Canada Dry humorist himself — Jack Benny!

JACK	Hello, half of one-percent of everybody … This is Ack-jay Any-bay talking or, as they say in France, Jacques Bennee … or, in Scotland, "It's a brae bricht moon licht aicht" … or do you like Jack Benny better? — I start the silliest things, don't I? Well, it takes up time, anyway, and every minute counts on this program.

But before we go any further, I want to make a public apology to George Olsen because last Monday night I made a very distasteful remark regarding George, and I'm terribly sorry. I said that Olsen was so close that when he pulled a five-dollar bill out of his pocketbook, Abe Lincoln got out and stretched … Well, I was entirely wrong as such was <u>not</u> the case. It was a <u>quarter</u>, and <u>Miss Liberty got off and stretched the other arm</u>.

I'm very sorry, George … those mistakes will never happen again.

Well, folks, yesterday was the first day of summer, so if any of you have been complaining about the heat before or perspired last week, it was all wasted … Summer is officially here, and it won't be long before fall draws on.

<u>And am I sore</u>! On my way to the Studio this evening, I stopped at a soda fountain and found five people drinking Canada Dry Ginger Ale by-the- glass, who had never

heard any of our programs. <u>That is not fair to us</u>, ladies and gentlemen. It may be fair to your thirst, <u>but not to us</u>. I mean, if you're going to continue doing that, we might as well stay home. Here we are, working our fingers to the bones …

MAN'S VOICE (ACCOMPANIED BY SNAP OF FINGERS)

<u>Come on</u>, seven!

JACK   I'll fade it …

Well, I'm afraid there's nothing we can do about it, so just go ahead and enjoy yourself … I don't know, George, it's hard to trust <u>anybody</u> nowadays.

Ethel will now sing, "Why Did You Come Along," dedicated to George Olsen and played by his No-Cover-Charge Orchestra.

2. WHY DID YOU COME ALONG? … ETHEL SHUTTA

JACK   Say, Ethel, did you see the fight last night?

ETHEL   What fight?

JACK   Why, the Big Fight!

ETHEL   I don't know… everybody here is getting along all right. Of course, Fran Frey had an argument with Paul Small yester …

JACK   All right, Ethel, never mind …

Well, ladies and gentlemen, I saw the Sharkey-Schmelling Championship Fight last night at the new Madison Square Bowl in Long Island. They call it a "bowl," but it's more like a blue plate…   you know, the blue plates on which they serve those forty-cent dinners? … Well, my seat was right where you'd <u>find the spinach</u> … on the edge of the plate. And I couldn't see very well because there were <u>a lot of beans</u> in front of me, and I had quite a hard time looking over <u>the noodles</u> … Are you getting hungry, hmmmm?

Yes, sir, I had a ringside seat … at least it was in the same county as the ring … And my father who lives in Waukegan, Illinois had a five-dollar seat and <u>didn't even have to leave home</u> … My cousin, Enoch, had a two-dollar seat and took a cruise via the Panama Canal to get there.

Well, anyway, it was a great battle … they tell me. What a fight! … what a fight! … what excitement! A boy woke me up in the seventh round by yelling: "CANADA DRY GINGER ALE!"

The fight was so close at the finish that the referee didn't know who to give it to. He looked around the ring for Dempsey, and couldn't find him … so he gave it to Sharkey … Congratulations, Mickey Walker!

There were a lot of erroneous reports this morning in the newspapers. … some gave the fight to Sharkey…others gave it to Schmelling. Of course, you can't go by the papers.

Now here's a clipping from the Buenos Aires Morning Castanet. It says:

"WE THINK THE WHOLE FIGHT WAS AN ARGENTINE TANGO … PLEASE STICK TO YOUR NATIVE DANCES.

WE STILL THINK FIRPO IS THE BEST MAN, AND THAT'S NOT A LOT OF BULL FROM THE PAMPAS."

Ah! Here's a clipping from Germany … the Hamburg Onion … er, Union. It says:

"VOS IS LOSE MIT YOU, MOCKS? … VY DID YOU

LET SHARKEY GIF YOU DOSE SOCKS, MOCKS? …

VELL, IT MAKES NO DIFFERENCE MIT US, MOCKS …

AUF WIEDERSEHN, MOCKS …"

Well, that was all about Mocks!

And here's one from the Daily Schnozzle, Durante, Mexico.

"GLAD TO HEAR THAT SHARKEY WON, AND THAT PROSPERITY WAS JUST AROUND HIS CORNER."

Well, anyway, folks, don't you believe the papers … let me describe what I saw …

Sharkey and Schmelling entered the ring to a great reception for Canada Dry Ginger Ale, made-to-order by the glass, as it was a warm night. They had just weighted in at the Commissioner's office, which was on the fourteenth floor of Primo Carnera … The referee, … Gunboat Smith, came in without his gun, and the fight started.

Well, the first four rounds were even … during the next three, everybody relaxed, including the fighters. Up to the time the referee was … unemployed … At the start of the eighth round, Sharkey and Schmelling both appeared fresh, but the spectators were groggy … In the middle of the round, Carnera entered the ring, wearing Tony Canzoneri on his lapel … He was all dressed up, and wore a ring on his fourth finger, with the Rock of Gibraltar in it … He came in very late and found the Four Marx Brothers sitting in his seat, and when Carnera sat down, five thousand people in back of him went home … This ended the eighth round.

Now the ninth and tenth rounds were even … even worse than the first four. But there was much excitement in the audience as Harry Lauder was discovered giving two cheers for Schmelling … So far, it was anybody's fight… but nobody wanted it.

The excitement really started with the last round. At the start of the fifteenth round, Sharkey and Schmelling exchanged blows in Schmelling's corner, Sharkey jabbed a long left into Tunney's stomach, who was sitting in the front row and wasn't even playing … In fact, he was reading Shakespeare's "MERCHANT OF VENICE," who was having a sale … Tunney became furious, but waited until the count of fourteen and threw his book at Tunney, making a triple play… TUNNEY to SHARKEY to SHAKESPEARE.

Someone threw a towel in the ring, which was a dirty Turkish trick.

At this time the famous ex-heavyweight, Tom Heeney was introduced in the ring. Sitting at the ringside were Heeney's three brothers … <u>Meeny</u>… Miney … and <u>Moe</u>.

Schmelling, who is also in the fight, is now very nervous and biting his fingernails. Sharkey, quick to realize the situation, shows Schmelling <u>the revised income tax rates</u>, knocking him colder than a mother-in-law's kiss.

NOW THEY'RE REALLY FIGHTING! … Schmelling comes to and hits Sharkey a terrific right hook, closing his eye tighter than Olsen's pocketbook … <u>Congratulations, George</u>! … But Sharkey comes right back with a left smash to Schmelling's jaw that <u>closed four banks in Vienna</u>   …The Kaiser, who was listening in on <u>the rattio</u>, heard this punch and <u>FELL OUT OF BED</u>.

The crowd went wild… the band played "Paradise," making the crowd wilder … Captain Hawkes, who was at the ringside, had a heavy bet on Sharkey, and become so excited that he made a <u>non-stop flight around Fatty Arbuckle</u>.

Then I went home …

Oh! Before I forget it, I'd like to mention that <u>our fighters</u>, Canada Dry and One-Round Circle, are now fighting at Coal Pail, Pennsylvania, for a shot at Sharkey's title.

And now George Olsen and his Overgrown Featherweights will play a request called, "Yeah Man," sung by <u>our</u> champion, Dick Hotcha Gardner. Get in there and sock it over, Dick!

3. YEAH MAN   DICK HOTCHA GARDNER

JACK   Ladies and gentlemen, we always try to keep our promise and bring celebrities to you as fast as we can get them.

You should have seen that parade in New York on Monday, when everybody paid that marvelous tribute to <u>Miss Amelia Earhart</u> … thousands and thousands of people lined the streets and showered her with ticker tape, confetti and thunderous applause. And she deserved it all, as it certainly was an outstanding achievement!

But with all due credit to our courageous heroine, Miss Amelia Earhart, we have with us tonight a young lady who also deserves <u>honorable mention</u> … A YOUNG LADY WHO NOT ONLY FLEW TO IRELAND, BUT ON REACHING IRELAND, IMMEDIATELY SWAM ACROSS THE ENGLISH CHANNEL AND GOT TO FRANCE JUST IN TIME TO WIN THE LADIES' OPEN GOLF CHAMPIONSHIP … What a flight! … what a swim! … what a game!

Pick up your French morning paper, and you will see for yourself the scores of this great flight … wonderful swim … and marvelous game. In the golf match, she went around the tough patie-de-fois-gras course, making the round of eighteen holes in twenty-one… seventeen holes in one and one birdie. NOW TOP THAT, all you golfers who talk a good game!

She was careless on the birdie hole, using a niblick on the divot. For the benefit of those of you who do not play golf, the divot is the fellow who <u>carries the golf clubs around from one hole to the other</u>.

And now we will have a few words from this champion of champions ... of champions ... MISS VIOLET RAY!

(ROUND OF APPLAUSE)

Miss Ray started her flying career very early in life. Her first experience was at the Aviation Counter in the five-and-ten cent store, where she sold <u>fly-paper</u>.

Miss Ray is here <u>in person</u> ... wearing a beautiful low-cut evening gown and is appearing here almost <u>in the flesh</u> ... Am I getting too flesh, customers? And now may I present ... VIOLET RAY ... which is certainly a <u>treat</u>-ment.

(MORE APPLAUSE)

MISS KELCEY	I am very happy to be here tonight, folks. And all I can say is that I owe all my success to Slippery Elm Bath Soap!
JACK (CONFIDENTIALLY)	Miss Ray, look at your part.
MISS KELCEY	Oh ... I owe all my success to CANADA DRY GINGER ALE ... made-to-order ... by the glass ... at all fountains.
JACK	There you are, folks...and we didn't even ask her.
MISS KELCEY	Yes, but you promised me that if I said Canada Dry ...
JACK	Tell the folks how you accomplished all these wonderful things.
MISS KELCEY	Well, I took a pound of ordinary flour ... added some water, and stirred it. Then I simply added the yolks of three eggs, and some sugar.
JACK	Well, that's very interesting. Did you have any trouble with fog or air pockets ... or did you run out of gas?
MISS KELCEY	No ... I just added half a pound of chopped nuts And a little cinnamon ... flattened it out with a rolling pin, and then ...
JACK	Now tell me about your swim across the Channel ... in order to keep the cold water from chilling you, did you have your body <u>well</u> <u>greased</u>? ...
MISS KELCEY	No... I just greased the pan, put the cake in and shoved it into a medium-hot oven.
JACK	I see... and you met no sharks on the way?
MISS KELCEY	No... I just let it bake until it was well-browned. Then I made some holes with a fork to keep it from puffing.
JACK	Well, you should have used your niblick. There was no excuse for a birdie in that hole ... Was any one very close to you in the golf tournament?

MISS KELCEY	No, of course not… I just added some whipped cream and a few cherries and it was ready to serve.
JACK	WHAT A FLIGHT! … WHAT A SWIM! … WHAT A GAME! … Do you think you would like to do the whole thing all over again, Miss Ray?
MISS KELCEY	Yes … but I'll need some more flour and eggs.
JACK	Thank you very much, Miss Ray. Here's my personal rubber check for seven dollars.
MISS KELCEY	Is it good?
JACK	Yes, ma'am … it's the greatest thing in the world for vulcanizing an inner tube.
MISS KELCEY	Thank you, Mr. Benny … B as in <u>Boloney</u>… E as in <u>Easy-to-Kid</u> … N as in <u>NO GOOD</u> …
JACK	All right, all right, Miss Ray, good-bye …
	And let me tell you, ladies and gentlemen, there are thousands and thousands of other people like Miss Ray, raving about Canada Dry Ginger Ale.
	And now George Olsen will play a novelty number called, "Bring Back Those Dear Old Circus Days," with vocal refrain by Fran Frey… thru the courtesy of Canada Dry … Ginger Ale… made-to-order … by the glass…

(OPENING BARS OF "CIRCUS DAYS" OVER LAST WORDS)

4. BRING BACK THOSE DEAR OLD CIRCUS DAYS　　　　　FRAN FREY

JACK	That was the last number on the sixteenth program on the 22nd of June. Are you indifferent … hmm? We want you to be sure and listen in next Monday night as we are going to have another big surprise for you. We are going to have a Baby's Night… and we want all your babies to listen in. I have to leave you now … and, as they say in Mexico, TIA JUANA go to bed? …
	Good-night, then.
ANNOUNCER	Now's the time to ask for a Canada Dry ice cream soda when you visit a soda fountain. It's a delicious drink — a real treat in this hot weather — night or day. Canada Dry is also available in bottles as well as made-to-order by the glass. You are invited to listen in again at this same time Monday night, when Jack Benny, Ethel Shutta and George Olsen will entertain. This is the National Broadcasting Company.

June 27, 1932

STATION	WJZ	PROGRAM	CANADA DRY GINGER ALE, INC.
	AND	DATE	MONDAY, JUNE 27, 1932
	BLUE NETWORK	TIME	9.30 - 10:00 P.M. (E.D.T.)

SIGNATURE - JOLLY GOOD COMPANY

1. I BEG YOUR PARDON, MADEMOISELLE   ORCHESTRA & FRAN FREY

2. A GREAT BIG BUNCH OF YOU   ORCHESTRA & ETHEL SHUTTA

3. IT WAS SO BEAUTIFUL   ORCHESTRA & PAUL SMALL

4. HUMMING TO MYSELF   ORCHESTRA & ETHEL SHUTTA & TRIO

5. COME AND SIT BESIDE THE SEA   ORCHESTRA & FRAN FREY

SIGNATURE - ROCKABYE MOON

SIGNATURE – JOLLY GOOD COMPANY

ANNOUNCER Ladies and gentlemen. Another half-hour of entertainment about Canada Dry Ginger Ale, now available made-to-order by the glass at soda fountains. George Olsen, Ethel Shutta and Jack Benny, the Canada Dry humorist, again perform for your enjoyment.

George Olsen opens the program with "I Beg Your Pardon, Mademoiselle."

1. I BEG YOUR PARDON, MADEMOISELLE   ORCHESTRA & FRAN FREY

JACK Hello… hello… hello, there George… hello, Ethel, how are you tonight?…hello, Kvetch!…

Pardon me just a moment, ladies and gentlemen… Say, were there any messages for me today? … mail, phone calls or anything?

MAN'S VOICE [Baldwin] What's the name, please?

JACK Benny … Jack Benny … you're my secretary, remember?

MAN'S VOICE Oh, yes … there's a letter here for you.

JACK Fan mail?

MAN'S VOICE Yes, from your tailor.

JACK Anything else?

MAN'S VOICE Yes, a phone call.

JACK Who from?

MAN'S VOICE Your tailor.

JACK Anything else?

MAN'S VOICE A telegram.

JACK	From my tailor?
MAN'S VOICE	Yes.
JACK	Well, tear up the phone call and destroy the messages … what else happened today?
MAN'S VOICE	Oh, there was a man here to see you about ten minutes ago.
JACK	A little short fellow?
MAN'S VOICE	Yes.
JACK	With a black moustache?
MAN'S VOICE	YES.

JACK AND MAN (TOGETHER)

> My tailor!
>
> Your tailor!

JACK	Did you tell him I sailed for Europe this morning?
MAN'S VOICE	Yes, and he said he will meet you in London tonight.
JACK	Well, this is no place to discuss business… I've got to talk to my students … hello, scholars! … are you lessoning? … This is Jack Benny talking… JACK as in lumber JACK … and BENNY as in tuppence, ha-BENNY … ARE YOU GIGGLING? … or aren't you a giggle-o? … hmm? … That calls for a slight pause to give you all a chance to hate me. Well, ladies and gentlemen, I find myself in another very peculiar position tonight, as <u>again</u> I have to apologize to George Olsen, and I'm getting mighty sick of it. Last Wednesday night, I said he took a quarter out of his pocket and Miss Liberty got off and stretched her other arm. Well, I was wrong again … I'm sorry, George.
GEORGE	Aw, that's okay, Jack.
JACK	What I really meant to say was that George had a rare old coin in his pocket … year 1881.
GEORGE	Well, what's funny about that? I've got a lot of old coins in my pocket.
JACK	I know… but they <u>were all new</u> when you put them in there.
GEORGE	Say, Jack, what makes you think I'm so tight?
JACK	Oh, I'm only kidding, George … just trying to get a couple of laughs at your expense. After all, what difference does it make <u>to me</u> if your money goes <u>into solitary confinement</u>?
GEORGE	Well, Jack I'm just a little careful, that's all … I'm saving for a rainy day.
JACK	Saving for a rainy day, eh? … Well, it rained all last week and you were still the same Olsen.

GEORGE	Well, I want to tell you one thing, Jack … I'm thinking of the future so that I can protect my <u>children</u>.
JACK	Of course, George, if you're going to have <u>forty or fifty</u> children, let's drop the whole thing.
	And now Ethel Shutta, who has been waiting here since nine o'clock this morning, will sing "A Bunch of You," played by George Olsen … and a bunch of the boys will whoop it up.

2. A GREAT BIG BUNCH OF YOU   **ORCHESTRA & ETHEL SHUTTA**

JACK	That was Ethel Shutta singing "A Bunch of You," played by George Olsen and his <u>Close</u> Harmonizers … do you get it?
	You know, folks, to hear me talk, you'd think George and I were deadly enemies. To be honest about it, we have been friends for a great many years. In fact, our friendship dates back to the year 1933 … er, 1923. Say, George, when did we start to become friends?
GEORGE	Any day now.
JACK	I see… and how things change … just to think <u>ten years ago</u> George Olsen used to work for me … and look at him now! Yes, sir, I was <u>his</u> <u>boss</u>. At that time I was the proprietor of a cafe just outside of Chicago … you know, one of those places where you get a nice dollar-dinner for seven dollars … BUT NO COVER CHARGE! Well, anyway, that's where George worked for four weeks and we didn't lose a customer! I used to pay him off every Saturday.
GEORGE	Now, Jack, wait a minute … I don't mind all the things you say about me when you're kidding because I realize it's all in fun. But don't tell people that I ever worked for you in a road house … because that's NOT TRUE.
JACK	What do you mean … it isn't true.
GEORGE	I mean just what I say … <u>I never worked for you in my life</u>.
JACK	But, George, I don't mean that you <u>worked for me</u> exactly … what I really mean to say is that we both worked in the <u>same</u> cafe … you're not ashamed of the fact that you worked in a cafe, are you?
GEORGE	No, I'm not ashamed of any place I've ever worked. But don't tell those people that I worked for you when you were just <u>an ordinary</u> <u>waiter</u> in that cafe, MR. BENNY!
JACK	Great fellow, George … always kidding.
GEORGE	No, I'm <u>not kidding</u> … I mean every word of it!
ANNOUNCER	Ladies and gentlemen, this fight comes to you thru the courtesy of Canada Dry Ginger Ale, made-to-order by the glass, at all fountains.
	Go ahead, boys.

GEORGE	Say, what do you mean by insulting me and telling people …
ETHEL (ENTERS SCENE QUICKLY)	
	Now, boys, boys … please! … Stop this arguing in front of the microphone … you ought to be ashamed of your selves … BOTH OF YOU!
GEORGE	Well, he's been making a lot of cracks about me that I don't like.
JACK	I have not, Ethel … I was only kidding.
GEORGE	You have, too.
ETHEL	Now, please, George … stay out of this … let me talk to Jack.
	Now, Jack, I'm sorry George lost his temper… But aren't you a little bit ashamed of yourself, too?
JACK	Oh gee, I didn't mean anything, Ethel. I thought George could take it.
ETHEL	Now wait a minute, Jack … I'm going to tell you something that I hope you will take in the right spirit and not feel offended. Promise me you'll understand.
JACK	I promise.
ETHEL	You've said a lot of little mean things about George and … if you only knew it … <u>he thinks the world of you</u>. He's always boosting you to the skies, and he's one of your greatest admirers.
JACK	Well, that's funny … he never sends me any <u>fan mail</u>.
ETHEL	Now, Jack, please be serious because I like you a lot and I'm just trying to help you, that's all. You know the thing that surprises me is that you are such a nice fellow … such a gentlemen … and <u>you can say</u> the sweetest things about everybody instead of getting laughs at their expense. Why, every time you introduce George, you're always kidding him … and you've hurt him terribly, Jack … you really have.
JACK	I'm sorry, Ethel.
ANNOUNCER	Ladies and gentlemen. This bawling – out comes to you thru the courtesy of Canada Dry Ginger Ale, made-to-order by the glass.
JACK (still in sulky mood)	At all fountains.
ETHEL	Now aren't you a little bit ashamed of yourself, Jack?
JACK	Yea … ah.
ETHEL	Well, try and be a sweet boy from now on, and tell George how sorry you are.
JACK	I'm sorry, George.
GEORGE	Aw, that's all right, Jack.
ETHEL	There now … that's much better.

JACK	Ethel, I want to thank you for this little lecture you've given me… you've made me realize how nasty I've been.
ETHEL	Aw, Jack, it was just for your own good.
JACK	Well, I appreciate every word of it… and <u>from now on</u> I'm going to be different.
ETHEL	I know you will, Jack.
JACK	I'm going to introduce George with a great deal of consideration … because he's a <u>swell fellow</u> and one of the <u>finest boys</u> I have ever been associated with.

And now, ladies and gentlemen, the next number will be "It Was So Beautiful," sung by Paul Small and played by George Olsen … a great musician … a liberal, honest, upright gentleman … one of the sweetest fellows that I've ever known … a man who is kind to everybody and worships his mother and father … a man who is kind to dumb animals … a man everybody loves and George loves everybody …

(On direct cue from Jack Benny, start introduction to number)

3. IT WAS SO BEAUTIFUL   ORCHESTRA & PAUL SMALL

GEORGE	Where's Jack?
JACK	Listen, old pal, will you introduce the next number? I feel so terrible about what I said and Ethel has spoiled my whole evening.
GEORGE	Here, take a glass of this Canada Dry Ginger Ale … you'll feel a lot better.
JACK	Do you think so?
GEORGE	Sure … here! take a sip. (SLIGHT PAUSE)

JACK (WITH TREMENDOUS FORCE)

LADIES AND GENTLEMEN! I feel great now … which is ANOTHER VICTORY for Canada Dry Ginger Ale, made-to-order by the glass at all fountains.

And you don't have to take my word for it … here's a note that we just received from our representative in Jersey:

(SOUND EFFECT: RATTLING PAPER)

Hear the note … hmmmmm? We wouldn't fool you.

Our representative tells you that he went to a factory in Newark, New Jersey where they manufacture <u>twiggots</u> and <u>muldrums</u>… He selected six men who work there … tied their hands securely behind their backs and locked them in a pitch-dark room. In fact, the room was <u>so dark</u> that you could hardly hear a plate drop … Our representative gave <u>each and every one</u> of these six men <u>three</u> articles … an umbrella … an elephant tusk … and a glass of Canada Dry Ginger Ale. They did as they were told, sampled each of the three articles, and unanimously declared that Canada Dry Ale was the best drink of the three!

And now Ethel Shutta will sing, "Humming to Myself," played by George Olsen and his Mickey the Misers ... let's go, boys!

4. HUMMING TO MYSELF   ORCHESTRA & ETHEL SHUTTA

JACK Well, ladies and gentlemen, there still seems to be a lot of controversy about the Sharkey-Schmelling fight— I mean, the Schmelling-Sharkey fight. No two people agree on the decision ... Sharkey says Schmelling won it... Schmelling claims Gunboat Smith won it... Italy blames it on Carnera ... the people in Siam blame it on their King ... the King blames it on our contest and our contest blames it on Canada Dry Ginger Ale, made-to-order by the glass ... SOME mix up, believe me!

Well, as I've told you before, I saw the fight, and all I can say is ... IT WAS A BALMY SUMMER'S EVENING,

AND A GOODLY CROWD WAS THERE ...

Well, the next day I saw the moving picture of the same fight.

The picture was all right, but I didn't like the cast. I think Walter Huston and James Cagney would have put up a better battle and thrown a few chairs at each other... I also think the picture lacked sex appeal, and it is my opinion that GRAND HOTEL is a much better picture.

Of course, I'm not crazy about the movies, anyway. I used to be in pictures and they weren't crazy about me either ... so we're even.

However, I'm getting away from the subject. It is not for me to say who won or lost the Sharkey-Schmelling fight. So we have brought here to the studio tonight four of New York's greatest fight experts ... four men who are conceded to be the highest authorities on the Art of Boxing... Let us hear their views.

Our first expert is no other than Homer T. Sass ... who is qualified to describe the punches as he has been employed on the T. & 0. Railroad as conductor and has punched tickets for thirty years. So he certainly is familiar with each and every punch ... Go ahead, Mr. Sass, describe the punches.

SASS Well, I'll tell you ... when a fellow gets on the train with a local ticket, I gave it the heart punch, which must be aimed well to hit the number. However, on a longer trip, the man receives two punches and holds his ticket until he is punched again. Of course, the Communist's ticket ...

JACK What do you mean by "Communists"?

SASS The people who communist from the suburbs to the city.

JACK Oh, you mean COMMUTERS!

SASS	Yes, pardon me … I'm now on the Canada Dry Limited … THIS TRAIN LEAVES IN THREE MINUTES FOR
	SARAZEN
	FARRELL
	CRUIKSHANK
	ARMOUR
	DEEGEL
	BOBBY JONES and
	ALL POINTS SOUTH
	ALL ABOARD …
	(MUSIC CUE: TRAIN EFFECT, FADING OUT IN DISTANCE)
JACK	Folks, I'm sorry that Mr. Sass had to leave, but he's a conductor. And trains and tide wait for no man.
	And now we have another expert… a man who is qualified to give you an accurate description as he has been a <u>fisherman</u> for fifty years and knows his <u>hooks</u> … MR. T. ANGLEWORM SMELT … and no relation to Schmelling … Tell us what <u>you</u> think of the fight, Mr. Smelt.
SMELT	Well, the TUNNEYS aren't running so good this season … I got a SHARKEY the other day and a few of those little BENNIE BASS and quite a lot of FLUKE.
JACK	All right, all right … that's only one man's opinion… he thinks the decision was a fluke …
	And now we have still another expert who is in the men's <u>hosiery</u> business. He will describe each and every <u>sock</u> of this big fight … I take pleasure in introducing Mr. Benjamin Listle Hose … What's <u>your</u> opinion of the fight, Mr. Hose?
HOSE	Well, that fight reminds me of a little story … there was a Swede and an Italian standing on the corner talking, when a good-looking young girl passed by. So <u>Pat</u> says to <u>Mike</u>, "Hasn't she got beautiful eyes"? And Mike says, "Yeah, but she's got a bad run in one of them!"
JACK	That's awfully good … and now, <u>last but not lost</u>, we will hear from a fellow who knows all about <u>uppercuts</u> as he used to be a <u>butcher</u> and is now manager of those two great fighters: <u>One-Round Steak</u> and <u>Kid Knee</u> … May I introduce to you, MR. J. VEAL CUTLET! … Well, Mr. Cutlet, what do <u>you</u> think of the fight?
	CUTLET (begins to laugh uproariously)
JACK	Well, that's the most accurate description we have heard yet…
	(LAUGHTER CONTINUES)
	What are you laughing at?

CUTLET	She had a bad run in one of them!
JACK	Okay, boys … thanks for coming up … And run, don't walk, to the nearest exit.
ANNOUNCER	Ladies and gentlemen, these four men sneaked in here thru the courtesy of Canada Dry Ginger Ale, made-to-order by the glass at all fountains.
JACK	With just the right amount of syrup.
	And before introducing the next number, I just want to say that after all the excitement of the Sharkey-Schmelling fight, little Gene Sarazen comes in on the last round with a 66, cutting my score in half … Congratulations, Gene!
	You know George Olsen and I were in the tournament, too. It's funny how they misspell names in newspapers. They had my name spelled KIRKWOOD and Olsen's name, DUTRO.
	And they even charged us green fees. Imagine that for an open golf tournament … oh, well, POLITICS!
	And now Fran Frey will sing, "Come and Sit Beside the Sea," played by George Olsen and his Mental Hazards. The drummer will play on the sand traps… Am I saying the wrong things? … hmmmm?
	FORE, George!

5. COME AND SIT BESIDE THE SEA   FRAN FREY

JACK	That was the last number of the seventeenth program on the 27th of June. Be with us on Wednesday night as we will have another surprise for you. You know, on nearly every program, you hear the phrase, "LADIES AND GENTLEMEN" repeated dozens of times … "Ladies and gentlemen – this" and "Ladies and gentlemen – that" … with absolutely no courtesy shown to the babies. There are 120 million individuals in this country – of which at least 20 million are babies. It's about time that a program was dedicated to this group. So WEDNESDAY will be a night for BABIES EXCLUSIVELY! All you grown-ups can go to bed early and leave the babies at the radio. Of course, if you really want to listen in, that's up to you. But it will still be Babies' Night!
	Well, I must leave you now. And, as they say in Cuba, did you HAVANA Canada Dry today?… Goodnight, then.
	SIGINATURE—ROCKABYE MOON
ANNOUNCER	Now's the time to ask for a Canada Dry ice cream soda when you visit a soda fountain. It's a delicious drink — a real treat in this hot weather — night or day. Canada Dry is also available in bottles as well as made-to-order by the glass. You are invited to listen in again at this same time Monday night, when Jack Benny, Ethel Shutta and George Olsen will entertain. This is the National Broadcasting Company.

June 29, 1932

STATION	WJZ	PROGRAM	CANADA DRY GINGER ALE, INC.
	AND	DATE	WEDNESDAY, JUNE 29, 1932
	BLUE NETWORK	TIME	9.30 - 10:00 P.M. (E.D.T.)

SIGNATURE - JOLLY GOOD COMPANY

1. HOW CAN YOU SAY YOU LOVE ME   "HOTCHA" GARDNER

2. HEY DIDDLE DIDDLE   TRIO & ORCHESTRA

3. IS I IN LOVE I IS   ETHEL SHUTTA & ORCH.

4. A BUNGALOW, A PICCOLO AND YOU   FRAN FREY & ORCH.

5. THE MILLS BROTHERS   QUARTET & ORCH.

6. GOODNIGHT, SWEETHEART   ETHEL SHUTTA & BOBBY BORGER

SIGNATURE - ROCKABYE MOON

SIGNATURE – JOLLY GOOD COMPANY

ANNOUNCER	Ladies and gentlemen. Another half-hour of entertainment about Canada Dry Ginger Ale, now available made-to-order by the glass at soda fountains. George Olsen, Ethel Shutta and Jack Benny, the Canada Dry humorist, again perform for your enjoyment, and you remember, this is <u>Babies' Night</u>.

George Olsen opens the program with "How Can You Say You Love Me?" "Hotcha" Gardner sings a chorus or two.

1. HOW CAN YOU SAY YOU LOVE ME　　　　　　ORCHESTRA & GARDNER

(Rattles – babies crying, etc. Orchestra plays "LONDON BRIDGE IS FALLING DOWN")

BENNY	Don't worry, folks … this is Just Babies' Night … hello, every baby … Cootsey, cootsey, cootsey, cootsey … this is Uncle Jack Benny talking … Benny … B as in LITTLE BO-HUNK-PEEP … E as in EAR-ly to bed and EAR-ly to rise … N as in NA-NA-NA-NA … another N as in the same thing … and Y as in yum-yum-yummy … Are you paying attention, babies? … hmmm?

Well, we're all here to play with you kiddies tonight … Poppa Olsen came over in a 1932 Kiddie Kar… with the chauffeur walking a block ahead … Cousin Ethel rode over in the rumble seat of a Tricycle… and Fran Frey, the Bogie Man, came over on a Scooter … Fran looks so cute tonight … he has on a little new white bonnet, tied with pink baby ribbon, and the prettiest blue rompers … how do you feel tonight, Fran?

FRAN (in high falsetto)	I feel like a two-year old.

JACK	Well, you look like 52.

FRAN	Can I help it if I worry?

JACK	All right, Fran … You'll help this program greatly by sitting down … Well, little off-springs, here's a letter that just came in from a <u>six-months</u> old baby in NIPPLE-ville, <u>O</u>-Kansas, regarding Canada Dry Ginger Ale. <u>It</u> writes us—

> "For the past five months I have been drinking milk out of the bottle and have been wondering why I couldn't <u>sleep nights</u> and was unable to <u>comprehend coherently</u> during the daytime" … this baby must have been Nicholas Murray Butler…

Well, anyway, it continues to say—

> "I have worried until I have <u>very little hair on my head</u>. So one day, as I was holding the bottle of milk in my hand, with the nipple in my mouth, I said to myself, 'Johnny, you've been a sucker long enough.' So I switched to your Canada Dry Ginger Ale, made-to-order by the glass, and NOW I am not only the best-looking baby in town, but feel stronger than ever and have obtained a good job <u>in the steel mills</u>. I am working <u>six</u> <u>days a week</u> and am the <u>main support of my family</u>.
>
> (Signed) <u>KIDDIE</u> from KANSAS CITY"

Another victory for the steel mills … er, Canada Dry Ginger Ale! Ah! It's letters like these that make letter like these … like letters like these … believe me.

And now Georgie-Porgie will play "Hi-Diddle-Diddle," sung by Skippy Fran … Snooky Rice … and Pudgie Borger … How anybody over six-months of age can listen to this, <u>I don't know</u>.

2. HI DIDDLE DIDDLE   ORCHESTRA & TRIO

BENNY: You know, little tots, as I look around the Studio, I see many baby celebrities here this evening. Of course a few phonies … which can't be helped … they're liable to sneak in any place.

Unfortunately, some of the infants had to leave early. <u>Babe Ruth</u> was here … but he had to <u>run home</u> as it was getting late. ANOTHER home run for the Babe.

We also had <u>Baby-faced</u> MacLarnan up here… and Mahatma Gandhi. Mahatma took advantage of this occasion just because he holds his wardrobe together with a <u>safety-pin</u>. However, we sent him away as he is over the age limit and that's what I call… taking <u>GANDHI from the babies</u>…

(BABY STARTS CRYING)

Aw, what's-matter wiz little ootsey-wootsey … Hah! Here's a little feller from over in Long Island, who is crying for ASTORIA …

And now we have a <u>surprise</u> for you … we have brought a little baby up here tonight … a <u>boy</u>, his father tells me … well, not exactly a baby … he's a year-and-a-half old and has two strikes on him already AS HIS NAME IS <u>Lucifer</u>. I understand that Lucifer has appeared in amateur theatricals like the Elk's Minstrels and things of that sort. He has a phenomenal voice for a child that age … mind you, <u>only a</u> <u>year-and-a-half</u>, and he is going to sing for you … Oh, I forgot to mention that Lucifer is the son of George Hicks, our announcer … Come here, Lucifer … say hello to the folks …

LUCIFER: Hello, everybody.

BENNY: Now tell everyone your name.

LUCIFER: My name's LUCIFER HICKS.

BENNY: That's a nice name … what are you going to sing for us, <u>my little</u> <u>man</u>?

LUCIFER (whispers)	What am I supposed to say now?
BENNY (whispers)	Say … I'm going to sing OLD MAN RIVER.
LUCIFER (repeats)	I'm going to sing OLD MAN RIVER.
BENNY	Old Man River … isn't that a rather difficult number for a little chap like you?
LUCIFER	No, not for me… <u>it's easy</u>!
BENNY	All right … Old Man River … give him a chord, George.
	(Strikes chord)
FRAN (in heavy voice – sings)	
	Old Man River, Old Man River … he just keeps arolling along, etc.
JACK	LUCIFER! … LUCIFER! …
FRAN (heavy voice)	What?
BENNY	Now here's a nickel … go out and buy yourself some rough-on-rats.
FRAN (heavy voice)	SCRAM, WILL YUH, BENNY?
JACK	Now, Lucifer. Uncle Jack kick teeth out… what <u>is</u> this younger generation coming to, anyway? … Well, don't blame Lucifer because you can't tell how a voice will come over the air.
	Oh, I forgot to mention that Junior is the <u>seventh son</u> of our announcer … which is ANOTHER victory for George Hicks, made-to-order, by the glass and sold at all fountains.
	Well, I'm sorry I started the whole thing. You can't trust babies … you don't know what they are liable to do next.
	(PHONE RINGS)
	Oh, pardon me, folks … hello, … oh, hello, baby … <u>MY BABY</u> … how is oo? … I said, oo … double o … yes, <u>baby</u> … did you have a good time last night, <u>babe</u>? … mean, <u>baby</u> … what time did you get home this morning? … no, you can't come up here now … this is BABIES' NIGHT … well goodbye, baby … see you later …
	That was <u>my</u> baby… 29 years old and still ga-ga.
	And now little Ethel will sing "Is I In Love, I Is," played by Daddy George Olsen and his Baby Elephants.

3. IS I IN LOVE I IS   **ORCHESTRA & SHUTTA**

BENNY	That was "Is I In Love, I Is," sung by <u>our baby</u>, Ethel Shutta.
	And now, I want all of you kiddies to listen in carefully as we have several nursery rhymes tonight, which many of you newcomers have never heard before. These

	rhymes come to you by special permission of Mrs. Mother Duck … or, Goose. Are you ready?
	Ethel, you recite the first one.
ETHEL	All right, Jack …
	Mary had a little lamb,
	Its FLEAS were white as snow,
	And every place that Mary…
JACK (whispers)	Ethel, you've got that wrong. It isn't FLEAS, but FLEECE!
ETHEL	Oh, FLEAS! … and all the time I thought it was FLEECE. Well, I'll start over again…
	Mary had a little fleece,
	Its lamb was white as snow,
	And every place that Mary went
	She … she … she …
BENNY	She ordered Canada Dry … isn't that cute?
	All right now, Ethel, it's my turn …
	Little Paul Small,
	Sat in a hall,
	Eating his Christmas pie.
	He put in his thumb, pulled out a megaphone,
	And said what a CROONER am I.
	Are you babies enjoying this? … Ethel, let's you and I do one together, Huh?
ETHEL	No, I don't wanna.
BENNY	Aw, come on, Ethel, nobody's listening in, anyway… on such a hot night as this, I'll start it …
	Where are you going, my pretty maid?
ETHEL	To the soda fountain, sir, she said.
BENNY	What are you going to buy, my pretty maid?
ETHEL	Canada Dry, by-the-glass, sir she said,
BENNY	And what is your fortune, my pretty maid?
ETHEL	My face is my fortune, sir, she said.
BENNY	I see that you're broke, then, my pretty maid.
ETHEL (with force)	I'm getting hungry, sir, she said.

BENNY (increasing in volume)

> I KNEW THAT WAS COMING, MY PRETTY MAID.

ETHEL (with still greater force)

> I'M SO HUNGRY I COULD EAT A HORSE, SHE SAID.

(GALLOPING OF HORSES' HOOVES)

BENNY   And <u>here's</u> your horse, my pretty maid …

Would you like <u>horse</u> radish, sir? she said.

(ETHEL LAUGHS)

ETHEL   What's the next line, Jack?

BENNY   All right, Ethel, let's drop the whole thing.

Little Bo-Peep.

Lost some sleep … and that's what is going to happen to <u>you babies</u> if you continue to listen in to this stuff.

I feel awfully silly tonight. Think I'll start life <u>all over again</u>. George! go out and get me a pair of <u>short pants</u>.

And now we are going to give you babies a <u>Limerick Contest</u> in <u>your</u> <u>own language</u>, in which you will have to fill in only <u>last line</u>. There is really no excuse for anyone not entering it as it will be made as simple as possible … Here it goes…

GA-GA-GA	GA-GA-GA	GA-GA-GA
GA-GA-GA	GA-GA-GA	GA-<u>GA</u>!
GA-GA	GA-GA	
GA-GA	GA—<u>GEE</u>! …	

Now all you have to do is fill in the LAST LINE, making it rhyme with GEE. The baby winning the <u>first prize</u> will receive a pair of golf knickers with a genuine imported safety pin … the winner of the second prize will receive <u>an all-day sucker</u> … and the winner of the third prize will receive a <u>half-day sucker</u>.

And now George Olsen, who is biting his nails, will play, "A Bungalow, a Piccolo and You," sung by Junior Fran, through the courtesy of Canada Dry – Ginger Ale – made-to-order – by the glass, etc.

(Music starts on cue "made-to-order")

4. A BUNGALOW A PICCOLO AND YOU

BENNY   Say, George, what have you got to offer for Baby's Night?

GEORGE   (Announces his specialty MILLS BROTHERS)

5. MILLS BROTHERS novelty   **ORCHESTRA & QUARTET**

JACK   And now for our bedtime story. Which one would you kiddies like to hear? … Little Red Riding Hood … or Jack and the Beanstalk … or Three Weeks? … Oh, you <u>would</u>, eh? Well, you'll get Little Red Riding Hood and <u>like it</u>. So let's go …

(SOUR FANFARE)

This isn't a contest, George.

Well, little offsprings … once upon a time there was a little girl who lived in the woods with her mother and father. She always wore a green sweater, a blue skirt and a yellow beret … so they called her little Red Riding Hood. I guess they called her that because her fingernails were always tinted <u>raspberry</u>.

Well, one day her mother asked her to take a basket of food over to her grandmother who lived five minutes from the station, according to the real estate agent … But, no kidding, it was a two-hour walk or twenty-five minutes by bus … First, Little R. R. Hood asked her brother, Little White Walking Pants to go with her, but he said no. So she took the basket and started out alone for <u>a tramp</u> in the woods. It doesn't give the name of the tramp, but it could be anybody in Olsen's band.

She finally arrived at her grandmother's house where she met a wolf at the door … which, in those days, was quite a novelty. Now Little Red Riding Hood had never seen a wolf before and, thinking it was a great big dog, she sang three choruses of ROVER, KEEP AWAY FROM MY DOOR! assisted, no doubt, by Fran Frey and Paul Small … This scared the wolf inside the house, whereupon he jumped into bed and covered himself with a crazy quilt made up of Olsen's fan mail, and played the part of the sick grandmother who was attending the opening of Texas Guinan's new night club …

Now wait until I turn the page …

So Little Red Riding Hood, unaware of this feature picture plot, walked right up to the bed … and <u>was she fooled</u>? YOU SAID IT, CHILDREN! Little Red Riding Hood asked, "Where's my grandmother?" but the wolf put on his spectacles and answered, "I am your grandmother … and what did you bring me, my dear?" "I brought you these sandwiches and some fruit and cigars." And the wolf said, "WHAT? No Canada Dry Ginger Ale, made-to-order by the glass at all fountains?"

(Ahem! I nearly forgot that.)

And, finally, Little Red Riding Hood got suspicious and said, "What sharp eyes you've got, grandma!" and the wolf said, "The better to see you with, my dear." And she said, "What a long <u>schnozzle</u> you've got," and the wolf said, "The better for talking pictures, my dear."

(Can you imagine, George, a wolf in a <u>Fox</u> picture? My! My! how they put it over on those kiddies!)

Then she came closer and said, "Grandma, what <u>large ears</u> you've got." And the wolf said, "And so has Clark Gable, my dear."

	And with that (<u>starts yawning</u>) little Red Riding Hood got sore … (more yawns) and the wolf jumped out of the bed, ad lib… and the sandwiches lived…
GEORGE	Hey, Jack! Wake up … wake up …
JACK	Oh, yes … and the grandmother lived happily ever after.
	And now George Olsen will play, "Goodnight, Sweetheart," sung by Ethel Shutta and Bobby Borger, thru the courtesy of Canada Dry – Ginger Ale… made-to-order, by the glass at all fountains …

(MUSIC STARTS ON CUE "MADE-TO-ORDER")

6. GOODNIGHT, SWEETHEART   ETHEL SHUTTA & BOBBY BORGER

(SIGNATURE- " ROCKBYE MOON")

JACK	That was the last number of the eighteenth program on the 29th of June … are you sleeping, kiddies? … I have to leave you now.
	(Starts singing—)
	So, go to sleep, my babies, my babies … Isn't that awful, Ethel?
ETHEL	You took the thought right out of my head.
JACK	So nightly-night, then.
ANNOUNCER	Now's the time to ask for a Canada Dry ice cream soda when you visit a soda fountain. It's a delicious drink – a real treat in this hot weather – night or day. Canada Dry is also available in bottles as well as made-to-order by the glass. You are invited to listen in again at this same time Monday night, when Jack Benny, Ethel Shutta and George Olsen will entertain. This is the National Broadcasting Co.

July 4, 1932

STATION	WJZ	PROGRAM	CANADA DRY GINGER ALE, INC.
	AND	DATE	MONDAY, JULY 4, 1932
	BLUE NETWORK	TIME	9.30 - 10:00 P.M. (E.D.T.)

[Ed note: cover page missing from original script]

SIGNATURE—JOLLY GOOD COMPANY

ANNOUNCER Ladies and gentlemen. Another half-hour of entertainment about Canada Dry Ginger Ale, now available made-to-order by the glass at soda fountains. George Olsen, Ethel Shutta and Jack Benny, the Canada Dry humorist, again perform for your enjoyment.

     George Olsen opens the program with "What, You Got No Trouble?"

1. WHAT, YOU GOT NO TROUBLE?   ORCHESTRA & FRAN FREY

ANNOUNCER And here's the Canada Dry humorist himself, — Jack Benny!

JACK Hello … of the people … by the people … and for the people… This is Independence Day, so let's forget politics for a while … Yep, people are shooting firecrackers today … George Olsen is Shooting craps… and this is Jack Benny, shooting off his mouth… and you ladies who have had three husbands, are you celebrating the FOURTH today?… hmmm? …Are you listening, babies?…oh, pardon me, that was <u>last</u> week.

     Well, I just looked at the calendar and noticed that it was the birthday of July the Fourth, one of our three great kings. His last battle was with Bismarck, the Third … whom he ate alive … or do you like anchovies? July the Fourth was a brother of Richard the Second, and his uncle was Olsen, the First, of Sweden.

     This year July 4th happen to fall on the fourth of July … which is much better than having it on September 9th … Let September take care of itself. Of course, in the olden days, July 4th fell on Louis, the 14th. Lots of things fell on Louis, the 14th … but the kid could take it.

     But what does the 4th of July mean? … It means that you have paid your rent <u>three days ago</u> … that <u>tomorrow</u> will be the fifth and that <u>yesterday</u> was the third.

ETHEL Jack, today is INDEPENDENCE DAY!

JACK Yes, Ethel, they all know that … I'm just trying to tell them some of the things they don't know.

	Of course this is Independence Day! Six of my dependents come over to spend the week-end … which means there will be independence for me today.
ETHEL	But you don't mind your relatives coming to visit you once in a while, do you, Jack?
JACK	It isn't that … I don't mind when <u>my</u> relatives come to visit me, but when they bring <u>their</u> relatives, that's carrying things a bit too far. Do you know that one car stopped in front of my house and <u>seven people</u> got out of the <u>rumble seat</u>? … I don't even want to think about it.
	And now Ethel Shutta will sing, "Talking to You about Me," in spite of George Olsen standing there with his stick … Say, George, instead of waving that stick, why don't you hold a fan in your hand? … at least you'll get a breeze out of it.

2. TALKING TO YOU ABOUT ME   ORCHESTRA & ETHSL SHUTTA

JACK	(SOUND EFFECT: slight explosion)
	What was that? Oh! … Say, a funny thing just happened. A firecracker exploded in Olsen's pocket and out flew three ten-dollar bills … a padlock and four fish hooks … Ah, well, George, it had to come out sometime.
	And, by the way, folks, our studio is filled with fireworks of all descriptions which we have brought to you thru the courtesy of Canada Dry Ginger Ale, made-to-order by the glass at all fountains … phew! I wish this product had a shorter name.
	Anyway, don't go away tonight … please stand by your radio as later — for the first time over the air — you are going to be entertained with fireworks! You will <u>hear</u> pink, blue and yellow firecrackers … please pay special attention to our yellow ones. And we promise you that a good time will be had by all. You will <u>see</u> torpedo <u>shots</u> and giant crackers, and probably hear them. Gene Sarazen is coming here to light up the niblick <u>shots</u>. Everyone here is in the holiday spirit and would like to take a <u>shot</u> at each other … The drummer is playing with two <u>sticks</u> of dynamite … and the trombone player is going to <u>blow</u> his brains out during the next number.
	Well, anyway, we believe that when <u>in Rome</u>, do as — what's that crack, Ethel?
ETHEL	Why … er … I think…
JACK	Never mind, Ethel … I got it. When in Rome, do as the Rome-anians … or something like that.
ETHEL	Say, Jack is it true that Canada Dry Ginger Ale is sold at all fountains, made-to-order by the glass, with just the right amount of syrup?
JACK	Shh! Ethel … not so loud.
ETHEL	Why, Jack?

JACK	We don't want people to be leaving their radios now and running to the nearest soda fountain for a glass of Canada Dry … Besides, Ethel, this is a holiday, and we don't want any advertising.
ETHEL	All right Jack, I won't say another word about Canada Dry Ginger Ale.
JACK	Yes … and nothing about made-to-order by the glass at all fountains, either.
	You know, this is a day when people want to forget business and advertising … they all want to be away at the beaches and in the country … I don't even know why we're here.
ETHEL	Jack, why didn't you go away for the week-end?
JACK	Oh, I never like to go away for the week-end unless I can spend <u>three</u> <u>or four months</u>!
ETHEL	But, Jack, I can't understand why you look so well. You're got the darkest coat of tan that I've ever seen.
JACK	Well, I spent all morning <u>under my car</u>.
(ETHEL LAUGHS)	
	I'm only kidding, Ethel … I spent two days at Atlantic City …Why, I saw you there on the boardwalk.
ETHEL	Then why didn't you come over and say hello?
JACK	Well, I was on my way to dinner … when I came back, you were gone … Then I put on my bathing suit and sat on the beach the rest of the day … that is, I sat there until a great big wave came along and <u>nearly</u> <u>wet</u> my suit, so I went home … You know, you have to be awfully <u>careful</u> around those beaches.
ETHEL	Wasn't there an awful crowd there Saturday and Sunday?
JACK	I should say so … It took me half an hour to get into the water.
ETHEL	Yes, I saw you swimming … I liked that stroke you use.
JACK	What stroke?
ETHEL	That stroke when you were swimming.
JACK	I wasn't swimming … I was <u>talking</u> to a friend of mine … Say, Ethel, I saw George teaching you how to swim … you know, when he had his arm around you in the water and —
ETHEL	I wasn't even <u>near</u> the water.
JACK	I'm sorry … pardon me, George…
ETHEL(begins to argue with George)	
	George, what do you mean by teaching a strange woman to swim? … the idea of putting your arms around her … who was she? … I demand to know … what does she mean to you, etc.

JACK (loud – to cover up Ethel's lines)

> AND NOW PAUL SMALL WILL SING, "SONGS FOR SALE," played by poor George Olsen and his orchestra … All right, Instructor Olsen, hop to it!

3. SONGS FOR SALE   **ORCHESTRA & PAUL SMALL**

ETHEL (still heard arguing)

> George Olsen, I'm surprised at you … I can't get over it … teaching a strange woman how to swim…

GEORGE — But honey, I didn't …

JACK — Ethel! … Ethel! … forgot it … why, I wasn't even down at the beach … Every time I buy a new pair of shoes, I put my foot in it … You're singing the next number, aren't you, Ethel?

ETHEL (annoyed) — Yes … and I don't want George to play it!

JACK — Now, Ethel, where's your sense of humor? Don't you know I was only kidding?

ETHEL — Well, I believe <u>you</u>, Jack … but <u>not</u> George.

JACK — If you were married to me, you wouldn't believe me, either … Tell me, Ethel, what number are you going to sing?

ETHEL — It's all about an ice-cream soda … made of Canada Dry Ginger Ale with ice-cream. Isn't that a delicious drink, Jack?

JACK — Yes, but the straw always gets in my eye.

ETHEL — Why, Jack, you had one with us only a few minutes ago … on our way to the studio.

JACK — Shh! Ethel … the sponsors may be listening in.

ETHEL — Well, anyway, speaking about sodas…

(right into number)

4. SIPPING SODA WITH SUZIE   **ORCHESTRA & ETHEL SHUTTA**

JACK — And now, ladies and gentlemen, I'm going to give you the real news of our Convention. After all, everything is quiet today … all places of business are closed … no newspapers printed … and you really don't know what is going on. Well, we're here to take care of our own customers. And if there is anyone listening in who is not one of our customers, just come in and keep under your hat…

Of course, both the Democratic and Republican Conventions are over, but our <u>own</u> Convention still goes on, in an effort to nominate a candidate for President on our Canada Dry Made-to-Order ticket. You remember we started this convention two weeks ago, but had to drop it on account of Babies' Night... because, after all, that is where we expect our heaviest vote.

I will start by reading the Minority Report on the 24th amendment ... which is equivalent to the sixth movement of the Unfinished Symphony ... As I am only given <u>three minutes</u> for reports, I shall now read you the <u>minutes</u>.

From the votes in the various sections, I learn that CINCINNATI gives us three <u>i's</u> ... that is, three i's in CINCINNATI, all dotted ... on the question of <u>reduced traffic</u>, three horses from MONTANA voted "Nay, nay, nay"   ... making a grand total of three "ayes" and three "nayes".

Eight delegates from Ellis Island <u>deported</u> ... I mean, reported that four left yesterday on the S.S. STEERAGIA while the other four left via the S.S. HOLLAND TUBE ... which is a draw for the U.S.A. and another victory for Canada Dry Ginger Ale...

GEORGE (quickly)   Made-to-order...

ETHEL (quickly)   By the glass...

PAUL   At all fountains.

(BREAK BY DRUMMER-dum-dum-dum-dum, da-da!)

JACK   Now in referring to the delegates from now on, I will not <u>waste time</u> by calling out the <u>full</u> names of the States, but will use only the <u>abbreviations</u>. For example, Massachusetts will be simply MASS ... and Georgia will be GA , and go forth...

Now for The reports — The States FLA ... LA ... and PA ... voted in favor of <u>peeling</u> a banana once, whereas the States of MIN ... KAN ... and TEX... believe in the REpeal of the banana.

Now the States of ARK ... CAL ... AND R.I. ... which is really bad grammar — it should be M.I. ... as in MINNESOTA ... are for Daylight Saving time, while the States of ALA ... MICH ... and MO ... three fine fellows ... are for bigger and better blue-plates ... that is, <u>less</u> plate and <u>more</u> meat.

Now the State of VT ... the State of VT ... Say, Ethel, how do you abbreviate VERMONT?

ETHEL   <u>VT</u>.

JACK   Well, the State of Vt ... Well, the State of MAINE sends us no votes, no-runs, three hits and two errors ... which reminds me ... speaking of Maine and its products, Paul Small, will now sing, "Cabin in the Cotton," played by George Olsen and his Fourth of July-ers.

5. CABIN IN THE COTTON   ORCHESTRA & PAUL SMALL

JACK   And now, ladies and gentlemen, the feature spot on our program … what you've all been waiting for … our FIREWORKS!

We have a man with us this evening who is the Champion Firecracker lighter … who has lighted firecrackers all over the world … and spent five years in a lighthouse … I take great pleasure in introducing to you Mr. J. PINWHELL PUNK … who will officiate as Master of Fireworks and control this <u>racket</u>. MR. PUNK!

(ROUND OF APPLAUSE)

Now, Punk…

PUNK   You made a mistake, Mr. Benny … The name's KLUNK.

JACK   I beg your pardon…MR. J. PINWHEEL KLUNK … Of course you know why you're here.

PUNK   No, I don't, Mr. Benny.

JACK   That's the idea, exactly … right in the spirit of our program … Now tell us, Mr. Dunk…

PUNK   It's Klunk.

JACK   I beg your pardon … MR. KLUNK, are you an American citizen?

PUNK   No … I was born here.

JACK   Well, it looks like I'm going to have trouble with you … tell us why they celebrate the Fourth of July by shooting off firecrackers?

PUNK   I don't know … I just light them, I don't listen to them.

JACK   Say, how long have you been lighting firecrackers?

PUNK   Oh, about twenty years.

JACK   And do you expect to continue in this business?

PUNK   Yes … until I get rid of all these matches … You see, I don't smoke.

JACK   You don't smoke … I see … Mr. Dunk … Punk … or Klunk, can you tell us what happened in 1776?

PUNK   What street?

JACK   Any street … here's an easy one. Who's the Father of our Country? (pause) Who's the Father of our Country? … Oh, you won't talk, eh?

PUNK   I'm no <u>stool pigeon</u>.

JACK   Well, go ahead and light the fireworks. And BE CARELESS!… The first one, ladies and gentlemen, will be a Roman Candle … now listen carefully…

(FIZZZZZZZ..POW!)

ORCHESTRA   Ah!

JACK   That was a Roman candle, ladies and gentlemen … wasn't that beautiful? Now some more…

(DRUM ROLL- CRASH!)

That was a triple cartwheel.

ANNOUNCER   Those fireworks come to you thru the courtesy of Canada Dry Ginger Ale, made-to-order by the glass at all fountains.

(BANG! BANG!)

MAN   OW!

JACK   That was the shooting of Dan McGrew … Some more?

(Pheeeeee – POP!)

That was the champagne of ginger ales…

(Pop! BANG!)

(EVERYONE LAUGHS)

Now what happened? … Olsen just burned his finger … isn't that funny?

(BANG! BANG!)

JACK   Ouch!

GEORGE   That was Jack Benny – someone set off a string of firecrackers in his pocket.

JACK   And now Bob Rice will assist in the celebration by singing, "When Gimbel Plays the Cymbal," played by George Olsen and his Wisecrackers, thru the courtesy of Canada Dry – Ginger Ale – made-to-order, by the glass…

(Music starts on "made-to-order")

6. WHEN GIMBEL PLAYS THE CYMBAL   ORCHESTRA & BOB BICE

JACK   That was the last number of our nineteenth program on the 4th of July. Did you have a good time, hmmm? … Well! I must leave you now. As they say in Washington, didya Tacoma bottle of Canada Dry? … Goodnight, then.

SIGNATURE — ROCKABYE MOON

ANNOUNCER	A glass of Canada Dry and your favorite sandwich make a delicious luncheon combination. Also try a Canada Dry ice cream soda when you visit a soda fountain. It's a real treat in this hot weather – night or day. Canada Dry is also available in bottles as well as made-to-order by the glass. You are invited to listen in again at this same time Wednesday night, when Jack Benny, Ethel Shutta and George Olsen will entertain. This is the National Broadcasting Company.

July 6, 1932

STATION	WJZ	PROGRAM	CANADA DRY GINGER ALE, INC.
	AND	DATE	WEDNESDAY, JULY 6, 1932
	BLUE NETWORK	TIME	9:30-10:00 P.M. (E.D.T.)

SIGNATURE - JOLLY GOOD COMPANY

1. OVER THE WEEKEND	HARMS	ORCHESTRA & ETHEL SHUTTA
2. ROSE ROOM	WATERSON, BERLIN & SNYDER	ORCHESTRA
3. HEAR THE LITTLE GERMAN BAND	MILLER	ORCHESTRA & ETHEL SHUTTA
4. SOMEONE TO CARE	REMICK	ORCHESTRA & ETHEL SHUTTA
5. MARGIE	WATERSON, BERLIN & SNYDER	ORCHESTRA & DICK GARDNER

SIGNATURE - ROCKABYE MOON

ALTERNATE

ALL THE WORLD IS WAITING FOR THE SUNRISE	HARMS

SIGNATURE – JOLLY GOOD COMPANY

ANNOUNCER	Ladies and Gentlemen. Another half-hour of entertainment about Canada Dry Ginger Ale, now available made-to-order by the glass at soda fountains. George Olsen, Ethel Shutta and Jack Benny, the Canada Dry humorist, again perform for your enjoyment.

George Olsen opens the program with "Over the Weekend." Ethel Shutta singing.

## 1. OVER THE WEEKEND	ORCHESTRA & ETHEL SHUTTA

ANNOUNCER	And now, folks. I give the mike to Jack Benny!

JACK	Hello, every sun burned body… Did you get tanned over the holidays?…hmmm? Well, I did. And say, girls, I like those new low-back bathing suits you're wearing. They're very attractive…hmmm…Besides. You are giving Adam a chance to get his rib back. Of course that's not a new idea, girls. Back in 1928, my girl from Newark used to be a bare-backed rider in a circus. And it's no fun riding on the back of a bear…<u>believe</u> me.

Well, let's get down to work. This Jack Benny talking…I as in pajama… A as in ankle…

HARRY & DOUG	All right, Jack, we heard that.

JACK	Thanks… Oh well, now Canada Dry Ginger Ale is made-to-order…

BARRY & DOUG	We heard that, too.

JACK	I see… All right, folks, I'll tell a story. Stop me if you've heard it… There was an Irishman… a Hebrew and a Frenchman sitting…

HARRY & DOUG	<u>Stop</u>!

JACK	Well, here's another one… There was a little fellow…

HARRY & DOUG	STOP!
JACK	I wish Floyd Gibbons were here. We might need someone to describe a riot … You know, this program is one big, happy family… one for all and all for themselves… All right, boy, bring me THEM fan mail.
HARRY B.	All of THEM?
JACK	No, not all… only THEM that said nice thing about me.
HARRY	We haven't any of THEM.
JACK	Okay, then… Give me some of THEM others… Ah! here's a letter from a lady in <u>Lukewarm Springs</u>… Arkan-<u>sota</u>… she types…writes… or scribbles:

"DEAR ELK or MOOSE"…hmmmm…

I am taking the liberty of writing you as we need your advice. My husband and I have been married <u>five years</u> this week, and we are celebrating our <u>golden</u> anniversary… as it seems like <u>fifty</u> … hmmm

All our friends are coming over to our anniversary dinner, and I would like to make a <u>special</u> dish for this occasion. It seems to me that I have heard you mention <u>Fran Frey</u> on several of your broadcasts. Please let me know on your Wednesday's program how to make a <u>Fran Frey</u>.

I'LL BE LISTENING

All right, Mrs. I'll-be-listening… In the first place, Fran Frey is not a dish. He's a reformed crooner who now sings … He also plays the saxophone… is good to his parents… sleeps between twin beds… and has a galloping mole on his neck … Of course, lady, you <u>might</u> be thinking of FRAN FREY POTATOES…Well, that's a dish of another sauce.

Now, I can help you out with that, Mrs. Listening… Listen closely…

Take Half a dozen eggshells… four <u>slightly used</u> tea bags… <u>empty</u> bananas… stir them well. And then spice with nine or ten watermelon seeds… place gently in a pail, and leave it in your backyard where the garbage-man <u>can't</u> miss it.

And <u>remember</u>, lady, we cannot enter into any correspondence regarding the result of this experiment.

Anyway, that's the way you make a <u>Fran Frey</u>… Next week I will tell you how to make a Paul Small.

(ASIDE)

George, I didn't know what to tell that lady. We'll have to get a cook-book up here.

And now the next number will be "Rose Room," played by Chef Olsen and his Too-many-cooks that will spoil the song … er, the broth.

2. ROSE ROOM　　　　　　　　**ORCHESTRA**

JACK　　　　You know, ladies and gentlemen, during the past week Canada Dry conducted another big test of its product. We sent our conductor of tests to the Bronx Zoo… which we thought was the Zoo-ological place to hold it… In this zoo, ladies and gentlemen, are to be found over two thousand wild and ferocious animals… birds of the forest… and bees that are out of beez-ness … one more crack like that, Jack, and we'll turn you out … Okay, Frank, it won't happen again… Well, go ahead, Jack…

Anyway, we took Canada Dry by-the-glass up to the Zoo where these animals are employed eight hours a day, posing for animal crackers… with only Saturday afternoon off to look out at the public and laugh… That's their sole diversion. After all, animals can't play golf… can you imagine a giraffe in knickers?

Well, to continue. We went thru the customary procedure of blind folding these animals and tying their hands securely behind their backs, and gave to each and every one a glass of Canada Dry Ginger Ale made-to order.

We gave a glass apiece to Mr. and Mrs. Lions… and their neighbors, Mr. and Mrs. W. Cats… wild is the first name… and to Mr. and Mrs. Wolf in the cage upstairs… and to the entire Fox family. You should see that Fox family grab their Canada Dry glasses and fill'em … You know, Fox Film… hmmm? I am sorry, Frank.

Well, folks, that was only three days ago, and already we have received the following testimonials:

First, here's a letter from Mr. and Mrs. I. Leo-pard. They say "Your Canada Dry Ginger Ale is not only a good drink, but certainly hits the right spot."…And you know how many spots there are on a leo-pard.

Here's one from Ben Lion… this is not the movie actor. It says: "I am a mountain lion and am glad that Canada Dry Ginger Ale is now sold by-the-glass at all mountains!"

Ah! here's one from Mr. and Mrs. Hippo Potomas. They write: HIPPO! HIPPO! HOORAY!   for Canada Dry."

Here is one from the fashionable Mrs. Ray N. Deer. "I tried your Canada Dry Ginger Ale with ice-cream… and find it is also good with anteloupe."…hmmmmmmm

Aha! here's one from a gorilla in the Monkey-House. He says: "Dear Mug: Dat Canada Dry Ginger Ale is de foist good drink I've had in toity years! Oh, those gorillas.

Another from the same address It reads: " Dear Mr. Benny… your Canada Dry Ginger Ale is very good. I love it with a dash of orchid ice-cream." Signed JIM PANSY… Ah! they even have them in the zoo… Another victory for Canada Dry Ginger Ale, made-to-order by the glass at all fountains.

And now George Olsen and his orchestra will play, " Hear the Little German Band." We have a rare treat for you as this number will be sung by a very famous, exotic

German movie star who happens to be visiting us this evening. She is under contract to…er…well, you know, she made those great picture called.. er… anyway, her name is… er… what's your name?

ETHEL(IN GERMAN DIALECT) EDEL SHUTTA.

JACK Marlene Detour… of course Miss Detour is always known for her two beautiful <u>eyes</u>… which she always shows in her pictures.

ETHEL Con ich sagen eine wort?

JACK Ja, Ja…but mak eet snapeeee…

ETHEL [there is a blank space in the script…perhaps she improvised]

JACK Well, all right, Ethel…er, Marlene…do your song.

3. HEAR THE LITTLE GERMAN BAND   ORCHESTRA & ETHEL SHUTTA

JACK Dot vos oxolent, Chorge… It's moosic like dot dot remints me uf ven I vas a liddle poy in de ceercus in Potsdam…

GEORGE What's-dam?

JACK Potsdam.

GEORGE Were <u>you</u> with a circus?

JACK Sure…I vos an acrobot… I used to make somersaltz…mit der Potsdam…Flotsdam… and Jetsdam Cercos…Und ve played Potsdam, Rotterdam und Amsterdam… and all dem big cities. Und ven you shpiel out de moosic, it remembered to me vot ve heard used to vunce in de ceercos parade…Are you fershtayen, Lansmen? hmmmm?

GEORGE So you like German bands, eh?

JACK Yis, Monahan…it's the divil himself in thin toones… I mean, yah, Meyer, der Deutscher moosic its grosartic … Boy! Turn those pages right.

GEORGE Say, Jack, you understand German pretty well. I suppose you spent some time there.

JACK Oh yes, George. You remember last year I was there for my run-down condition?

GEORGE Oh yes…did you take the baths at Baden-Baden?

JACK I was run down, George…<u>not dirty</u>. But what I liked about Germany is the music they play there. You know, not <u>hot</u> cha or <u>cold</u> slaw… it's real music … written by masters like Wagner… Gounod… Strauss… Liszt… and Beethoven… Say, George, do you know "<u>Ill</u> Trovatore?"

GEORGE Yes.

JACK	Well, he's much better now… Take that fellow Beethoven, for example. There's a man can write music.
GEORGE	Jack, I'll bet you don't ever know what Beethoven wrote.
JACK	I don't, oh? Why, he wrote "Mendelsohn's Wedding March." But I don't think it will be much of a hit, George.
GEORGE (LAUGHS)	Beethoven didn't write that. Mendelsohn wrote "Mendelsohn's Wedding March."
JACK	No, I think you're wrong, George. Let's call him up.
GEORGE	Call him up? Why, he's been dead over a hundred and fifty years.
JACK	What?… Sammy Beethoven!… well, what do you know about that?… tck…tck…tck…tck…
GEORGE	Well, anyway, Jack, I'm glad to know you like high-class music.
JACK	Yes, sir. And there's no one I'd rather hear than that great tenor, Gigolo.
GEORGE	You mean gigli…G-I-G-L-I.
JACK	I'll kill the guy who types these sheets… Yes, George, I'm fond of good music.
GEORGE	Well, I'll play some opera for you… have you heard the sextette from "Lucia" lately?
JACK	No… what station are they on?
GEORGE (imitating Jack's style of delivery)	Oh well… ladies and gentlemen, George Olsen, who wouldn't give a nickel to see Old Man River marry Mississippi… will now play, "Someone to Care," with vocal chorus by Paul Tightwad Small.
JACK	Thanks, George… you took the words right out of my mouth… and this comes to you thru the courtesy of (To the melody of Sextette from "Lucia") Canada Dry Ginger Ale… made-to-order by the glass… at all fountains…

(Music starts on "At all fountains")

(Mocking sound)

    nyeh…nyeh…nyeh…nyeh…

4. SOMEONE TO CARE   ORCHESTRA & PAUL SMALL

JACK	Ladies and gentlemen, this program is in a very generous mood this evening. We are going to start something that is sure to interest all our radio customers. We realize that the weather has been terribly warm this year, and that you'd be rather be outdoors. So as a special inducement to keep you listening into our program during the

summer season, we are going to give you Profit-snaring…Sharing… coupons. Now let me tell you how this works:

The first coupon will be a 1/16th certificate… which is a Harvard Crimson color… or a sort of <u>nose red</u>.

The next coupon will be the 1/8th certificate… in a sort of Memphis <u>blue</u>.

Then comes the one-quarter certificate in a color chosen by Ethel… A sort of Zane <u>Gray</u>.

This is followed by the one-half certificate which is sort of a Bowling Green … and then the <u>full</u> certificate, or one full coupon, which is a sort of George <u>White</u>.

ANNOUNCER   These coupons come to you thru courtesy of Canada Dry Ginger Ale…

ANNOUNCER & JACK (together)

made-to-order by the glass.

JACK   I wish he wouldn't do that while I'm talking…

Now here's how you get these Coupons… it's very simple and <u>only</u> takes up <u>your time</u>… Of course, we will have to trust each other in this little transaction, as you know we cannot give you coupons over the radio.

If you will listen carefully to our <u>full</u> program, you will be entitled to a <u>full</u> certificate… which your printer will no doubt make up for you very reasonably.

If you listen to Olsen's numbers <u>alone</u>, you get the 1/16th certificate. But don't expect anything for listening in to Paul Small… as we have no <u>small</u> coupons… or little <u>kew</u>pies.

Now if you listen <u>to me</u>… give yourself <u>seven full</u> certificates. It's worth it!…

(ROUND OF APPLAUSE)

Jealous! So, folks, take advantage of Daylight Saving Time and <u>save</u> our coupons. Let me tip you off a few of the useful gifts which you will receive…

For <u>16,000</u> coupons or 7,000 certificates…you will receive a pair of LADIES baseball stockings… with two runs in one… three runs in the other… two men on base and none out… Nice, isn't it?

Now for <u>960,000</u> coupons or 70,000 certificates… which should cover something like <u>1400 broadcasts</u>… you will receive a pair of MEN'S golf stockings … with the eighteen holes in them.

For only <u>17,512</u> coupons, you will receive <u>absolutely free</u>, mind you, <u>a Wonder Clock</u>… in which the minute hand is missing and you will <u>wonder</u> what time it is.

For <u>20,165</u> coupons, you will receive a GENUINE Canada Dry made-to-order sold at all <u>FOUNTAIN PEN</u>.

Now for <u>one million, five hundred thousand coupons</u>… you can have your head examined with absolutely no expense to you… by our personal physician… J. Annapolis Baltimore… M.D.

Now, folks, these are just <u>a few</u> of the valuable articles we are giving away on this little profit-sharing plan. We just want to show you that we have a heart as big as the heart of Maryland.

Oh, I forgot to mention that for <u>ten million</u> certificates, our junkman will give you <u>ten cents for each hundred pounds</u>… which will bring you in a tidy sum. Just think! you might be young now… but think of the <u>future</u>… by saving our coupons till you are <u>ninety-five</u> years old, you can become independent for life… And <u>who</u> will you owe it to?

ANNOUNCER   You will become independent thru the courtesy of Canada Dry Ginger Ale made-to-order by the glass, sold at all fountains.

JACK   And now Dick Hotcha Gardner, who is <u>very independent</u>, will sing an old favorite, "Margie," played by George Olsen, the coupon saver… and I wish I had <u>his</u> coupons… <u>coupon</u> my word, I do.

6. MARGIE   **ORCHESTRA & DICK HOTCHA GARDNER**

JACK   That was "Margie" thru Georgia… And that was the last number on the 20th program on the 6th of July.

I hope you will all be with us on Monday night, as Monday will be AMATEUR NIGHT…Yes, ladies and gentlemen, AMATEUR night… Hah! I heard what you said… you said <u>Monday</u> night!…hmmm.

And as they say on our coming program, AM-AT-YOUR (AMATEUR) SERVICE! So good-night, please.

SIGNATURE – ROCKABYE MOON)

ANNOUNCER   Whenever you're thirsty – and especially on these hot days – remember that a glass of Canada Dry or a Canada Dry ice cream soda will give you a wonderful pick-up. Ask for Canada Dry at the nearest soda fountain. It is available made-to-order by the glass as well as in bottles. You are invited to listen in again at this same time Monday night, when Jack Benny, Ethel Shutta and George Olsen will entertain. This is the National Broadcasting Company.

July 11, 1932

STATION	WJZ	PROGRAM	CANADA DRY GINGER ALE, INC.
	AND	DATE	MONDAY, JULY 11, 1932
	BLUE NETWORK	TIME	9:30-10:00 P.M. (E.D.T.)

SIGNATURE - JOLLY GOOD COMPANY

1. THE WORLD IS WAITING FOR THE SUNRISE	ORCHESTRA
2. I WANT TO GO HOME	SHUTTA
3. THAT'S HOW WE MAKE MUSIC	ORCHESTRA
4. I KNOW YOU'RE LYING BUT I LOVE IT	SHUTTA & FREY
5. THREE GUESSES	FREY

SIGNATURE - ROCKABYE MOON

SIGNATURE – JOLLY GOOD COMPANY

ANNOUNCER Ladies and gentlemen. Another half-hour of entertainment about Canada Dry Ginger Ale, now available by the glass at soda fountains. George Olsen, Ethel Shutta and Jack Benny, the Canada Dry humorist, again perform for your enjoyment.

George Olsen opens the program with "THE WORLD IS WAITING FOR THE SUNRISE."

1. THE WORLD IS WAITING FOR THE SUNRISE   ORCHESTRA

ANNOUNCER O. K. Jack, you're next.

JACK Say, Hicks, this is Amateur Night – isn't it?

ANNOUNCER Yes.

JACK Well, I don't suppose anybody will be listening in to this. I'd better call up a friend of mine and be sure that we have at least <u>one</u> listener.

Hello, Operator … Operator … give me FOREST … Tree… Tree… Tree… Hello, Mr. Bush?… This is Jack Benny… No, BENNY … "B" as in Bonehead … No, not Prendergast … BENNY … A … B … No, not Abe Benny … Jack Benny, that's it … What's that? … Oh, you don't know him! … You must be listening to the wrong number.

(SOUND EFFECT: CLICKING OF RECEIVER)

Hey, Operator … you gave me the wrong number … Give me Forest … Tree … Tree … Tree … Hello, Bush? … Jack Benny. Say, I want you to listen in tonight. We're having Amateur Night … No, not Ham … <u>Am</u> … Amateur Night. What? It'll <u>be ham</u>? All right, no wisecracks. You're not such a good tailor, either … Say, how's everything at home? <u>Oh</u> … Well, congratulations … Your wife … two … <u>three</u>? … Well, well… how's she doing? …

Can you imagine that?... his wife bid <u>three hearts</u> and it looks as though she'll make it...

Well, be sure to listen in tonight ... Good-bye, Bush.

(SOUND EFFECT: HANGS UP PHONE)

Let's get started with our program ... Hello, anybody ... <u>and Mr. Bush.</u> This is Amateur Night ... and have <u>we got</u> amateurs? You know what an amateur is ... it's a <u>Jack</u> of all trades and an <u>Olsen</u> of none ... But aren't we all? ... hmmmm?

Well, this will be very much like a vaudeville show ... First, we're going to give you our News Reel ... or <u>Pathetic Weekly</u> ... All the latest news events. And don't forget, folks, we're only <u>amateurs</u>.

The first bit of news is that Sharkey won the World's Heavyweight Championship ... Good boy, Sharkey! ... Latest news from the Convention in Chicago is that Roosevelt has a good chance of getting the nomination ... Our <u>own</u> Candidate for President on the Canada Dry Made-to-Order Ticket has double-crossed us and taken a job as <u>a street cleaner</u>, as he doesn't care which branch of the government he works for. He said he would sooner wear a <u>white</u> suit than live in the <u>White</u> House.

Here's more news ... we have received word that Gene Sarazen is in great form, and it looks very much as though he will win the British Open Golf Championship! He will then try for the National Open ... We personally do not think he has a chance for either.

ANNOUNCER	But, Jack, he won both of them already.
JACK	He did? ... Well, folks, disregard our latest bit of news ... Our ace news reel man reports that Amelia Earhart has landed safely in Ireland. Of course, this is not yet official ... It is also rumored that King Alphonso has left Spain ... <u>without his hat</u> ... And last, but not least, there is a report that George Olsen is going to join our Canada Dry program ... Say, George, if you're here, will you play the next number? What's it going to be?
GEORGE	"I Want to Go Home."
JACK	It's all right with me, George, ... Ethel, you're in on this.

2. I WANT TO GO HOME   ETHEL SHUTTA

JACK	That was fine, George ... right in keeping with our program ... Is there anything else you would like to contribute?
GEORGE	Yes, I'd like to tell a story as long as it's Amateur Night.
JACK	I kind of felt that ... go ahead.
GEORGE	What's the difference between a cup of coffee ... A Chinaman ... and a lot of flies?

JACK	That's awfully good, George. Now I'll tell one.
GEORGE (LAUGHS)	But, Jack, I haven't told you the answer yet … What's the difference between a cup of coffee … a Chinaman … and a lot of flies?
JACK	I don't know. What is the difference?
GEORGE	The Chinaman and the cup of coffee are <u>both</u> yellow.
JACK	I drink <u>black coffee</u>.
GEORGE	I mean coffee <u>with cream</u> in it.
JACK	So far, that's fine, George. But where do the flies come in?
GEORGE	Thru the window when you keep it open.
JACK (LAUGHS)	That's awfully good, George. But this is Amateur … not <u>Revival</u> Night.
GEORGE	But, Jack, I told it just the way you gave it to me.
JACK (VERY QUICKLY)	The next number, ladies and gentlemen … Oh, I forgot. Now the first contributor to our non-professional program will be … Mr. J. Leather Lung … who claims to be an <u>amateur announcer</u>, and comes to you direct from the Union Depot where he has been announcing for the past ten years and has never missed a station … May I present to you Mr. J. Leather Lung … who will announce and advertise our product in his own stupid … own clever way. MR. LUNG!…
(CHORD)	
ASH	Hello, everybody … this train leaves in five minutes for (mumbles) Yankels … Neural … Osnig … Armen … Alamee … <u>and</u> <u>all points north</u>.
JACK	Hey, wait a minute. What's this? … Don't be plugging <u>those</u> products on our program.
ASH	I'm only tuning up … I'll be ready in a minute.
JACK	All right, let's see what you can do with <u>our</u> product. And <u>remember</u> … our sponsors are listening in.
ASH	Ladies and Gentlemen, this program comes to you through the counter of … of the courtesy by the glass … sold by Ginger Ale … at all by the courtesy of the Canada Dry fountains … You can now buy the courtesy by the glass … I mean, you can now buy Canada Dry by the courtesy of the glass, made to the fountain, by the order … <u>How was that</u>?
JACK	What are you talking about?
ASH	Don't you understand English? … That's the way I announce my trains.
JACK	Well, no wonder people who want to go to Albany get off at Kansas City.

ETHEL	Why, Jack, he's just trying to tell the public that Canada Dry Ginger Ale made-to-order by the glass, is now sold at all fountains.
JACK	Is that what he was trying to say?
ETHEL	Yes, but he forgot to mention that it's also good with ice cream. That's what you missed, Jack.
ASH	Aw, she don't know what she's talking about.
JACK	I see ... Is that all you're going to do?
ASH	No, I want to introduce the next song.
JACK	What is it?
ASH	It's all about golf ... it's the Caddy Song.
JACK	What's the Caddy Song?
ASH	(SINGS) Caddy me back to old Virginie ... this will be played by that cheap guy, George Olsen ... Well, how was that?
JACK	That wasn't bad ... it was all right. I think that with the right amount of training and good living, you ought to make a pretty good announcer ... in time ... a long time.
ASH	What do you think I ought to do?
JACK	Well, I'll tell you, Lung ... go back to the station ... call out your trains ... and stand in front of one of them ... Make it the Express!
ASH	Thanks, Mr. Benny, ... that's what I call a friend.
JACK	Now, let me see ... who else have we here? ... Ah! here's another gentleman. Mr. er ... er ... say, who are you?
FRAN (TOUGH VOICE)	I'm Erlanger Claw, the Lion-tamer!
JACK	Oh, you're a lion tamer! ... that ought to be quite a novelty... Did you bring your lion?
FRAN	Ain't you guys got a lion up here?
JACK	No.
FRAN	Say, why do you ask guys to come up here if you ain't got no lion.
JACK	George see that we have some animals up here on Wednesday ... Ah! there's a sweet-looking little girl, waiting to go on ... Come here, my pretty miss ... Isn't she cute? ... What do you do?
MIND-READER (IN GRUFF VOICE)	I'm a male impersonator.
JACK	Can you impersonate a man running down the steps?

MIND-READER (WITH DETERMINATION)   Why, of course!

JACK   There are the steps.

(SOUND EFFECT: THE BEAT OF A WOMAN'S FEET RUNNING DOWN STEPS)

Kvetch! Close that door … this must be another program … We will now return to our Canada Dry program, and George Olsen will repeat, " THAT'S HOW WE MAKE MUSIC" for the fifteenth time … for the benefit of a man in Siberia who hasn't yet heard it … George, you don't mind if I don't listen to this.

3. THAT'S HOW WE MAKE MUSIC   ORCHESTRA

JACK (SINGS)   That's how we make YOU SICK … And now, ladies and gentlemen … and <u>Mr. Bush</u> … the next amateur artist to appear this evening is Mr. … er … Mr. … er … say, what's your name, son?

BAKER   Olsen … Hotcha … Benny.

JACK   Well, Olsen Hotcha Benny … that's a familiar name. You didn't leave out anything, did you?

BAKER   Yes, Paul Small.

JACK   Say, where are you from?

BAKER   Fran Frey … Ohio.

JACK   Of course, you're an amateur artist … but what's your vocation?

BAKER   I got a job every <u>four years</u>.

JACK   <u>Every four years</u>? … what do you do?

BAKER   I put "<u>29</u>" on the month of February.

JACK   I imagine you must be kept pretty busy … What do you do in the way of entertaining?

BAKER   Oh, I imperson-<u>ate people</u>.

JACK   How many?

BAKER   I imperson-<u>ate people</u>.

JACK   I hate to kick your teeth out on this nice program … go ahead.

BAKER   My first impersonation will be that of a <u>flea</u>.

JACK   A FLEA?

BAKER	Yes.
JACK	Well, maybe this is just what radio has been waiting for … Go ahead, imitate a flea.
BAKER	Bzzzzzzzz … How's bzzzzzzzzzz… How's bzzzzzzzzzzzz…
JACK	That flea has a lot of endurance – hasn't it?
BAKER	That's the <u>male</u> flea … Now, the female flea … bzzzzzz… How's bzzzzzzzzz … How's bzzzzzz.
JACK	What's the difference?
BAKER	There's <u>no</u> difference. That's what I'm trying to show you.
JACK	I see … are you <u>insured</u>?
BAKER	Only for collision.
JACK	Well, that's all you need … What else can you do?
BAKER	I'd like to sing a song that I wrote myself … with <u>eight other people</u>.
JACK	Would you like to have the orchestra accompany you?
BAKER	I ain't going any place.
JACK	I see, that's what <u>you</u> think … go ahead! George, have the piano player follow him on this.
BAKER	Yeah, give me the vamp.

(PIANO STARTS VAMPING)

(BAKER STARTS HIS SONG…)

> I got a girl named Nelly,
> Nellie is my girlie's name.
> Everyone else calls her Nelly
> 'Cause Nelly is my girlie's name…

JACK	The name of this song is Nelly.

> Her name is Nelly … Nelly…
> My girlie's name is Nelly.
> Nelly is my girlie's name.
> It could be Fanny or Elsie,
> Sadie, Dot or Katarina,
> But Nelly is my girlie's name.
> Her name is Nelly, Nelly,
> And oh, what a figure!
> Nelly is my girlie's name.

	She has but two teeth in her mouth!
	One points north and the other points south,
	<u>B U T</u>
	Nelly is my girlie's name…

(da-da-dum-dum-da)

	They call her Nelly, Nelly, Nelly-Nelly-Nelly,
JACK	Nelly is <u>his</u> girlie's name…

	It could be Pittsburgh or Sammy,
	Lena or Salami,
	But Nelly is my girlie's name.

ANNOUNCER (SOFTLY)	Nelly comes to you thru the courtesy of Canada Dry Ginger Ale made-to-order by the glass at all fountains…

JACK [singing over the announcer] They call her Nelly, Nelly, Nelly-Nelly-Nelly,

'Cause Nelly is my girlie's name.

(LOUDER)

She has a figure — oh me, oh my,
Like the straw in glass of CANADA DRY.
But Nelly is my girlie's name…

(da-da-dum-dum-da)

Her name is Nel-el-hi … Nel-el-hi…

(SOUND EFFECT: TWO LOUD SHOTS ARE HEARD – SILENCE – THEN A DULL THUD.)

JACK	And now, ladies and gentlemen — <u>and Mr. Bush</u>, George Olsen will play another request number, "I Know You're Lying, But I Love It," sung by Ethel Shutta and Fran Frey … <u>without Nelly</u>.

4. I KNOW YOU'RE LYING, BUT I LOVE IT.   SHUTTA & FREY

JACK	We have here tonight a little female wizard who is an amateur mind reader. … She has X-ray eyes and on a bright day can see clearly thru a glass … a psychic genius … seizes all and tells nothing … a woman of a thousand eyes … and hooks on the back of her dress … I now take great pleasure in introducing the Arabian seeress … MISS ALLAH BAMAH.

(START ORIENTAL MUSIC: OBOE AND TAMBOURINE … CONTINUE VERY SLOWLY UNDER DIALOGUE)

What are you going to do, Miss Alah-mode … Allah Bamah.

MIND READBR	First, I must be thoroughly blindfolded … then I wish you would pass thru the audience and I'll tell you each and every object that you pick up. All you have to do is ask me what it is.
JACK	There … your eyes are now securely handcuffed … <u>sees all,</u> <u>knows all</u>
MIND READER	And I must now go into a trance
JACK	That's better that Walter Winchell … he goes into a <u>transom</u> … Ladies and gentlemen … and <u>Mr. Bush</u> … Allah is now gazing into the <u>crystal</u> … of my watch … Allah, you mustn't go into my pockets … All right, Allah, are you ready?
MIND READER	Yes.

(OBLIGATO MUSIC CEASES)

JACK (IN A LOUDER VOICE)	This man is a musician … what is he holding? … Come, come … this should be easy for one of your <u>sex</u>.
MIND READER	A <u>sex</u>-ophone.
JACK	Wonderful! … this man here is holding up a coin … what is this coin?
MIND-READER	It's a … It's a…
JACK	Come on now, Allah … don't let them <u>buffalo</u> you.
MIND-READER	A nickel!
JACK	Marvelous, marvelous … tell me now, what is this man wearing in his tie?
MIND-READER	Gravy.
JACK	You're wrong … concentrate! … Don't let this <u>stick</u> you.
MIND READER	Mucilage.
JACK	Wrong again … think, Allah! … What is this man wearing in his tie? Don't let this <u>stick</u> you.
MIND READER	A pin.
JACK	Terrific! … You should be with Houdini.
MIND READER	You should be with Napoleon.
JACK	Here's a middle-aged gentleman standing up. Tell me, Allah, what is his <u>first</u> name. Don't let it get your goat.
MIND READER	Billy.
JACK	I get it … billy goat … Allah, you're uncanny.
MIND READER	Well, you're not so good-looking yourself.

JACK	What's this lady drinking? … this should be <u>made-to-order</u> for you, Allah.
MIND READER	Canada Dry Ginger Ale.
JACK	Give us the full plug, Allah.
MIND READER	Made-to-order, by the glass, at all fountains.
JACK	Here's a fellow sitting with his girl. He's trying <u>to seize</u> her … what's <u>his</u> first name?
JACK & MIND READER (TOGETHER)	Julius…
JACK	I know that one, too, Allah … Here's a little lady wearing two things. What are they?
MIND READER	Louder.
JACK	This lady is wearing two things … are you <u>hearing</u>?
MIND READER	Earrings.
JACK	Stupendous!
MIND READER	Is she wearing them, too?
JACK	Allah, stick to your lines. (ALLAH SCREAMS) Allah! What's the matter, Allah?
MIND READER (LOUD)	I had a purse when I came in here with nine dollars in it, and I don't know where it is.
JACK	I thought you were a mind-reader.
MIND READER	I can't find my umbrella. (CONTINUES TO SCREAM)
JACK	Don't raise your voice … just leave your address and we'll send it.
MIND READER	My address … it's … it's … I've even forgot my address.
JACK	Well, just forget…

(SHE LETS OUT A PIERCING SCREAM. BAKER STARTS SINGING CHORUS OF "NELLY"

ASH ANNOUNCES: "THIS TRAIN STOPS AT YANKELS … NEURAL … OSZNIG … ARMEN … ALA-MEE … AND ALL POINTS NORTH)

George, you better go into the next number.

5. THREE GUESSES   **FRAN FREY**

JACK	That was the last number of the twenty-first program on the 11th of July. I'm going to ask you kindly to forget tonight's program as you can't depend on amateurs. … Just think of Canada Dry Ginger Ale made-to-order, by the glass, and be with us

on next Wednesday Night. (PHONE RINGS) Pardon me ... the phone ... Hello ... Hello ... oh, you Bush! ... how did you like our program? ... What? ... when does it start! ... Say, Bush, trade in your radio for a muzzle ... Good night, Bush.

SIGNATURE – ROCKABYE MOON.

ANNOUNCER   Whenever you're thirsty and especially on these hot days – remember that a glass of Canada Dry or a Canada Dry ice cream soda will give you a wonderful pick-up. Ask for Canada Dry at the nearest soda fountain. It is available made-to-order by the glass as well as in bottles. You are invited to listen in again at this same time Wednesday night, when Jack Benny, Ethel Shutta and George Olsen will entertain. This is the National Broadcasting Company.

July 13, 1932

STATION	WJZ	PROGRAM	CANADA DRY GINGER ALE, INC.
	AND	DATE	WEDNESDAY, JULY 13, 1932
	BLUE NETWORK	TIME	9:30-10:00 P.M. (E.D.T.)

SIGNATURE - JOLLY GOOD COMPANY

1. STUCCO IN THE STICKS — PAUL SMALL & SHUTTA

2. ROAMING FOR ROMANCE — ETHEL SHUTTA

3. EAT, DRINK AND BE MERRY — FRAN FREY

4. SYMPHONY OF LOVE — PAUL SMALL

5. GET YOURSELF A CUP OF SUNSHINE — FRAN FREY

SIGNATURE - ROCKABYE MOON

SIGNATURE — JOLLY GOOD COMPANY

ANNOUNCER Ladies and gentlemen. Another half-hour of entertainment about Canada Dry Ginger Ale, now available by the glass at soda fountains. George Olsen, Ethel Shutta and Jack Benny, the Canada Dry Humorist, again perform for your enjoyment.

George Olsen opens the program with "ROAMING FOR ROMANCE," Ethel Shutta singing.

1. ROAMING FOR ROMANCE   ORCHESTRA & SHUTTA

ANNOUNCER All right, Jack, here's your public.

JACK Hello, summer customers … <u>some are</u> here … <u>some are</u> there … <u>some are</u> in the country … <u>some are</u> listening … <u>some are</u> not … this is Jack Benny silly-quize … I mean, sillella … sola … <u>yeah</u>, JACK BENNY. Do you remember last Monday we had Amateur Night? Well, what can you expect from <u>amateur</u> amateurs? So tonight we bring you back our own gang of <u>professional</u> amateurs.

And now … Say, Hicks, is there anybody listening in on a hot night like this? I think I'd better play safe and call up some friends of mine again.

HICKS All right, Jack — you know best. Here's the phone.

JACK If anybody happens to be turning a dial and I'm on, pardon me.

(CLICKING SOUND)

Operator … Operator … give me ORANGE THREE FOUR FIVE … Yes, Orange Three Four Five … Oh, I see, wiseguy-ESS … where can you get oranges, <u>three for five</u>? … That's the phone number. Get it for me.

Hello, is this you Dracula? How are you? … This is Jack Benny. Say, Draccy, I want you to do me a favor, will you? Stop scaring people just for one night and listen in to our program … Yeah, do that … How's the wife, Draccy? Oh, she's working, eh? … What's she doing? Uh-huh, I see. Haunting a house for some wealthy people … Well, that's a pretty tough job … because I've been <u>haunting</u> a house at the Beach all summer, but the rents are too high … Oh, you <u>heard</u> that. Well, I'll see you soon, Draccy. We'll go out together and have lots of fun … you know, fire shots at each other … Well, so long.

(HANGS UP PHONE)

Nice feller, Dracula, but he's not living right. If he doesn't take care of himself, he'll soon start looking like Fran Frey.

And now, Fran, who didn't hear that last crack, will sing "EAT, DRINK AND BE MERRY," played by George Olsen and his Boogey-men.

Say, Fran, I meant to ask you something … where did you get that name, <u>Fran</u>? It's awfully cute … really.

FRAN   Well, I don't know Jack. Probably because I'm everybody's fran.'

JACK   I see. It looks as tho I'm going to have trouble with you, too. You know <u>Amateur</u> Night is over.

FRAN   Well, I'll tell you, Jack. I'm really one of <u>twins</u>. First, they were going to call me Francis. Then they decided to divide the name between my twin sister and myself. So they called <u>me</u> Fran … and <u>her</u>, Sis. Get it … <u>Fran-cis</u>?

JACK   Oh, you call your sister <u>Sis</u>? … That's an odd name, … hmm. In spite of that name, tho, I think you're going to get some place. Because, after all, there are a lot of great people by the name of Fran. For instance, <u>FRAN</u> Klin Roosevelt … then there is <u>FRAN</u> Kie and Johnny … clever those Chinese … and then there's <u>FRAN</u> Kenstein … and…

FRAN (LAUGHS HEARTILY)

JACK   Say, what are you laughing at? That wasn't so funny.

FRAN   Orange … three four five…

JACK (IN DISGUST)

Play, George.

2. EAT, DRINK AND BE MERRY   FRAN FREY

JACK   That was "EAT, DRINK AND BE MERRY," sung by Orange Three Four Five … I mean, Fran Frey.

Before we go any further, I want to show you that there is absolutely no gratitude in this world. Here's a letter … <u>just look</u> <u>at it</u> … Yes, it has a 3-cent stamp on it. When people want to pan you, the cost means nothing.

It's from a lady in <u>Ottawa</u>, Canada … Dry … Ginger … Ale … well, I might as well go thru with it … made-to-order, by the glass, sold at all fountains … and good with ice cream. I'm sorry I said that, but I'm glad of it.

Well, anyway, this letter reads:

"Radio's Latest-Pain-in-the-Neck,

Dear Mr. Benny (hmmm)

I've been listening to your broadcasts. In fact, haven't missed one of the entire twenty-one programs, and hate them all. I heard your Ladies Night, Babies' Night and Amateur Night. Now I would suggest that you have an Off Night … stay off the microphone … On this night, as a special request, take the Road to Mandalay, and do not detour … I would also suggest that you play games like Hide-and-Seek and lose each other. And, furthermore, "

Well, all right, Madam. There's no need reading these other sixteen pages … Folks, you can see what this lady is driving at. I don't have to have a building fall on me … this lady does not like us. Anyway, she signs her name, Mrs. J. Welland Canal.

Well, Mrs. Canal, I hate to dignify such letters as yours with an answer, but I'm going to make a rule to the exception and tell you why we can not have an Off Night.

A farmer who had a vegetable patch, owned a very faithful old horse that had a bad habit of sitting on vegetables. As soon as this horse would see any kind of a vegetable, he would sit down on it and you could not budge him. Strange to say, his favorite vegetable was succotash, altho at times he was partial to corned beef and cabbage … if you didn't remove the cabbage.

Well, to continue with this narrow-tive, one day the farmer decided to sell the animal to a friend of his … which he did. He also told the friend of the horse's peculiarity … sitting on vegetables. But the man said it was all right with him, as he had no vegetable patch, and took the horse away. now on the way home, they had to pass over a creek … no, not the fellow who runs a restaurant … a creek full of water. Lo and behold! the horse, without warning, sat right down in the middle of the creek and would not get up. He tried for hours to get the horse out of the water, but the animal would not budge. So the man went back to the farmer from whom he had bought the horse and said, "I thought you told me this horse only sits on vegetables. Well, right now he's sitting down in the creek and I can't get him out of the water." So the farmer said, laughingly, "Oh, I forgot to tell you … today is Friday, and every Friday he sits on fish."

And so, Mrs. Canal, that is why we cannot have an Off Night.

Say, any more fan mail?

HICKS	Here are two for Mr. Frey.
JACK	That's FRAN mail … we won't bother with it.
FRAN	(LAUGHS) He sits on corned beef and cabbage…
JACK	And now Ethel Shutta and Paul Small will sing a duet, "Stucco in the Sticks" while I will sit-o around the Studi-o.

3. STUCCO IN THE STICKS   **ETHEL SHUTTA AND PAUL SMALL**

HICKS   Ladies and gentlemen, owing to the humidity, Jack Benny and his cohorts have just left for the Anywhere Soda Fountain for a drink. However, we are prepared for all emergencies, and will turn you over to the fountain.

(GENERAL CROWD NOISES AND ACTIVITY AROUND FOUNTAIN. CONVERSATION CONTINUES SOFTLY "What will you have, please?" 'Glass of Canada Dry'. Right away, Madame", etc. UNDER FOLLOWING SCENE)

ETHEL (SALES GIRL) What's yours, Madame?

DOROTHY (FIRST CUSTOMER)   I want <u>five</u> cents worth of jelly beans for a <u>seven</u>-year old girl.

ETHEL   I have nothing smaller than a size six.

DOROTHY   Never mind, I'll take chewing gum.

ETHEL   Will you chew it here or take it with you?

DOROTHY   No, send it to me and <u>charge it</u>. (PAUSE – TO CLERK) Give me a Canada Dry.

2ND CUSTOMER   Say, Miss, will you loan me a marshmallow? I want to powder my nose … Service! Service! … please give me five cents' worth of rock candy for my little boy.

(SOUND EFFECT: 3 HEAVY BANGS)

     Don't throw it at me … Say, is your peanut brittle?

ETHEL   Well, what do <u>you</u> want, Madame?

HARRY CONN (to clerk)   Give me a glass of Canada Dry.

PAUL SMALL (clerk) With ice cream?

HARRY   I'm thirsty … not hungry.

JACK (enters quickly) Well, it looks as tho we're going to have trouble <u>with you</u>, too.

HARRY   Hello, Mr. Benny … have a drink on me.

JACK   I'll have one, but I'll pay for it.

HARRY   No, you don't. It's on me.

JACK   Don't argue. We'll flip a coin … here, you flip it and I'll holler.

HARRY   Okay with me. What is it?

JACK   Heads!

HARRY   "Heads" is right … <u>you win</u>! … Wait a minute, Mr. Benny. This coin has <u>two</u> heads on it.

PAUL   What will you have?

JACK	Make mine a large glass of Canada Dry.
HARRY	Me, too.
PAUL	Say, Mr. Benny, I hear you are playing the Capitol Theatre next week.
JACK	Yes, did you see my name in front of the theatre?
PAUL	No, there was a fly standing right there … but I'm coming over to see you Mr. Benny.
JACK	Thanks.
PAUL	Can you give me the passes <u>now</u>?
JACK	Come on! … hurry up with that large glass Canada Dry … Ooh, here comes Olsen. (UNDERTONE) Look the other way … make believe we don't see him.
GEORGE	Hello, boys … I see you're having a drink.
JACK	This town is full of strangers.
GEORGE	Come on, fellers … have a nice large glass <u>on me</u>.
JACK	It can't be you, George.
HARRY C.	Sure, Mr. Olsen … I'll have <u>ice cream</u> with mine.
GEORGE	Come on, Jack. Order something … I'm buying.
JACK	You are? Certainly … I'll have <u>steak and onions</u> with mine.
PAUL	There you are, gents.
JACK	Say, George, I want to apologize for the things I said about you … You're all right … Say, Clerk, fill this up again … You know, George I'm only kidding when I say things about you.
GEORGE	That's all right, Jack … have another … come on, gang, have another one on me.
CROWD	Sure — okay, George, Etc.
PAUL	What will you have?
VOICE	CANADA DRY…
SECOND VOICE	Large Canada Dry.
THIRD VOICE	Canada Dry.
PAUL	And what will you have, sir?
FOURTH VOICE	I'll have … I'll have…
JACK	A Canada Dry … Let's give three cheers for Olsen … Hooray! hooray! hooray! Well, I'll see you later, George.
GEORGE	Oh, wait a minute, Jack.

JACK	Oh-oh!
GEORGE	Can you imagine that? I left all my money in the Studio. I haven't a cent with me. Take care of the check, will you, Jack?
JACK	I was afraid of that.
GEORGE	So-long, see you later.
CROWD	So long, Mr. Benny … <u>thanks, George</u>.
JACK	Don't mention it … here you are, Clerk.
PAUL	Shall I take it all out of this?
JACK	Yes, all of them. And, listen … then next time I come here and Olsen walks in, put me in a booth with about a hundred feet of barbed wire around it … so long.
PAUL	Wait, Mr. Benny … that glass belongs <u>to us</u>.
JACK	Oh, pardon me.
GEORGE HICKS	Ladies and gentlemen, Olsen and his Band are now back at the Studio and will play "Symphony of Love," sung by Paul Small.

4. SYMPHONY OF LOVE   PAUL SMALL

JACK	Hello, everybody … this is Saphead Jack Benny again.
GEORGE	Oh, Jack, I owe you some money … here it is.
JACK	Oh, it's all right, George.
GEORGE	No, take it, Jack.
JACK	It's all right, George. Besides, it was <u>eighty</u> cents … not seventy.
GEORGE	Aw, go ahead and take it.
JACK	Never mind, George … well, this has got to stop sometime, Give me that dough … and say, Clerk, never mind the <u>barbed wire</u>.
	And now, ladies and gentlemen, the biggest event of the year … This comes to you <u>without warning</u> … the biggest surprise on the radio since Kingfish went to work for Amos 'N Andy … without the courtesy of Canada Dry Ginger Ale.
	So tonight, for <u>no reason whatsoever</u>, without making you figure out double cross-word puzzles or the habits of a lady bug … we are giving away a hundred and fifty thousand dollars in gold … <u>count it</u> …
	one hundred and fifty thousand … There are no strings attached to this gift … we don't ask you to leave your right eye with us … take your finger prints … or keep

	you guessing for months … We simply want to get rid of this as it is too big a bundle to be carrying around in this hot weather … And after all, <u>you can't</u> <u>stop anybody</u> from wanting to give away a hundred and fifty thousand dollars.
	To show you that there is no favoritism in these awards, we have here a group of men known for their honesty, integrity and great records as citizens.
	The first man is the Honorable Jay T. Loan … President of the Bonnie Banks of Scotland … Say Something, Mr. Loan.
HARRY CONN	Sumpthin'.
JACK	Ah! Another gentleman of character … Mr. Morris J. Plan … Secretary of Mortgages … say something, Mr. Plan.
HARRY CONN (different voice)	Ahem.
JACK	And last, but not <u>leash</u> … least … J.K. Leash, Esquire … secretary of his wife's Pomeranian … Say something, Mr. Leash.
HARRY CONN	Woof!
JACK	I expected that … Now get together, gentlemen, and figure out who shall get this money … Go into a huddle, gents.
6 ORCHESTRA BOYS	(ad lib – using football terms)
JACK	The boys are now in deep, <u>quiet</u> thought … Ah! here they come with the slips containing the names of the neediest cases. We will read them immediately, give the money away and call it a day … Now, gentlemen, did you come to an agreement as to who shall be the beneficiaries?
HARRY C.	Aye!
JACK	Are these the names?
HARRY C	Aye!
JACK	Are you sure these are the people you want the money given to?
HARRY C	Yes.
JACK	Keep it dignified.
HARRY C	Aye!
JACK	Now before announcing the names, in order to make this official, we will hear from the Royal Buglers.

(BUGLE SOUNDS "Assemble" Call)

	Now the first award of ninety thousand and no cents-dollars goes to John T. Rockefellow … who is badly in need of money as he is down to his last golf ball. He strangely happens to be here tonight, so here's the money, John … Congratulations!
FRAN (rube voice)	Thanks … I owe it all to Canada Dry Ginger Ale, made-to-order.
JACK	That wasn't necessary at all … but very good. Keep it in … And the second award of forty thousand and no cents-dollars … I'm reading this from a check … goes to Mr. Honey Dew … Mr. An-dew Melon … who also anticipated this and is here with us tonight. Here you are, Andew … ten, twenty, thirty, forty and a hundred aces.
FRAN	I owe it all to…
JACK	And the third prize of twenty grand … bucks … dollars … goes to J. T. Morgan's brother … Tomorrow Morgan.
ORCHESTRA BOYS	(congratulate the winners)
JACK	Now there you are, boys … That's a load off my mind … give me the baton, George … All right … all together…

(THREE VOICES SING: "Happy Days are Here Again" – followed by "HOORAY!")

	Good-night, everybody…
ORCHESTRA BOYS	Good-night … so long, Jack…

(FADE OUT SOUND)

FADE IN:

ETHEL	Hey, Jack … wake up … wake up.
JACK	Ethel … where am I?
ETHEL	In the N. B. C. Studio.
JACK	Gee, Ethel, I must have fallen asleep … I had the funniest dream … I dreamed I gave a hundred and fifty thousand dollars away … can you imagine that? Say, George, (yawns) … will you introduce the next number, please?
GEORGE	The next number, ladies and gentlemen, will be, "Get Yourself a Cup of Happiness." Okay, let's go, boys.

5. GET YOURSELF A CUP OF HAPPINESS   ORCHESTRA

JACK	That was the last number on the twenty-second program on the 13th of July. Say, George, I've got to go way uptown tonight, and I was just wondering whether you could let me have a dollar until Friday?

GEORGE	What? ... after the way you've been talking about me?
JACK	Aw, George, I didn't mean those things ... I'm going out with a new girl tonight, and where can we go with only <u>eighty cents</u>?
GEORGE	All right ... here, Jack.
JACK	Thanks, George ... See you Monday, ladies and gentlemen ... Good-night...

HEY, TAXI!

SIGNATURE – ROCKABYE MOON

ANNOUNCER	Whenever you're thirsty – and especially on these hot days – remember that a glass of Canada Dry or a Canada Dry ice cream soda will give you a wonderful pick-up. Ask for Canada Dry at the nearest soda fountain. It is available made-to-order by the glass as well as in bottles. You are invited to listen in again at this same time Monday night, when Jack Benny, Ethel Shutta and George Olsen will entertain. This is the National Broadcasting Company.

July 18, 1932

STATION	WJZ	PROGRAM	CANADA DRY GINGER ALE, INC.
	AND	DATE	MONDAY, JULY 18, 1932
	BLUE NETWORK	TIME	9:30-10:00 P.M. (E.D.T.)

SIGNATURE - JOLLY GOOD COMPANY

1. SLEEP COME ON AND TAKE ME	PAUL SMALL
2. UNDER THE OLD CROW'S NEST	ETHEL SHUTTA
3. TALKING TO YOU ABOUT ME	ETHEL SHUTTA
4. O. K. AMERICA	FRAN FREY
5. RHUMBATISM	DICK GARDNER

SIGNATURE - ROCKABYE MOON

SIGNATURE – JOLLY GOOD COMPANY

ANNOUNCER   Ladies and gentlemen. Another half-hour of entertainment about Canada Dry Ginger Ale, now available by the glass at soda fountains. George Olsen, Ethel Shutta and Jack Benny the Canada Dry Humorist, again perform for your enjoyment.

George Olsen opens the program with "Sleep, Come On and Take Me." Paul Small singing.

1. SLEEP COME ON AND TAKE ME   ORCHESTRA & PAUL SMALL

ANNOUNCER   O.K., Jack, don't keep the American people waiting.

(VAMP MUSIC)

JACK (SINGS)
Here we are again,
Ethel, George and me,
All good friends, but terrible company.

    We went out last night,
    Ethel, George and Me.
    We ate like horses,
    And George left me the check.

Di-dee-di-dee-di,
Di-dee-di-dee-di,
Seven courses,
And George left me the check,
Di – dee – di – dee – di…

GEORGE (INTERRUPTING)   Hey, Jack, Jack.

JACK   Di-dee-di-dee…

GEORGE   Say, Jack, that stuff has gone <u>far enough</u>. Now don't think I'm a sorehead, but if you can't tell the truth, please don't mention my name at all. I do <u>most</u> of the spending on this program. The least I deserve is an even break. <u>Now get that straight</u>. Lay off of me.

JACK	Di-dee-di-dee-di … Ladies and gentlemen, what the Swedish gentleman was trying to tell you is, that Canada Dry Ginger Ale is made-to-order by the glass and sold at all fountains.
GEORGE	I don't want to hear any more about my being a tightwad … I'm sick and <u>tired</u> of it.
JACK	The gentleman further states that Canada Dry Ginger Ale, made-to-order by the glass, is good for that tired feeling.
GEORGE	I didn't say anything of the kind. You've got a lot of <u>nerve</u>, telling people that I'm tight.
JACK	And <u>furthermore</u>, he says that it is soothing for the <u>nerves</u> … and delicious with ice cream.
GEORGE	All right, Jack you win.
ETHEL	Oh, Jack…
JACK	Hello, Ethel.
ETHEL	Say, Jack, I saw you last night at the Capital Theatre, with all those movie stars … and I thought the show was just dandy.
JACK	Thanks, Ethel. How did you like my act?
ETHEL	You looked very handsome in those white trousers, blue coat and…
JACK	I know, Ethel … but how did you like <u>my act</u>?
ETHEL	And that yellow tie you wore, looked just lovely from where I sat.
JACK	Ethel, I've always had those clothes. But how did you really like <u>my act</u>?
ETHEL	But what I liked most of all, Jack, was the gentlemanly way in which you conducted yourself when <u>nobody</u> applauded.
JACK	Ethel, you might mean well, but you're not doing me any good. As a matter of fact, I <u>was applauded</u> every time I made my exit.
GEORGE	Sure, everybody applauded <u>then</u>.
JACK	Stand by, ladies and gentlemen … this won't go much further.
ETHEL	We're going to see you at the theatre <u>again</u> tonight.
JACK	Do me a favor, Ethel. Sit in the <u>last row of the balcony</u> and let me know how my <u>collar button</u> looks from there … And now, by way of intermission on this program, George Olsen will play, "Under the Old Crow's Nest." It will be sung by Ethel Shutta, who goes to a theatre just to sit down … Come, come, Ethel…
ETHEL (WHISPERS)	Jack, I'm not quite ready yet. Say something to keep the program going.
JACK	Canada Dry Ginger Ale made-to-order by the glass…

(MUSIC PICKS UP ON CUE: "made-to-order").

2. UNDER THE OLD CROW'S NEST   ORCHESTRA & ETHEL SHUTTA

JACK   Say, Ethel, that's an awfully cute number you just sang. I never heard it before.

ETHEL   Why, Jack, I sang it here only a couple of weeks ago.

JACK   You did? … Oh, that must have been the night I was <u>unconscious</u> and gave away the hundred and fifty thousand dollars.

ETHEL   You know, Jack, <u>eighteen</u> out of those twenty checks came back.

JACK   They did?

(POSTMAN'S WHISTLE BLOWS)

HARRY CONN (POSTMAN)
               Two letters for Mr. Jack Benny.

JACK   Ah! there are <u>the other two</u>.

ETHEL   Say, Jack, I wish you'd tell that story you're telling at the theatre this week.

JACK   Which one?

ETHEL   You know, the one about the two Marathon runners.

JACK   Sure, I'll tell it. That would be kind of apropos right now … with the Olympic Games going on. Well, Ethel, if I tell it, promise not to laugh?

ETHEL   I promise.

JACK   Well, anyway, there were two Marathon runners making a non-stop run between New York and Chicago. Well, they started out from Columbus Circle, New York and ran as far as <u>Poughkeepsie</u>. When they turned around, they happened to see a <u>third</u> man running behind them … just a few feet behind them. He was a kind of a silly-looking guy, so they didn't say anything. They kept on running. Well, they got as far as <u>Buffalo</u>. They turned around again and saw this same guy still chasing them, so they finally stopped and one of the runners yelled over to him, "Hey! what's the idea of following us all the way from New York?" And the guy says, "Shh! Don't say anything … I'm a <u>stowaway</u>." Is that the story, Ethel?

ETHEL (DOES NOT LAUGH)
               Jack, is that the same story you told in the theatre?

JACK   Yes … you told me you laughed at it.

ETHEL   I did … I laughed at everything except "The <u>stowaway</u>." I don't know what that means.

JACK   Well Ethel, a stowaway is an uninvited guest on a <u>Trans-Atlantic</u> liner.

ETHEL   What does <u>Trans-Atlantic</u> mean?

JACK	George, play the next number while Ethel goes to Night-School … Say, George, is there a dictionary around here somewhere?
GEORGE	Why?
JACK	I think we're biting off more than we can chew on this program.

3. TALKING TO YOU ABOUT ME   ORCHESTRA & ETHEL SHUTTA

JACK	That was "Talking to You about Me," sung by Ethel Shutta … And now, ladies and gentlemen, we are again keeping our promise to you by bringing you novelties over the air whenever we <u>can't</u> help … er, <u>can</u> help it. So <u>tonight</u> we are glad to welcome to our Studio hundreds of foreign and American Olympic stars, who are on their way to Los Angeles to seek fame in those great Olympic contests. They have graciously consented to make only one appearance before entering the hard tests of endurance in California. And that appearance <u>is here only</u>. HERE THEY COME…

(SOUND OF FEET MARCHING AS ORCHESTRA PICKS UP MARCH TEMPO, GRADUALLY DIMINISHING IN VOLUME) (MUMBLING OF VOICES)

> They are now entering the Studio … each and every one an athlete of renown … swimmers … divers … hurdlers … runners … butchers, bakers and candlestick makers. How are you, boys?

(SEVERAL SPEAK TOGETHER)

FRENCHMAN	Comman-tally vous, Monsieur Bennee?
GERMAN	Wie gates, Herr Benny?
SPANIARD	Coma esta-Usted, Senor?
ITALIAN	Allo, Benny.
GREEK	Tie kannes, calla?

ANOTHER VOICE (DISTINCT)

> Ello hay, Enny-Bay?

JACK	Ah! from <u>Pig Latinia</u> … Let me introduce these champions to you. <u>First</u>, I want you to meet the three <u>Pole</u> Vaulters … <u>from Poland</u>. They hope to defeat the <u>North Pole</u> and the <u>Pole from the South</u>, and expect to finnish no <u>Warsaw</u>-than second … Those Poles broke into a vault … I mean, into the vault-game five years ago … and got out just in time for the main events. Don't confuse these <u>vaulters</u> with <u>Vaulter</u> Vinchell … I take great pleasure in introducing the Messrs. <u>Timothy J. Snach-nach-a-chowski</u> … Number 2, E. Thorgersen <u>Zebot-tskit-ski</u> … and Number 3, <u>J. Mortimer Sliv-o-vitch</u> … They will tell you what they expect to do at the Olympics.
POLISH FELLOW	Zavita … Mazurka … Scatchaka … Poolka.

JACK	Just a word, boys. Ah! that was very nice of you to say that about us.

(TRIPPING SOUND)

Oops! look out … Mr. Sliv-o-vitch just stumbled over a drumstick … and he's a pole vaulter. Oh, well … Next I will introduce two runners from Saucepan, Greece … They are entered in the running at the Olympics … where they will run a restaurant during and after the games … I take great pleasure in introducing Mr. Indian-apoulus, Indiana … and his wife, Mrs. Minnie-apoulus … Say something, Cincinnatus … er, Indian-apoulus.

GREEK (WITH ACCENT)

Wan russ biff … one hopple dumpling … one cocoanuts pie … cups coffee … one nacktie vid gravvy…

JACK   That's what I call a regular dinner … All right, folks, just one word. You know it's bad taste to throw guests out…

And now, ladies and gentlemen, a squad of well-dressed athletes are here from Check-suitia … which is right near Two pair of Pantsia … They are entered in the Checko Games … aren't you?

CHECKO (HARRY CONN)
Chess.

JACK   Pardon me … the Chess Games. Their spokesman wishes to say something.

CHECKO (HARRY CONN)

Canada Dry is ah gooten trink, mein frient … Bro solt iss kafen and trinken, and zie gezunt.

JACK   Thank you, thank you … He just said they are glad to be here and hopes that, while in this country, no Slovako will slip them a rubber-checko.

And now a gentleman from Norway … Mr. Lute Fisk … a swimmer. He has mastered the crawl stroke by getting home to his wife at three a.m. … He wears a half medal for swimming half-way across the English Channel … and hasn't been seen since … But here he is, and don't ask us why.

Ah! we also have here some of our National Champions … I see some office runners from Alban-ia, New Yorkia … And there are two wrestlers from Tussle … I mean, Tulsa, Oklahoma.

Come over here, boys … we also have some taxi-drivers who will run in the hundred-meter races. Those men have run a hundred meters up to seven-fifty flat for one mile. Their records, so far, are fifteen for the first quarter … and five for each additional quarter. And the boys don't claim to know it all … they take tips … They are now in training—

(SOUND EFFECT: HONKING OF AUTO HORNS)

Mr. Havrilla is here … with bulging muscles and rarin' to go—home. He will run in the 760 kilocycles for the N.B.C. … which, no doubt, means some club or other.

Say something, everybody.

(MUMBLING OF VOICES)

George Olsen will now play a number for our guests ... after which they will entertain you with their various feats. You will see their <u>last</u> workout before entraining for the Coast.

Olsen and his boys, who won all the <u>Swedish matches</u>, will play for you, "Okay, America!" with vocal refrain by Fran Frey. OKAY, GEORGE!

4. OKAY, AMERICA   **FRAN FREY**

JACK   And now for the big event ... <u>the Finals</u> ... deciding who shall really go to the Coast for the Olympic Games. First, we have Miss <u>Ima Fish</u> ... in fancy dives. Are you ready, <u>Ima</u>?

MISS FISH (DOROTHY ROSS)
         <u>Ima-ready.</u>

JACK   The first dive will be the <u>Bread-knife</u> Dive!

(DRUM ROLL – followed by SPLASH – ROUND OF APPLAUSE)

         The next dive will be the Standing – Sitting – Stretching – Yawning – Leaning – Resting – Standing Dive.

(SEVEN THUMPS ON SPRINGBOARD)

         Ah! How she handles that springboard.

(DRUM ROLL – FOLLOWED BY SPLASH —

         What's happened to her? She hasn't come up yet ... Well, we can't waste time.

         The next entry, folks is Lady <u>Godiva</u> ... who will start the proceedings with a triple <u>somersault</u> and, at the same time, crochet a muffler for Fran Frey's saxophone ... OKAY!...

(SHORT DRUM ROLL)   ONE!...

(SECOND DRUM ROLL)   TWO!...

(THIRD DRUM ROLL)   THREE!...

(SPLASH — ROUND OF APPLAUSE)

         What a fight! ... er, what a <u>dive</u>! ... Very well done ... And, Fran, here's your muffler.

         Latest bulletin from our Tank ... Miss Fish hasn't come up yet.

	And now Lady Godiva will do the eight-and-a-half by the six-and-<u>three-quarters</u> … dive.
ANNOUNCER	These dives come to you thru the courtesy of Canada Dry Ginger Ale, made-to-order…
(SPLASH)	
JACK	<u>That</u> was our announcer, Mr. Havrilla … He just fell into the tank … <u>And I didn't push him</u>.
	And now, ladies and gentlemen, a rather difficult feat in which this little lady will attempt to dive from the <u>hundred-foot board</u> into the tank … with a glass of Canada Dry Ginger Ale in each hand … <u>without spilling a drop</u>!
(APPLAUSE – SHORT DRUM ROLL)	
	Ah! She has stopped a second to powder her nose…
(LONGER DRUM ROLL)	
	<u>There she goes</u>!
(HEAVY THUD, followed by GLASS CRASH)	
	Aha! there are the two glasses of Canada Dry Ginger Ale, filled to the top. But where is she? … Say, Referee, what was the time on that?
REFEREE (FRAN FREY) (IN WHISPER)	Three hours, four minutes and thirty-two seconds.
JACK (WITH AUTHORITY)	The time was five and one-fifth seconds … Ah, here she is … now she will dive from a height of <u>two hundred</u> feet … with a <u>made-to-order counter</u> on her back.
LADY GODIVA (ETHEL SHUTTA – IN HEAVY VOICE)	<u>Say, what do you think I am</u>?
JACK (QUICKLY)	And now for the hammer-throwing finals! … We have here the lady champion hammer-thrower, <u>Miss Ethel Shutta</u> … who holds the record for throwing a hammer a hundred and fifty feet and hitting George Olsen … who happens to be her husband … <u>Good boy, Ethel</u> … I'll buy you that medal.
	Next, ladies and gentlemen, the <u>Twelve Bulgarian Sleep Walkers</u> who will…
TRAINER (JOHN WIGGIN – WITH AUTHORITY)	Stop! Say, what's the idea of keeping these athletes up at this hour of the night? They are about to enter the greatest test of their lives, and orders are to get then in bed <u>by nine o'clock</u>.
JACK	Well, who asked them to come up here? They're <u>Olsen's</u> friends, not mine.
TRAINER (WIGGIN)	I'm the director of athletics … and I think <u>you</u> should be entered in the Olympic Games … You're the Champion <u>Bull-thrower</u> of the World! … Come on, athletes … forward MARCH!…

(MUMBLING OF VOICES – STAMPING OF FEET AS THEY MARCH OUT. ORCHESTRA PLAYS EXIT MARCH)

JACK Can you imagine that? He thinks the <u>Olympic Games</u> are more important than the Canada Dry program … Oh, well, it takes all kinds of people to make a world.

Say, George, you're still with us, aren't you?

MISS FISH (DOROTHY ROSS)
Oh, Mr. Benny, is it all right for me to come out of the tank now?

JACK Yes, Ima … Come out from under the table and brush yourself off … And now George Olsen and his Pool-room Athletes will play … say, George, what's that new number you're going to play?

GEORGE OLSEN We will now play for you a brand-new number called "Rhumba-tism", written by that well-known team of Revel and Gordon … Let's go!

5. RHUMBA-TISM   ORCHESTRA AND DICK GARDNER

JACK That was the last number of the twenty-third program on the 18th of July. Be with us on Wednesday night as we will present a very unusual program. The title is … <u>BOARDER'S NIGHT</u> … How many of you give a thought to the poor lone boarder. He has three prunes for breakfast … sleeps in the spare-room … eats boloney for his supper … And who thinks of him? Well, WE <u>DO</u>. So on Wednesday night, we will honor him on our program.

As they say to a fellow who gets a bargain … <u>good-buy</u>!

ANNOUNCER Whenever you're thirsty – and especially on these hot days – remember that a glass of Canada Dry or a Canada Dry ice cream soda will give you a wonderful pick-up. Ask for Canada Dry at the nearest soda fountain. It is available made-to-order by the glass as well as in bottles. You are invited to listen in again at this same time Wednesday night, when Jack Benny, Ethel Shutta and George Olsen will entertain. This is the National Broadcasting Company.

July 20, 1932

STATION	WJZ	PROGRAM	CANADA DRY GINGER ALE, INC.
	AND	DATE	WEDNESDAY, JULY 20, 1932
	BLUE NETWORK	TIME	9:30-10:00 P.M. (E.D.T.)

SIGNATURE - JOLLY GOOD COMPANY

1. SONG OF INDIA — ORCHESTRA

2. LET'S GO OUT IN THE OPEN AIR — ORCHESTRA & ETHEL SHUTTA & FRAN FREY

3. LITTLE FRAULEIN — ORCHESTRA & PAUL SMALL

4. SUCH IS LIFE — ORCHESTRA & ETHEL SHUTTA

5. SCAT SONG — ORCHESTRA & DICK GARDNER

SIGNATURE - ROCKABYE MOON

SIGNATURE – JOLLY GOOD COMPANY

ANNOUNCER Ladies and gentlemen. Another half-hour of entertainment about Canada Dry Ginger Ale, now available by the glass at soda fountains as well as in bottles. George Olsen, Ethel Shutta and Jack Benny, the Canada Dry Humorist, again perform for your enjoyment.

George Olsen opens the program with "Song of India".

1. SONG OF INDIA   **ORCHESTRA**

ANNOUNCER Ladies and gentlemen, this is Boarder's Night … the night dedicated to people who are away from their homes and live in boarding-houses. And now Jack Benny will guide you thru this mess. All right, Jack, you're on … good luck!

JACK Hello, <u>every boarder</u> … this is Jack Benny talking … the fellow who was here Monday Night. Remember … the fellow without the moustache? … hmm? Well, anyway, this is <u>Boarder's Night</u> … and only people who sleep in hall bedrooms and have at least three prunes for breakfast, are allowed to listen in … also those who have the three—room apartments known as parlor, bedroom <u>and sink</u>. However, <u>I suppose there will be the usual number of intruders</u> … just as we had on Babies' Night when <u>ten million</u> grownups tuned in … by mistake. After going to all that expense and trouble arranging a Babies' Night, we asked over two hundred infants in various parts of the country if they listened on that gala night. They don't even remember the incident. Why, only this morning I asked a baby in the crib if she heard our Babies' Night. She stuck her little head out of the crib and this is what she said:

"Altho my brain was functioning clearly on that singular occasion, the idiosyncrasies in which you so flagrantly indulged were infinitely beneath my aesthetic tendencies."

Baby! you're talking thru your hat … No more cradle programs for us. And that is <u>why</u> we are having a Boarder's Night tonight. Are we prepared? Ha! ha! … can a canary croon?

BALDWIN <u>NO</u>!

JACK	Kvetch, throw the gentleman out.

(SOUND EFFECT: DULL THUD)

Now I would like to have you boarders meet a lady who has been conducting a boarding-house for the past <u>thirty-two years</u>. And if all these prunes that she served for breakfast in those thirty-two years were placed end to end, they would go about half-way around George Olsen's bankroll … And those are <u>some</u> prunes.

I now take pleasure in introducing Miss <u>Kitchenette Zinc</u>.

MISS ROSS (IN HEAVY GERMANIC ACCENT)

Halloa, efreybodec.

JACK	Now, Miss Zinc, tell us what your boarders do for pastime?
MISS ROSS	De trink Canada Tri Gingherale by-de-glass.
JACK	What?
MISS Ross	De trink Canada Tri Gingherale by-de-glass.
JACK	Funny, I can't understand you … what do they do?

MISS ROSS (IN DISGUST)

De use Schmaltz' toothbicks.

JACK	There you are, fellers … <u>another victory for Canada Dry</u>.
MISS ROSS	Bardon me, Mr. Pennec, I got some tree-minute boilet ecks on de vire, and de've been dere an hour alreaty … I gotta, run avay.
JACK	All right, thanks for coming up, Miss Zinc.

The next number, boarders … and ladies and gentlemen, is called, "Let's go Out in the Open Air." It will be sung by Ethel Shutta and Fran Frey, and will be played by George Olson who thinks a landlord is a <u>public enemy</u>. Go ahead, George.

2. LET'S GO OUT IN THE OPEN AIR   **ORCHESTRA & SHUTTA & FREY**

JACK	Since announcing that tonight would be Boarder's Night, we have received thousands of letters inquiring about it. Here's a letter from a boarding-house keeper in Shower … <u>Bath</u>, Maine … This letter reads … <u>all right, wait till I open it</u> … it reads:

"WJZ BENNY,

Care of Station Canada Dry.

Dear <u>Cur</u>: (Imagine spelling <u>Sir</u> with a "<u>C</u>")

I listened in to your program the other night when you told a lady how to make a Fran Frey. I followed your rules closely, made the dish and served it to my fifteen boarders. I am now very anxious to keep the seven survivors, as boarders are hard to get these days. I have often heard you mention "Hotcha Gardner" on your program, which sounds very appetizing. Please advise me how you make it. Will be listening in Wednesday night.

(signed) Mrs. SALLY PHANE

All right, Mrs. Phane, tune me in clearly … and listen. In the first place, this dish does not have to be a Hotcha Gardner. It could just as well be a Hotcha Dumpling … or a Hotcha Tamale … Now which do you prefer, Mrs. Phane?

MISS ROSS   I like it very plain.

JACK   Say, is this a radio or a telephone?

But, first of all, what is Hotcha? … It comes from that Latin gambling phrase, "I gotcha" … and as in that other Latin word, "watcha" … like "watcha-doing tonight?" … See? … Watcha … gotcha … hotcha … Now what other program could give you this valuable information? You said it … plenty of them.

All right, then, now in making a hotcha gardner, you take the whites of two second-story yeggs … beat these yeggs up until help arrives … them you add a tumbler of somersault … the acrobatic kind … and season with a pinch of writing pepper. (Be sure to write on only one side of the pepper.) Then you put this on your range and hold the high note … Now in order to time this so it does not burn, I would suggest that you hum two choruses of "Paradise" … or "Lullaby of the Leavings."

Of course, that is only the "cha." It is easily made into a "Hot-cha" by putting Gardner in the pot, accompanied by Paul Small and Fran Frey.

Is that clear, Mrs. Phane? … Now please be sure and let us know how many boarders you will have left next week … as we will have another dish for the remaining few.

Say, was that right, Hotcha?

GARDNER   Aw, don't bother me. I'm reading a book.

JACK   There you are, Madam … just as I told you … Next week, if you will listen in, we will tell you how to make an Ethel Saute … with sport dressing.

And now, boarders, when you hear the three little chimes, George Olsen and his boys will play, "Little Fraulein." It will be sung by Paul Small.

(SOUND EFFECT:

3 DISTINCT COW BELLS

What chimes? … Boys, is there nothing you can do right?

ORCHESTRA   Nothing!

JACK	Play, George…

3. LITTLE FRAULEIN ORCHESTRA & SMALL

JACK	We have <u>another</u> surprise for you … even for us. Tonight we bring you for the <u>first time</u> on the air one of the well-known <u>boarders</u> of the world … the <u>Mexican Border</u>. He comes direct to you from Rio <u>Grand</u> … Street, where he is a well-known door-mat … I mean, <u>mat-a-dor</u>. His daily pastime is <u>fighting</u> <u>the bull</u>! … And now may I present to you Mr. …er … what's <u>your name</u>, sir?
RALPH ASHE (with Spanish accent)	
	I am Uncle <u>Don</u> Pedro … from <u>Don</u>town … and who are <u>you</u>?
JACK	I am <u>Don</u> good and tired from playing golf.
ASHE	The <u>Golf</u> of Mexico, Senor?
JACK	All right, <u>I'll</u> tell the jokes on this program, Pedro … I suppose you came here prepared to entertain your fellow-boarders tonight?
ASHE	S<u>i</u>e S<u>i</u>e, senor.
JACK	You mean, <u>see, see</u>, senor.
ASHE	Yes … see, see, senor … what's the diff'rance?
JACK	Of course you're a <u>real</u> Mexican, aren't you Pedro?
ASHE	See … I was born in <u>Mehchico</u>.
JACK	Born <u>where</u>?
ASHE	<u>Mehchico</u>.
JACK	<u>Mehchico</u> … is that the way they pronounce it down there?
ASHE	See … See.
JACK	Well, I was born in Brook<u>chl</u>yn … Anyway, it <u>mex</u> no difference. Tell us, Pedro, what are you going to do to entertain us tonight?
ASHE	I weel do like I do in Mehchico … I will fight <u>de bool</u>.
JACK	<u>You will fight the bull</u>? … Did you hear that, you lucky customers? … a bull fight <u>right in this studio</u> … Say, Pedro, did you bring the bull with you?
ASHE	I always have heem with me.
JACK	All right, folks, we'll have to clear out the studio. We're going to give our customers a <u>real</u> bull fight … <u>Nothing</u> is too good for our customers.

(SOUND EFFECT: Scraping of feet, moving chairs, etc.)

TRUMPET CALL

JACK   Scram, everybody!

Ladies and gentlemen, you are about to witness a <u>fight to the</u> <u>finish</u> … between Don Pedro, the <u>Mexican Border</u> … and Joe Bull … of <u>Bull</u>, Montana … I know what you're thinking of, you little customers, you.

This fight will be refereed by those four Mexican football players … One <u>Don</u> and three to go.

Here they come into the ring … the first to enter is the Matador … and his little brother, <u>Cuspi</u> … who will second him. All right, <u>Senor Olsen</u>.

(ORCHESTRA PLAYS OPENING BARS OF "TOREADOR"
SONG FROM THE OPERA "CARMEN.")

SOUND EFFECT: BULL'S HOOFS.

FRAN FREY (bellowing) Ma-ax! … Ma-ax!…

JACK   AH! here comes the <u>bull</u>.

PAUL (loud)   AND HOW!

SOUND EFFECT: GONG

JACK   They are now in the center of the ring. The bull looks confident, but Don says it is <u>meat</u> for him … Jack Benny talking and Canada Dry Ginger Ale is paying.

ORCHESTRA BOYS (ad lib)   Hooray! … bravo! … Boo! … etc … etc.

JACK   Don grabs the bull by the horns, but the bull tears out of a clinch and chases Don around the ring.

ASHE (muttering)   Sacramento!

FRAN   MA-AX … MA-AX … MA-AX … MA-AX.

JACK   Ah! he's paging the Four <u>Maax</u> Brothers … Well, it looks like the Don is <u>don</u> … But <u>no</u>! … he steps to the right and escapes a wild uppercut from the bull.

ASHE   Sacramento!

JACK   The bull is running away! … Don is after him with his sword … And how that bull can take it … <u>What's this</u>? … they break and meet in the center. The bull leads a long hoof to the jaw, nut Don counters to the <u>sirloin</u> with mashed potatoes … <u>what a mash</u> … THEY BREAK AGAIN…

SOUND EFFECT: GONG

ORCHESTRA BOYS (ad lib)

HOORAY! … BRAVO! … DON PEDRO! … BOO!

JACK (quickly)   just as the gong brings the <u>first</u> round to a close.

	Cuspi is working over Pedro … while the bull is over in his corner, looking over the <u>stock ticker</u>.
	And now I will give the mike to … No, I will <u>not</u> plug any product between rounds…
PAUL SMALL (HIGH VOICE)	
	Get your Canada Dry Ginger ale, by-the-glass … etc. etc.
BALDWIN (HEAVY VOICE)	
	You can't enjoy the bull fight without a glass of Canada Dry Ginger Ale made-to-order, etc. etc.
THOMAS	Here, boy! give me fifteen glasses.
SMALL & BALDWIN (REPEAT THEIR LINES)	
JACK	That noise is just something that they <u>happen</u> to be selling … sounds like Canada Dry Ginger Ale to me … But who knows? Anyway, it's a swell drink with…

(SOUND EFFECT: GONG RINGS)

(Mumbling of crowd)

	<u>ROUND TWO</u>! … Kid Chocolate steps into Berg … I mean, Don steps up to the bull with a knife and fork … but the bull is in <u>rare</u> <u>condition</u> … He steps away. Now they are feinting … the bull is now <u>charging</u> Pedro … I don't blame him. Who wants to work for nothing? … <u>And now they are clashing</u>…
ANNOUNCER (INTERRUPTING)	
	Jack … Jack! … here's a note from the sponsors.
JACK	A note from the sponsors, eh? … Pardon me just a moment, folks … So <u>that's</u> what the sponsors want … Okay, I'll give it to them…
	They are still fighting … and the bull sidesteps by courtesy of Canada Dry Ginger Ale … they are now battling hoof to toe … by courtesy of Canada Dry Ginger Ale … there goes a <u>right to the</u> <u>bull's eye</u> … by courtesy of Canada Dry … another right … now a left … by courtesy of Canada Dry … Pedro is down to the floor … by courtesy of … a left … by courtesy of … the bull … Canada Dry … Don Pedro … by courtesy … (Gives a heave) Ah!…
ANNOUNCER	Ladies and gentlemen, Jack Benny has just collapsed … thru the courtesy of Canada Dry Ginger Ale … which is now sold by-the glass at all fountains.
	Well, the <u>fight is over</u> … and the bull is the winnah!
ORCHESTRA BOYS	BRAVO! … HORRAY! … CHEERS, etc.
ANNOUNCER	And now <u>the bull</u> will say a few words to the radio audience.
FRAN FREY (imitating bull)	Hello, ma-a-a … I'll be right ho-oome.

ANNOUNCER	George Olsen and his Orchestra will now play, "Such Is Life", sung by Ethel Shutta.

4. SUCH IS LIFE   **ORCHESTRA & ETHEL SHUTTA**

JACK	And now, <u>boarders</u>, stand by … we have a bedtime story for you. Of course when I was a boarder, I never went to bed before three a.m., and I'm not asking <u>you</u> to go to bed. Just listen to our bedtime story and you'll easily fall asleep … Of course, if you happen to be asleep already, that's <u>your gain</u> and <u>our loss</u>.
	Once upon a time there were three little hunters who went into the woods to shoot some dice … Dice are two little spotted animals who gallop along at the snap of your fingers and the word "ha!" … Now the first little hunter saw a pair of dice … which are just like leopards only they are <u>red with white spots</u> … Now the way to handle these dice is to grab them and shake them up … which this little hunter did, depositing <u>two bits</u> on the ground to catch <u>two other bits</u> … Just then, there was a groan as he looked into <u>snake eyes</u>…

ORCHESTRA BOYS (SNORE)

JACK	What's that?
ETHEL (WHISPERS)	That's a swell bedtime story, Jack, but not so loud. George and the boys are already asleep.
JACK (STARTS TO YAWN)	Well, so the policeman bid <u>one club</u> … the umpire bid <u>a diamond</u> … and the undertaker bid <u>one spade</u> … and the dummy bid them all <u>good-night</u> … what a fight for honors!…
ETHEL	Jack, for heaven's sake, don't you fall asleep.
JACK	Pardon me, Ethel … so Eeeny said to Meeny, you stay here and Miny Moe … as the traffic is very heavy and he's liable to get run over. Just then little Boy Blue came along in a high-powered car and almost ran over Moe, and he said, "Little Boy Blue, come blow your horn" … and Little Boy blew … I think <u>we</u> ought to blow, Ethel.

(TERRIFIC SNORING HEARD)

	Even the bull is asleep.
ETHEL	No, that's <u>George</u>.
JACK	We'll have to take George up as he has to play "The Scat Song" from the <u>Scat</u> and the Fiddle. It will be sung by Hotcha Gardner … who will sing it in his sleep.

5. SCAT SONG   **HOTCHA GARDNER**

JACK	That was the last number on the 24th program on the 20th of July. Were you <u>bored</u>, boarders? … hmmm? And next Monday we're going to have a Request Night, in

which we will do everything that we have been requested … well, of course, net <u>everything</u> … just the pleasant things … Must leave you now, and as they say in Mehchico … Say, Ethel, what do they say in Mehchico?

ETHEL   I don't know Jack.

JACK   Well, good-night, then.

SIGNATURE – ROCKABYE MOON

ANNOUNCER   Whenever you stop a soda fountain for a refreshing drink or a sandwich ask for a Canada Dry Ice Cream Soda or a glass of Canada Dry … Remember it is now available made to order by the glass as well as in bottles. Next Monday night at this same time Jack Benny, Ethel Shutta and George Olsen will again entertain you. This is the National Broadcasting Company.

July 25, 1932

STATION	WJZ	PROGRAM	CANADA DRY GINGER ALE, INC.
	AND	DATE	MONDAY, JULY 25, 1932
	BLUE NETWORK	TIME	9:30-10:00 P.M. (E.D.T.)

SIGNATURE - JOLLY GOOD COMPANY

1. DRUMS IN MY HEART — ORCHESTRA

2. YOU CAN'T TELL LOVE WHAT TO DO — ORCHESTRA & ETHEL SHUTTA

3. LISTEN TO THE GERMAN BAND — ORCHESTRA & ETHEL SHUTTA

4. LITTLE BLUE CANOE — ORCHESTRA & PAUL SMALL

5. BUGLE CALL RAG — ORCHESTRA

SIGNATURE - ROCKABYE MOON

SIGNATURE – JOLLY GOOD COMPANY

ANNOUNCER   Ladies and gentlemen. Another half-hour of entertainment about Canada Dry Ginger Ale, now available by the glass at soda fountains, as well as in bottles. George Olsen, Ethel Shutta and Jack Benny, the Canada Dry humorist, again perform for your enjoyment.

George Olsen opens the program with "Drums in My Heart."

1. DRUMS IN MY HEART   ORCHESTRA

ANNOUNCER   Okay, Jack, you're on!

BENNY   Hello, anybody… this is Jack Benny, a gentleman, a scholar and a man of letters … I mean, <u>fan mail</u>. … As you all know, this is Request Night, and we have received one million, ten hundred and eleven – ty five thousand, twelve hundred and eighty-four letters, with different requests from our faithful listeners. In fact, if all of our fan letters were placed end to end, they would reach further than you could <u>throw an elephant</u>.

In these requests, thousands have <u>asked</u> us to do different things, while others have <u>told</u> us to do different things. … Oh, well, you can't talk to a customer. The customer is always right.

One wise guy writes this request: He says—

"Hey, Jack!

You have worked very hard for twelve weeks. Why don't you go away for a vacation? You need the rest and <u>so do we</u> … I would suggest that you take a long hunting trip in the wilds of Africa and <u>lose your gun</u>."

(Signed) CONSTANT LISTENER

All right, Consty, we get it ... why don't you go down to the beach and pull a wave over your head?

Here's a letter that I received from twins in Walla Walla, Washington, Washington... It's another request letter and reads...

"Dear, Dear ... Jack, Jack ... Benny, Benny...

(Darn that Walla Walla)

We would like to have Olsen, Olsen play Lullaby, Lullaby of the Leaves, Leaves ... We'll be listening, listening in Walla Walla.

(Signed) Helen, Helen.

I'd hate to take those girls to dinner ... Imagine, in times like these, ordering a steak, steak.

Well, tonight, ladies and gentlemen of the radio audience, you are running this program and don't blame us... We have picked out the cream of the requests and you will now get the milk of the program.

Incidentally, Canada Dry, the champagne of Ginger Ales – I suppose you've tried it ... most everybody has – is paying for this.

Now the next number will be, "You Can't Tell Love What to Do," played by George Olsen, sung by Ethel Shutta and requested by two requestrians who have radios on their saddles. All right, Ethel.

2. YOU CAN'T TELL LOVE WHAT TO DO   ORCHESTRA & SHUTTA

JACK	And now, ladies and gentlemen, we have had a very peculiar request for tonight's program ... asking me to lead the orchestra and let George Olsen be the master of ceremonies. The party who sent us this letter figured that he might help our program a lot and surely can't hurt it any. I think that's a very good idea, George ... don't you?
GEORGE	Well, we can try it.
JACK	You know, George, I've been watching you lead that orchestra for twelve weeks now and I want to know one thing ... what's difficult about it? The boys don't even look at you. I mean, no matter what number you direct, they play what they want. I think it's a cinch.
GEORGE	All right, Jack, if you think it's so easy to lead an orchestra, let's change places. You direct the next number and I'll be the master of ceremonies.
JACK	All right, George, give me the stick ... From now on, boys, we're going to have real music. Remember, when I count two, we start the next number.

GEORGE	Jack, watch out for the retards and the crescendos.
JACK	Oh, are they with us? … Hey, Tom, cut out the smoking. Throw away that cigar.
FRAN	That's my oboe.
JACK	Pardon me. … Say I don't want any outsiders around here. Who's that fellow sitting on the piano stool?
GEORGE	Why, that's the <u>piano player</u>.
JACK	Oh, I'm sorry. Say, George, you have a new man in the orchestra tonight … haven't you?
GEORGE	Yes, Jack … how did you know?
JACK	I noticed that he was in <u>tune</u> during the first number … Go ahead, George, introduce me. <u>You're</u> the master of ceremonies.
GEORGS	Okay, Jack. Ladies and gentlemen, this is George Olsen speaking. The next number will be, "Happy Days are Here Again." It will be played by Jack Benny who is tighter than a battleship rivet. In fact, Benny kept half a dollar in his pocket so long, <u>the eagle forgot how to fly</u>.
JACK	(LAUGHS) Ha, George, I'll bet you've been saving that for a year. … And now, folks, I want to show you how easy it is to lead an Orchestra… Remember, boys, when I count <u>two</u>, start… All right! one… <u>two</u>…

(FIRST VIOLIN STARTS TUNING UP)

(LAUGHS AGAIN) A little embarrassing   Take it again, boys… now, one, TWO!
(THIS TIME TWO VIOLINS AND CELLO START TUNING UP)

JACK	Boys! Boys! we're <u>all</u> going to play. It's a fine time to be tuning up. Well, at least they're <u>interested</u>. George. … Let's start again… ONE … TWO!

(THIS TIME THE ENTIRE ORCHESTRA STARTS TO TUNE UP)

Well … Canada Dry Ginger Ale, made to order by the glass, is sold at all fountains. And you'll like it, too.

George, are you <u>sure</u> this is the right stick?

GEORGE	Yes, Jack, it's the same one I use. Try again.
JACK	Boys! … please … professional courtesy … ONE! … TWO!

(ENTIRE ORCHESTRA AGAIN TUNES UP)

GEORGE	Wait a minute, fellows.

(BOYS STOP)

Jack! Jack! … give me the stick and let me start the number for you. Then when I get the boys going, I'll give you the stick again… All right, come on, fellows.

(BOYS START "HAPPY DAYS ARE HERE AGAIN" – finish half a chorus)

JACK   All right, George, I'll take the stick now.

(The minute Jack starts directing, orchestra goes into discord.)

JACK (disgustedly)

    Oh well, George pays these boys … not me …

    The next number, ladies and gentlemen, will be, "Listen to the German Band," requested by another pair of twins from <u>Baden-Baden</u>, Germany, Germany. It will be sung by Ethel, Ethel … and played by George, George.

    You're certainly getting double entertainment tonight, folks.

3. LISTEN TO THE GERMAN BAND   ORCHESTRA AND SHUTTA

JACK   Hello … Hello … this is Jack Benny again, the <u>former</u> Orchestra leader.

    Well, folks, we have some more extraordinary requests from the various communities, asking us to say something about their respective cities. In fact, to give their home towns a boost … which we are only too glad to do. We will try to do it <u>in song</u>.

JACK   Now the first request comes from that well-known resort, Venice, California. Ethel, let's you and I sing about <u>Venice</u>. (Introductory music)

ETHEL(Sings)   "Pale moon shining on the fields below,

      Darkies singing sweet and low,

      Please don't tell me 'cause I know…

JACK   <u>VEN-ICE</u> sleepy time way down South … All right, Ethel, that's enough for Venice.

    Our next request comes from Akron, Ohio … Come on, Paul, you take this one. Sing about <u>Akron</u>. (Introductory music)

PAUL(Sings)   <u>AKRON</u> give you anything but love, baby…

JACK   That's enough, Paul … no favoritism. Just a word for each city.

ANNOUNCER   Jack, here's one request from Winnipeg…

JACK   Ah! Here's one from TROY, New York. Now that ought to be easy. Ethel, you take this one … from <u>TROY</u>. All right, George. (Introductory music)

ETHEL(Sings)   You <u>troy</u> somebody else,

      I'll <u>troy</u> somebody else…

(Sings)	All right, Ethel. I would suggest that you folks <u>troy</u> another program … I'm glad Schenectady didn't write in.
	Now here's a very peculiar request coming from a man who used to live in <u>Lima</u>, Ohio and moved to <u>Orange</u>, New Jersey, who wants us to sing about <u>Lima and Orange</u>, making it tough for us, eh? … All right George, <u>I'll</u> take this one.
	"<u>LIMA</u> dreamer … <u>ORANGE</u> we all?" (Introductory music) Eh! I guess that's bad, eh?
ANNOUNCER	Jack … Jack … <u>WINNIPEG</u>.
JACK	Now here's a request from the capital of New York state … ALBANY… Fran, see what you can do. Sing something nice about <u>Albany</u>. (Introductory music)
FRAN(sings)	ALBANY … Why don't you take ALBANY,
	Can't you see …
JACK	We're trying to please you … All right, Fran, that's enough for Albany.
ANNOUNCER	Jack, what about Winnipeg?
JACK	All right … all right … I'll sing about Winnipeg. (NO MUSIC THIS TIME)
	(Sings) WINN<u>IPEG of my heart</u>, I love you … Now stay away from me. And now, ladies and gentlemen, here's our last request. It comes all the way from the Far East, asking us to mention that strange Oriental country, <u>China</u>. All right, George, I'll do this one … Are you listening, China?
(Introductory music)	CHINA … CHINA Harvest Moon up in the sky, I ain't had no lovin' since Hong Kong, Pekin or Shanghai…
ANNOUNCER	Jack, here's a note from the sponsors.
JACK	Oh, a note from the sponsors, eh? … "Jack Benny, cut out all that nonsense. If you're going to sing about anything, sing about Canada Dry Ginger Ale made – to – order by the glass." All right, sponsors … Let's give it to them, George.
(Introductory music)	
JACK & ETHEL(sing)	"I LOVE A GLASSY OF CANADA DRY, IT'S CLASSY, AND IT'S SOLD AT THE COUNTER … LARGE AND SMALL. IT'S TASTY AND DELICIOUS, SO, SPONSORS, THERE'S YOUR WISHES … IT'S GOOD WITH ICE CREAM, TOO. (ORCHESTRA JOINS IN) Oh! CANADA DRY! …
JACK	That, ladies and gentlemen, concludes our musicale. And now Paul Small will sing, "Little Blue Canoe," played by George Olsen and his Street Peddlers.

4. LITTLE BLUE CANOE **ORCHESTRA & SMALL**

JACK　　　　We have another request this evening from a very well-to-do family who are vacationing at Rubbish-by-the-Sea. … They write us a long letter, telling us to cut out our Amateur Nights as <u>twenty – five in a row</u> is over – doing it … Their tastes run to art, classic literature and opera.

　　　　　　Well, anyway, we're here to please <u>everybody</u>. We anticipated this letter and had an <u>opera singer</u> up here this evening, so get out your <u>opera</u> glasses, folks … I now take great pleasure in introducing to you a young lady who comes to you direct from the <u>Aborn</u> Opera Company … and she's <u>a – born</u> singer … Jack Benny said that, and he's <u>not</u> sorry.

　　　　　　This little lady is a protege of that famous opera singer, Marion Talley who, as you all know, quit the opera to take up <u>farming</u>. Now this … little lady intends to do the same except that she will take up <u>plumbing</u> … as her pipes are in such fine condition … She has an excellent <u>range</u> … which runs by <u>gas</u> or <u>electricity</u> … and all her <u>notes</u> are ten days <u>overdue</u>.

　　　　　　She studied <u>ten</u> years in Paris … <u>twelve</u> years in Berlin … <u>nine</u> years in Budapest … and <u>four</u> years in vain … I mean Spain … <u>And she's still a student</u>!

　　　　　　<u>These</u> are the kind of people we bring to you! … Of course, this young lady is not what you would call " a beautiful girl." In fact, it will take a voice like Galli Curci's <u>to square it</u>.

　　　　　　And now may I present … that standing, sitting <u>diva</u>…

ETHEL (whispers)　　It's pronounced "deeva", Jack.

JACK　　　　All right, Ethel … they laughed at it … And now may I present that coloratura <u>mezzanine</u> – soprano, Miss <u>Lorraine Gitus</u>.

(ROUND OF APPLAUSE)

MISS CARYL (in affected tones)

　　　　　　How do you do, ladies and gentlemen.

JACK　　　　Oh, I forgot to mention that Miss Gitus sings in many languages. She speaks French, German and Spanish fluently … and you should hear her say "Good morning" in <u>Algebra</u> … by the way, Miss Gitus, how are you getting on with your Greek?

MISS CARYL　　Oh, <u>he's</u> all right.

JACK　　　　<u>That</u>, ladies and gentlemen, gives you a rough idea of what to expect. Now let's hear from you, Miss Gitus.

MISS CARYL　　What would you like? Do you like " La Paloma" or "La Boheme"?

JACK　　　　Why mention <u>cigars</u> when this is the Canada Dry Ginger Ale made-to-order program? … I suppose you've tried a glass, folks … most everybody has…

MISS CARYL　　For my first selection, I will sing " Il Bachio" which, In English, means the Kiss.

JACK	Well, that's good in <u>any</u> language.
MISS CARYL	And during the cadenza, I will imitate a <u>flute</u>.
JACK	That will be darned sweet of you … You say you will do this <u>during</u> the cadenza.
MISS CARYL	Yes.
JACK	Remember, folks, this is <u>not</u> the Cadenza Milk Program, but the <u>Canada Dry Ginger Ale</u> program … are you ready, Miss Gitus?

(Introductory music)

PAUL SMALL (in falsetto, stars song – strikes sour note.)

MISS CARYL	Oh, pardon me … this is my <u>first</u> time on the air.
JACK	Pardon me … but this will be your <u>last</u> time … Go ahead now, don't be nervous.

PAUL SMALL (starts to sing again)

JACK (ad libs)	Folks, if you had a bad radio, it isn't our fault … It came out of here sweet…

PAUL SMALL (Strikes a high note – unable to go on)

MISS CARYL	Oh, I'm sorry.
JACK	Here, take a sip of this Canada Dry Ginger Ale, and I'm sure you'll feel better.
ANNOUNCER	Now, ladies and gentlemen, Canada Dry Ginger Ale made-to-order by the glass takes away that tired feeling and refreshes you. It can be bought at all fountains…
JACK	All right, Mr. Wallington, you're interrupting the artiste.
	And now, ladies and gentlemen, I want you to hear the same voice <u>after</u> taking a drink of Canada Dry Ginger Ale.

PAUL SMALL (sings as badly as before)

JACK	Notice the change? … That's funny, <u>I don't</u> … well, I guess it's <u>just the voice</u>.
MISS CARYL	And now I'll imitate the <u>flute</u>.

(FLUTE SOLO)

JACK	Marvelous! … can you do a saxophone?
MISS CARYL	I'll try…

(SAXOPHONE SOLO)

JACK	Wonderful! … how about the <u>drums</u>?

(DRUM SOLO)

What a voice!

PAUL SMALL (reprises song)

JACK (adlibbing)   Now just a bit softer, please… I think you're standing a little too close to the microphone … back a bit … not quite so loud… back, back,… softer… softer…

(Singing stops altogether)

MISS CARYL   Why, Mr. Benny, you're backing me through the door.

JACK   You're telling me! … Say Kvetch, close the door.

(SOUND EFFECT: DOOR SLAM)

     Our next request is for all of us to move out of the building. And while we pack, George Olsen and his Gingeralians will play, "Bugle Call Rag" … which nobody requested.

5. BUGLE CALL RAG   ORCHESTRA

JACK   That was the last number of the 25th program on the 25th of July. And I hope you will all be listening in next Wednesday night as it will be the last program on our first series. And I'm mighty glad that everybody is drinking Canada Dry Ginger Ale, made – to – order by the glass. And do you know <u>why</u> I'm glad? … well, there has been a rumor … do you get it? … Well, see you Wednesday.

SIGNATURE – ROCKABYE MOON

ANNOUNCER   Whenever you stop at a soda fountain for a refreshing drink or a sandwich ask for a Canada Dry Ice Cream Soda or a glass of Canada Dry. Remember it is now available made-to-order by the glass as well as in bottles. Next Wednesday night at this same time Jack Benny, Ethel Shutta and George Olsen will again entertain you. This is the National Broadcasting Company.

     (WHILE ETHEL SHUTTA IS SINGING

     "ROCKABYE MOON" JACK INTERRUPTS—

JACK   Oh, Ethel, Ethel… we've just received another request from one of our best cities … <u>Dover</u>, New Hampshire … the letter came a little bit too late. Can you think up something quickly?

ETHEL(Sings)   Let's talk is DOVER …

JACK   Thanks, Ethel, that's it … well, good-night.

July 27, 1932

STATION	WJZ	PROGRAM	CANADA DRY GINGER ALE, INC.
	AND	DATE	WEDNESDAY, JULY 27, 1932
	BLUE NETWORK	TIME	9.30 - 10:00 P.M. (E.D.T.)

SIGNATURE – JOLLY GOOD COMPANY

1. MARCH ON TO OREGON   ORCHESTRA

2. WHILE THEY DANCE AT THE MARDI GRAS   ORCHESTRA & PAUL SMALL

3. WE'RE ONLY WALKING IN THE MOONLIGHT   ORCHESTRA & ETHEL SHUTTA & FRAN FREY

4. HARVEST MOON   ORCHESTRA & EHTEL SHUTTA

5. WITH SUMMER COMING ON   ORCHESTRA & PAUL SMALL

SIGNATURE – ROCKABYE MOON

SIGNATURE: JOLLY GOOD COMPANY

ANNOUNCER Ladies and gentlemen. Another half-hour of entertainment about Canada Dry Ginger Ale, now available by the glass at soda fountains, as well as in bottles. George Olsen, Ethel Shutta and Jack Benny, the Canada Dry humorist, again perform for your enjoyment.

George Olsen opens the program with "March On to Oregon."

1. MARCH ON TO OREGON   ORCHESTRA

ANNOUNCER Before going any further, I want to congratulate Jack on this first series of twenty-six programs, and I am very happy to announce that it will be continued for at least thirteen more weeks. I have not been announcing on this program, but I have been listening in…and, Jack, I just want to say that I have <u>enjoyed every one of them</u>. Congratulations, Jack.

JACK Thanks, Jimmy, for reading those words as they are written. And before going any further, I want to congratulate George Olsen for his splendid music which gave this program its pep… George, I never realized how good you were until last Monday when I tried to lead your orchestra, and <u>anybody</u> who can lead that gang deserves credit… Congratulations, George.

GEORGE Thanks, Jack. And before playing our next number, I want to congratulate Ethel Shutta for her excellent vocal support, and I also want to say that…

ETHEL Thanks, George… And I want to congratulate Fran Frey for his assistance in these vocal numbers, and –

FRAN Don't mention it, Ethel… I think that Paul Small deserves a lot of credit for… for…

PAUL Thanks, Fran…and I must congratulate Hotcha Gardner for singing those hot numbers and —

GARDNER Thanks, Paul…and I want to say something about the orchestra who have helped materially to make this —

CROWD (ad libbing)	Thanks, … thanks, that was great, etc.

(SOUND EFFCT: CANARY WHISTLE)

JACK	That's the <u>studio canary</u> congratulating the goldfish for being able to stay here for thirteen weeks. And now I want to –
ANNOUNCER	This waste of time comes to you through the courtesy of Canada Dry Ginger Ale, which is now sold at the fountain by the glass. And everybody's drinking it, or we wouldn't be here… All right, Jack, your public awaits.
JACK	Hello, <u>several</u> people… that was James Wallington announcing… the big <u>butler</u> and <u>door</u>man from the West…and this is Jack Benny… The big <u>hay</u> and <u>feed</u>man from the East… hay and feedman… when a girl passes on the street, I holler "Hey!" and then I have to feed her… <u>get it</u>?
ANNOUNCER (groans)	Oh, Jack… please!
JACK	You didn't like that one, eh, Jimmy?
SADYE (laughing)	Oh, I think that's <u>awfully</u> funny.
ANNOUNCER	Pardon me, Miss… but the guests are not allowed to make comments during our program.
SADYE	I think Mr. Benny is the <u>cutest</u> thing.
ANNOUNCER	SHH! Miss… please!
JACK	Well, anyway, this is a great night for us, and we're all very happy to be here.
ANNOUNCER	Jack, don't mind that little girl interrupting, but she's been coming up here to see you two or three times, and seems to be kinda anxious to meet you.
JACK (with force)	I know, Jimmy… but <u>business is business</u>. We're doing a program now… We can't have anyone up here interfering… (whispers) Who is she?… Do you know her?… (again with force) We haven't time, Jimmy… this is <u>business</u>… (again whispers) Is that <u>her</u> standing over there? Ooooh!…
	The next number, ladies and gentlemen, is a request from New Orleans for Paul Small to sing, "While We Dance at the Mardi Gras," played by George Olsen and the boys.
	(whispers) Jimmy, she's cute, isn't she?… Go ahead, George.

2. **WHILE WE DANCE AT THE MARDI GRAS** **ORCHESTRA & SMALL**

JACK	Gee, that's a great number, Paul… I enjoyed that.
ETHEL	Say, Jack, did you see all those telegrams that came for us tonight?

JACK	Yes, kind of nice, isn't it?
ETHEL	Why don't you read them?
JACK	Aw, I'd like to, Ethel… but I'm afraid it might sound like we're conceited. Say, Jimmy, do <u>you</u> think I ought to read these telegrams aloud?
ANNOUNCER	Certainly … your public is entitled to it.
JACK	I hate to have them think we're boosting Canada Dry Ginger Ale up here.
ANNOUNCER	They won't think that… go ahead and read them.
JACK	All right, then… now here's a telegram from a family in Detroit, Michigan. It says…

> "DEAR CANADA DRY:
> WE HAVE HEARD ALL OF YOUR TWENTY-SIX PROGRAMS
> AND WE TAKE OFF OUR HATS TO… AMOS 'N' ANDY."

Well, I imagine they <u>keep</u> their hats on when they listen to us.

Here's another wire. It reads –

> "DEAR CANADA DRY GINGER ALE NOW SOLD AT ALL FOUNTAINS"

That's all it says…Oh, well… the <u>ten words are up</u>… Well, thanks for what you left out.

Oh, here's a very wonderful tribute from Mr. John L. Dumb-bell, who runs a health resort. It reads –

> "DEAR TO WHOM IT MAY CONCERN:
> FOR YEARS I HAVE BEEN TRYING TO BUILD UP MY PEOPLE
> PHYSICALLY BY GETTING THEM TO BED EARLY. STOP. THEY
> HAVE HEARD ONE OF YOUR BROADCASTS AT NINE THIRTY
> AND NOW GO TO BED AT <u>SEVEN O'CLOCK</u>. THANKS"

Oh well… early to bed and early to rise… makes you miss lots of Canada Dry's.

Ah! A wire from that famous inventor who made all this possible – <u>Marconi</u>!

He says –

> "I INVENTED WIRELESS WHICH IS NOW RADIO…AND AFTER
> LISTENING TO YOU FOR THIRTEEN WEEKS AM SORRY I
> STARTED IT."

I get it, Marc…trying to <u>Mussolini</u> on my jokes.

Well, well… here's a cable from SCOTLAND… It's sent to our cable address:

> "JACK-BEN-OLS-CAN-DRY' and says

"UP HERE IN SCOTLAND WE'RE ALL DRINKING CANADA DRY BY THE <u>GLASS</u>-GOW"

SADYE	Oh I think that's <u>swell</u>.
ANNOUNCER	No comment, Miss… please.
SADYE	He says the <u>funniest</u> things.
ANNOUNCER	Quiet, <u>please</u>.
JACK	Now here's another telegram from the Twelve Little Listeners in —
SADYE (laughing)	When you drink Canada Dry, where does the <u>glass go</u>? That's the funniest joke… Oh, I <u>must</u> tell that to my mother.
JACK	<u>That</u> isn't what I said, Miss… I said: they're all drinking it by the <u>glass</u>-gow.
SADYE	I don't care <u>what</u> you said… I think you're <u>swell</u>.
JACK	Thanks… now will you kindly sit down until our program is over?
SADYE	Yes, Mr. Benny… you don't mind if I call you <u>Jack</u>… do you?
JACK	Of course not.
SADYE	Thanks, Mr. Benny.
JACK	What's <u>your</u> name?
SADYE	My name's Mary Kurtzinger Livingston… But just <u>Mary</u> to you.
JACK	I'm awfully glad of that… these are only half-hour programs, you know. Say, by the way, <u>where</u> do you live?
SADYE (quickly)	Oh, I live in Plainfield… you get on a bus, then you get off at the second stop-light… walk three blocks to you left… then you cut thru the cemetery and over the hill… then up the road until you see a little red house…and you go right thru the field… and <u>THERE YOU ARE</u>!
JACK	There <u>you</u> are… not <u>me</u>… Well, it was sweet of you to come up here, Mary. Now why don't you sit down quietly and listen to the rest of our program?
SADYE	All right, Jack.
JACK	I'm sorry, ladies and gentlemen, but these little interruptions are bound to occur. And now Ethel Shutta and Fran Frey will sing, "Walking in the Moonlight" …and while they do this number, we will prepare for our big banquet in the studio, which our sponsors have so thoughtfully arranged for us this evening. Oh George, … please don't mind any little noise you might hear during the next number…you know, waiters, guests, dishes rattling and things like that…

3. WALKING IN THE MOONLIGHT   ETHEL & FRAN

SOUND EFFECT: General commotion; moving of chairs…dishes, glasses and silverware rattling.

CROWD — mumbling, greeting each other, etc.

JACK   What time is it, Jimmy?

ANNOUNCER   Nine forty-five.

SOUND EFFECT: Assorted auto horns, trolley car bells, etc.

JACK   Ah! The limousines are arriving for the banquet…do you think we can take care of <u>all</u> these people?

ANNOUNCER   I think so, Jack. You'd better stay at the door and greet the guests. I'll help here.

SADYE   Can I help, Jack?

JACK   No, no, no… oh yes. Mary, you check the ladies' wraps and things.

MARY [it really says this]   I'll do anything for you, Jack…because I think –

JACK   All right, Mary, here they come.

(MORE AUTO HORNS — PEOPLE TALKING)

GEORGE (whispers)   Look at those evening gowns…some swanky crowd…eh, boy?

JACK   Yes, sir… here come Mr. and Mrs. Who-Aster… nobody asked her, but here she is… How do you, <u>Mrs. Who</u>?

DOROTHY ROSS (gruff voice)   Say, when do we eat?

JACK   Yes, it's a charming evening.

SADYE (quietly)   Your wraps, ma'am…

SOUND EFFECT: Footsteps passing, people talking, ETHEL SHUTTA greeting people.

JACK   Waiter, show the lady to her seat.

BALDWIN   This way, Madame.

JACK   Well, well, well!… I am so glad to see you, Mrs. Gotta-Feller… <u>what's his name</u>? Good evening!

ETHEL SHUTTA (in grand manner) How do you do?

JACK   You're looking fine…Mrs. Gotta-Feller, meet Sir James Wallington, Earl of Announce…

ETHEL   Not Get-Rich-Quick-Wallington!

JACK   No, this is Go-Broke-Slow-Wallington.

(VOICES TALKING AND LAUGHING)

ANNOUNCER	May I show you to your seat, Madame?
DOROTHY & PAUL (together)	How do you do, Mr. Benny?
JACK	Oh, how are you, Mr. and Mrs. Anaconda Copper?…I didn't expect to see you… Well, well!…and Mr. Worthington Pump. You're looking great.
BALDWIN	Thanks, Jack.
JACK	Ah! Here come Mr. and Mrs. Electric… how are you, <u>General</u>? (ad lib) Welcome to our Canada Dry Banquet… eat, drank and be <u>MERRY</u>.
SADYE	Did you call me, Jack?
JACK	No, I said…<u>be merry</u>. But you can take the lady's wrap.
SADYE	All right, Jack… I'll do anything you say, because I –
JACK	Never mind, Mary, not now. Ah! Here comes that little society debutante, Miss <u>Casaba Mellon</u>…
DOROTHY ROSS (grand manner)	How do you do?
JACK (mimicking her)	How d'yuh do? Well, well, … Mr. and Mrs. <u>Hoover</u>… well, old Pete Hoover of Chicago… hello there, Pete! …and hello, Tessie.
PAUL AND DOROTHY (together)	Hello, Jack. How are you?
JACK	Say, George, who's that <u>distinguished</u>-looking gentleman over there…in that full-dress suit?
GEORGE	I don't believe we know him… Must be one of the crowd from Newport.
JACK	Good evening, sir! How do you do? My name's Jack Benny… I don't think I've had the pleasure of meeting you.
FRAN FREY	I'm one of the waiters. Where do I go?
JACK	George! Tell him where to go.
FRAN (shouting – heavy voice)	Get your Canada Dry Ginger Ale at the fountain… you can't enjoy this banquet without a glass of Canada Dry… everybody's drinking it… step right up to the fountain!
JACK	Say, Fran… we're not <u>selling</u> Canada Dry tonight… we're <u>giving</u> it away.
FRAN	Oh yeah? Well, what shall I do with this nine dollars I took in?
JACK	Give me two and return the rest… George, will you entertain the guests while they are getting seated?
GEORGE	Sure, Jack.

JACK	A brand new song… Harlem Moon… Ethel, help us out.

4. **HARLEM MOON**   **ETHEL SHUTTA**

ROUND OF APPLAUSE. Buzzing of voices – dishes rattling, etc.

BALDWIN	Waiter, bring me a glass of Canada Dry.
DOROTHY	Fill this up again.
ANNOUNCER	The banquet is now in full swing… the hall is filled to capacity and promises to be the biggest affair of the year. I am now turning the mike over to Jack Benny, our toastmaster.

(ROUND OF APPLAUSE)

JACK	Guests…ladies and gentlemen… <u>and George Olsen</u>… I am very happy to see you all here this evening, and we will now proceed with a toast to the champagne of Ginger Ales… <u>Canada Dry</u>…
	Here's to the guy who drinks Canada Dry, Even as you and I. And here's to the glass that's sold at the fountain When…when…when the moon comes over the mountain.
CROWD	Hooray! Hooray for Jack Benny, etc.
SADYE	I think that was <u>swell</u>.
JACK	Now we have several after-dinner speakers here who will say a word or two on conditions in—

[[Page 15 is missing from the microfilmed script in the NBC Masterscripts Collection at the Library of Congress, the only known existing copy of this script]]

JACK	[this is in progress] … Here they are folks…Olsen jabs a fork at Pot Roast…but <u>misses</u> and stabs Hotcha Gardner in the knuckles…Gardner reaches a long left out for the salad…Olsen crosses a right for the beans and the waiter ducks…Paul Small reaches for an uppercut of beef and gets his sleeve in the butter…Tunny Fish is now on the table but looks fresh on toast…Olsen just came out of a clinch with Asparagus and looks tired, but is coming back for more…<u>How he</u> <u>can take it</u>!…away from the other people…Wallington just put some cigars on the table…and Olsen is right on the ropes…I mean, the cigars… Olsen bawls out Gardner and Gardner hits him with a fowl…

(SOUND EFFECT: FIGHT GONG)

As the bell ends the first round, and the food. The time for this was two minutes and forty-eight seconds. Olsen wins and is now the <u>Gravyweight</u> <u>Champion</u> of the <u>World</u>!

(SOUND EFFECT: BANGING OF SILVERWARE ON DISHES AND GLASSES)

JACK: And now we will hear from that great maestro, the Honorable George Olsen, who can play anything Shakespeare ever wrote.

(SOUND EFFECT: MORE BANGING OF SILVERWARE)

GEORGE: Ladies and gentlemen, this reminds me of the time I was in Africa – and I – I— I—

JACK: Thanks, George… And now we will hear from that charming debutante, Miss Van… Trucking-Van.

PAUL (falsetto voice): When I first came here from Iowa, I was considered a wallflower. Women laughed at me, and the men shunned me. I didn't know what to do. Friends advised me to drink water—

JACK: Canada Dry.

PAUL: I mean, Canada Dry…which I have now been drinking for two years. I am still a wallflower, but I am not thirsty any more, and I owe it all to Canada Dry.

\(APPLAUSE)

JACK: Now, Miss Trucking-Van, you said that of your own free will, didn't you?

PAUL: No, you gave me a dollar last week to learn it.

JACK: ANOTHER victory for Canada Dry… And now I wish to take advantage of this occasion and say a few words regarding Canada Dry Ginger Ale made-to-order by the glass… Unaccustomed as I am to public speaking—

FRAN: Well, good-bye, everybody…

DOROTHY: Good night… I had a lovely time.

(OTHER VOICES: Good-bye, etc.)

JACK: When I was a boy of six, I was considered a very weak child—so much so, that when my car broke down, I couldn't even push it up a hill—

BALDWIN: Well, see you again, Jack. Thanks for asking me up…

ETHEL: Good-bye…

JACK: And I think Canada Dry has done more for me than anything—

OTHER VOICES: Good-bye… had a grand time, etc.

JACK: And in my opinion Canada Dry was like a mother to me…

(SOUND EFFECT: Auto horns in distance, crowd saying good-bye, etc. Someone calls! Chauffeur!

ANNOUNCER: George, you better play the next number. They're all walking out on Jack.

5. **WITH SUMMER COMING ON SMALL**

JACK …and that is why I like Canada Dry Ginger Ale.

SADYE Mr. Benny… I mean, Jack… I'm going home now.

JACK All right, good-night, Mary. I'm glad you came up. Come up again sometime.

SADYE Monday night?

JACK Monday – er—er—oh, all right. Goodbye.

SADYE I thought you were <u>swell</u>… good-bye, Jack.

JACK That was the last Mary… I mean the last number on the 26th program on the 27th of July. I want you all to listen in Monday night as we are going to have another surprise…NOVELTY NIGHT… We are going to show how many things can be done over the radio that you never thought possible… We, either. In fact, we don't even know how we're going to do them…
But time will tell… Well, we'll see you Monday night… <u>Reserve a dial early</u>. And as they say in Walla Walla… Good-night… good-night!

SIGNATURE – ROCKABYE MOON

ANNOUNCER Whenever you stop at a soda fountain for a refreshing drink or a sandwich ask for a Canada Dry ice cream soda or a glass of Canada Dry. Remember it is now available made-to-order by the glass as well as in bottles. Next Monday night at this same time Jack Benny, Ethel Shutta and George Olsen will again entertain you. This is the National Broadcasting Company.